THE MYTHISTORY OF KAJIR RONGHANGPI

The Mythistory of Kajir Ronghangpi

The Making of Kaziranga National Park

Edited by

DHARAMSING TERON
VULLI DHANARAJU

MANOHAR
2026

First published 2024
Reprinted 2025, 2026

ISBN 978-93-6080-067-3 (hardbound)
ISBN 978-93-6080-792-4 (paperback)

Published by
Ajay Kumar Jain *for*
Manohar Publishers & Distributors
4753/23 Ansari Road, Daryaganj
New Delhi 110002

Typeset by Ravi Shanker, Delhi 110095

Printed and bound in India

Contents

Preface

Kaziranga National Park, a recognized UNESCO World Heritage Site and a renowned national park in India, is widely recognized for its exceptional efforts in wildlife preservation and for being home to the greatest population of One-horned rhinoceroses. It is situated on the southern bank of the Brahmaputra River and has a border with the Karbi Anglong district of Assam. Kaziranga is closely intertwined with the socio-cultural customs of the Karbis. The Karbis holds great significance as an indigenous community in the north-east India, primarily residing in the two hill districts (Karbi Anglong and West Karbi Anglong) of Assam. They can also be found in various districts of Assam, including Nagaon, Sonitpur, Morigaon, Kamrup, Golaghat, N.C. Hills, and Cachar, albeit in small numbers. Historically, the present Kaziranga National Park has been populated by the Karbis. The National Park is closely associated with distinctive and rich customs, traditions, and oral literature of the Karbis.

Kajir Ronghangpi, a prominent 'mythical legendary' figure in the oral traditions of the Karbi people, was associated with the etymology of Kaziranga. The name Kaziranga has several origins, but all agree that it is derived from the Karbi term *Kajir Arong*, which means "territory of Kajir." (The "land of Kajir Ronghangpi"). This book highlights the importance of oral tradition and folklore in providing valuable insights into the history and cultural heritage of a region, particularly by revealing the hitherto unexplored history of Kaziranga National Park.

Kajir Ronghangpi holds an honored place in the social memory of the Karbis, being commemorated and preserved through songs, rituals, and performances. Her influence led to the establishment of the renowned Kaziranga National Park. Presently, the oral tradition of Kajir Ronghangpi holds a significant place in the collective memories of the locals in the surrounding areas of the park. Though the oral tradition of Kajir Ronghangpi is frequently imagined in the memories of Karbis, it has not been systematically documented, resulting in a shift in the political narratives of the current territorial history of the Kaziranga National Park.

The Karbi cultural domains have been built with their "cognitive" and "relational space" notions, which always show their values, feelings, beliefs, and perceptions. It is important to remember that stories are always told by people, about people, and for people, and thus the derivations of the great mythical legend Kajir Ronghangpi are not only about the territory of the Kaziranga National Park, but also about the oral tradition of the people who have lived there for centuries. As a result, the stories and attributions of these people must be researched and documented using "orality". Unfortunately, the local territories have not been constructed with 'interactive ideas' of the community rather they are constructed by "meta-historical ideas" which are often contested in the making of "local history". Hitherto, the argument is, the tradition of Kaziranga National Park is not merely a "passive ground" upon which events unfold, cultures amalgamate, and social processes take shape. It is part of the entire process that produces oral traditions and oral discourse of the community.

Kaziranga National Park is the centre of biodiversity where the local people and their ecological systems have highly been influenced by Kajir Ronghangpi's tradition. She also played a vital role in the conservation of the flora and fauna, especially the local rhinos. Such tradition can be seen in the oral narratives of the Karbis. Recently biodiversity has been transformed due to changes in the relationship between people and ecology, the government's perceptions towards flora & fauna, deforestation, *Arnam Keso* (sacred groves), climate change, growing demand for natural resources, etc. In this context, this book tries to explore the local ecosystems that have been produced by the tradition of Kajir Ronghangpi and her people who struggle to continue the tradition for making their history.

Another important aspect of this book is to explore the cultural heritage of the Kaziranga National Park. Heritage is often constructed by the local ecological or cultural values which cannot be separated from "space" and "time" that has been carved by the locals. But such heritage can be altered when the claims or attributions of the people are forcibly changed (changes in "space" and "time") due to "hegemonic ideas" perpetuated by the so-called state with modern "territorial ideas" or boundary making. Yet, Kajir Ronghangpi's heritage is a vibrant process in the construction of the identity of the Karbis and their history. In this context, this book aims to reaffirm the ecological, cultural, and spatial concepts of Kajir Ronghangpi, which can be elucidated by examining the oral narratives (myths, folktales, legends, and other forms of knowledge) of the Karbis. This book provides a critical review of the oral traditions of the Karbis, providing an alternate perspective on how the Kaziranga National Park can be "re-invented" by considering the insights of the "Mythistory of Kajir Ronghangpi".

10 May 2024 DHARAMSING TERON
Diphu VULLI DHANARAJU

Acknowledgements

Like any other scholarly work, this book is a collaborative effort. This book is the outcome of the international conference on "Oral Tradition of the Karbis: Memorizing Kajir Ronghangpi –The 'Rhinoceros Lady'" (as part of the annual commemoration of the 'The Rhinoceros Lady' on 5th December) held on July 27-29, 2023 by the Art & Culture Department, Karbi Anglong Autonomous Council (KAAC), Diphu in association with Assam University, Diphu Campus, Centre for Karbi Studies, and Diphu Govt. College, Diphu. At the very onset, we would therefore like to extend thanks to all the chapter contributors. Without these chapter contributors' support, this book would not have been a reality in this form.

We would like to express our heartfelt gratitude to Dr.Tuliram Ronghang, Hon'ble Chief Executive Member, KAAC, Diphu, for his keen interest and incredible support in publishing this book. We are grateful to the Karbi Anglong Autonomous Council for their full support in publishing this book without hardship. We also thank Mr. Surjya Rongphar, Hon'ble Executive Member, i/c Art & Culture, KAAC, for his support in the completion of this book.

We owe an intellectual obligation to Mr.Elwin Teron, Chief Advisor, CEM, KAAC, and an intellectual figure in Karbi Anglong, for his academic guidance and support. Without his enormous generosity and scholarly support, this book would not have been conceivable.

We wish to express our sincere thanks to Prof. Rajive Mohan Pant, Vice Chancellor, Assam University, Silchar, Prof. Sivasish Biswas, Pro-Vice Chancellor of Assam University, Diphu Campus, Maggie Katharpi, General Secretary, Centre for Karbi Studies, and the Principal, Diphu Govt. College, for their academic and administrative assistance in completing this book. We also owe an intellectual debt to Dr. Michael T. Haneise, Associate Professor, UiT Arctic University of Norway, for his academic support in completing this book.

We extend thanks to Mr. Mukul Kumar Saikia, Principal Secretary of KAAC, Mr. Si-im Taro, Member Secretary of KAAC, Ms. Rani Terangpi, Deputy Director of Art & Culture, KAAC and Mr. Dilip Kathar, Art & Culture Department, KAAC, for their valuable administrative assistance in the successful completion of this book.

We extend our thanks to Ms. Girbani Deka for her thorough proofreading of the book and to Mr. Ranjan Engti for designing cover page (picture) of the book.

We want to take this opportunity to thank the Karbi folklorist and the people with whom we conducted oral interviews for the narrative in the surrounding area of Kaziranga National Park. These oral narratives serve as the foundation for constructing the arguments laid out in the introduction. The argument presented in the introduction chapter would not have been possible without the outstanding generosity and support from these people.

No words are left to express our gratitude to the Manohar Publishers, New Delhi for their keen interest in the publication of this book.

DHARAMSING TERON
VULLI DHANARAJU

Introduction

The Mythistory of Kajir Ronghangpi – The Rhinoceros Lady

DHARAMSING TERON and VULLI DHANARAJU

The 'mythistory' of Kajir Ronghangpi, in its various local versions and variations, though sketchy, is still alive in the collective Karbi memory. The story travelled with Karbi ancestors as they migrated and settled in various locations whether in the Khasi and Jaintia Hills, Kamrup, North Cachar (where once they were numerous), in the plains in Nowgong, and in the north of the Brahmaputra in Darrang.[1] Karbi presence from Kaliabor to Kaziranga as noted in colonial account[2] is reiterated and acknowledged by the 'large-scale impact of Karbi language elements'[3] in the topography of Kaliabor which partly accommodates the Kaziranga National Park. The persistence of the story of Kajir Ronghangpi, spawning its retellings over generations, has given it an aura of an enduring myth. Kaziranga today is synonymous with a *rongman* – literally an 'abandoned village' of Karbi ancestors who once thrived here before the colonial conservation drive dispossessed them a century or so ago – stirring up a deep sense of loss, longing and nostalgia. The myth of Kajir Ronghangpi which inspired the naming of the Kaziranga National Park is not just a fabulous story – it has wider implications for Karbi history and conservation.

The title of this book was chosen based on the arguments presented therein. The etymology of 'Kaziranga' can be traced back to the 'mythistory' of Kajir Ronghangpi, who was historically regarded as a 'rhinoceros lady.' The main argument of this work is to trace the etymology of 'Kaziranga' based on the 'mythistory' of Kajir Ronghangpi. The oral tradition of Kajir Ronghangpi is honored, deified, and kept alive in Karbi social memory through songs, rituals, and oral discourses. She inspired the designation of the world-famous Kaziranga National Park, which was once in the heart of huge Karbi settlements. Though the oral tradition of Kajir Ronghangpi is frequently visualized in local memories, it has not been systematically recorded, resulting in a shift in the political narrative of the current 'territory of the Kaziranga National Park'. The Karbi cultural domains have been built with their 'cognitive' or 'relational space' notions, which always indicate their values, feelings, beliefs, and perceptions. It is important to remember that stories are always told by people, about people, and for people, and thus the derivations of the great myth of Kajir Ronghangpi are not only about the territory of the Kaziranga, but also about the oral tradition and ritual of the people who have lived there for centuries. As a result, the stories and attributions of these people must be researched and documented using orality. Unfortunately, the local territories have not been constructed with 'interactive ideas' of the community rather they are constructed by 'meta-historical ideas' which are often contested in the making of 'local history'. Hitherto, the argument is, the tradition of Kaziranga National Park is not merely a passive ground upon which events unfold, cultures amalgamate, and social processes take shape. It is part of the entire process that produces oral traditions and oral discourses of the community.

Kaziranga National Park is the centre of biodiversity where the local people and their ecological systems have highly been influenced by Kajir Ronghangpi's tradition. She played a vital role in the conservation of the flora and fauna, especially the local rhinos. Such tradition can be seen in the oral narratives of the Karbis. Recently biodiversity has been transformed due to changes in the relationship between people and animals, the government's perceptions towards flora and fauna, deforestation, sacred groves (*angry gods*), climate change, and growing demand for natural resources etc.

This book also delves into the local ecosystems shaped by the tradition of Kajir Ronghangpi and her people, who are dedicated to preserving their cultural heritage. Delving into the cultural heritage of the Kaziranga National Park is another crucial aspect of this book. Local heritage is shaped by the ecological and cultural values intertwined with the specific 'space' and 'time' of the community. But, such heritage can be altered when the claims or attributions of the people are forcibly changed (changes in 'space' and 'time') due to 'hegemonic ideas' perpetuated by the so-called state with modern 'territorial ideas'. How Kajir Ronghangpi's traditions have played a significant role in the making of modern Kaziranga National Park is the main focus of the present compilation.

CONCEPTUALISING MYTHISTORY

> Ever since Herodotus declared in Histories that to preserve the memories of the great achievements of the Greeks and other nations he would count on their own stories; historians have debated whether and how they should deal with myth. Most have sided with Thucydides, who denounced myth as 'unscientific' and banished it from historiography.[4]

Looking at the statement above, different groups of historians have engaged in discussions regarding the possibility of constructing historical narratives using myths. History is all about a 'perspective'. Historians often view writing history as a 'scientific activity'. However, in recent times, some historians have begun exploring 'mythistory' as an approach to writing history.[5] History as an academic discipline is different from 'mythistory'. Historians are constantly re-evaluating the past, exploring new inquiries, uncovering fresh sources, and discovering new insights in old documents to provide a fresh perspective on understanding history. It is important to understand that our knowledge and perceptions about history are constantly evolving. Collective memories change over time for different reasons. This can be observed in the context of the etymological inquiry of 'Kaziranga' discussed in the following paragraphs.

It can be quite challenging to define 'myth' in the context of 'mythistory'. The fundamental definition, as understood by researchers in mythology and anthropology, refers to 'sacred stories from traditional cultures typically featuring supernatural entities, and so on.'[6] The term, 'myth' can also encompass the supplementary narratives that evolve from one generation to another. Theodore Reik (1957)[7] says myth is 'not a story told as history but history told as story…' In other words, it is a narrative of a real experience in the past. What we call myth today is not an imaginary tale but a real-life experience of the primordial society. Karbi myths reflect every facet of Karbi life. The cultural past of the Karbi people is narrated through myths, legends, and folk tales passed down through generations, resembling a narrative about history. Dharamsing Teron (2008)[8] a prominent oral historian and one of the editors of this book, presented arguments referring to Karbi history:

> …there was a time when a Karbi forefather could speak in endless verses-the language he so fluently used to express his world-views, his religion, and to communicate with his exotic surrounding and his descendants. The Karbi forefather's verses, sung in simple repetitive tones but in strict metrical order, told tales of creation of the universe, the origin of the first Karbi parents, the elaborate wedding and funerary rituals, the ordeal of migration and so on. In fact, the vast repertoire of Karbi oral tradition touches upon every aspect of the tribe's ways of life. In spite of the lack of documentation, these verses have managed to survive in rural areas till date. The Karbi 'history', therefore, continues to be trapped in the realm of myths, legends and hearsays.

However, the word, 'myth' is commonly linked to negative connotations, often used interchangeably with falsehood, fables, or false information. Scholars define the term 'myth' as something complex and significant. The academic use of the word is related to the human endeavor to categorize and comprehend constant yet mysterious facts about oneself and the world we inhabit.[9] Scott E. Robinson (1991)[10] made a convincing argument about the influence of myth in society, highlighting its dual nature. Myth has therefore been used in both positive and negative contexts for particular reasons. For example, 'The myths of major religions are often considered to be moral and beneficial to society,' states Harold M. Foster, 'but the myths of 'Nazi Germany were incredibly destructive.'[11]In this context, as suggested by William McNeill,[12]it is proposed that:

> Myth and history are close kin inasmuch as both explain how things got to be the way they are by telling some sort of story. But our common parlance

reckons myth to be false while history is, or aspires to be, true. Accordingly, a historian who rejects someone else's conclusions calls them mythical, while claiming that his own views are true. However, what seems true to one historian will seem false to another, so one historian's truth becomes another's myth, even at the moment of utterance.

McNeill accomplishes the article by stating, 'Mythistory' is what we actually have a useful instrument for piloting human groups in their encounters with one another and with the natural environment.' Also, he contends, 'to be a truth-seeking mythographer is therefore a high and serious calling, for what a group of people knows and believes about the past channels expectations and affects the decisions on which their lives, their fortunes, and their sacred honor all depend.' These are poetic phrases, and McNeill is describing a world myth that the poet is no longer only responsible for building, but also the historical scholar. In his article, Peter Heehs[13] argues that myth and history are often seen as opposing methods of explanation. Yet, myth and history offer distinct perspectives on the past of different cultures. Defining history is hardly easier than defining myth, but a historical approach necessarily involves both establishing a chronological framework for events and comparing and contrasting rival traditions in order to produce a coherent account of history.

In *Mythistory*, Joseph Mali (2003)[14]re-examines the oldest controversy in historiography in the context of generating the 'perspectives'. Challenging the conventional dichotomy between myth and history, Mali argues for a historiography that integrates both and acknowledges the significant impact of myth on shaping personal and cultural identities. He believes that historiography ought to disclose rather than eliminate these 'fictions', showing how they have impacted historical events. Mali offers a new perspective on modern historiography by connecting it with the traditional concept of 'mythistory.' He uses the term 'Myth' in a broader sense to refer to non-rational influences on human history, such as tradition, the irrational, and the subconscious. He does not distinguish between myth as a narrative or collection of legends, 'myth' as the authoritative conformity of a tradition[15], and a general term for the fundamental non-ethical forces. But he does not provide a clear definition of the term 'myth' in his work *Mythistory*. This can be largely understood with the following statement offered by John Foster's (2008) article review:

> That the term, 'mythistory' does not imply a blurring of the metaphysical boundaries between history and myth. Mali does not argue for historiography to be reduced to the ontological status of myth, nor for it to be elevated to the normative status of myth, nor, most importantly of all, that myth and historiography are interchangeable terms.

In adherence to McNeill's [16] argument, Mali advocate for modern historiography to examine not just what occurred (history) or what people think happened (myth), but the process through which both impact the creation and continuation of historical significance ('mythistory')[17]. The blending of myth and history, known as the 'mythistorical', is a narrative style that merges classical historiography with modern recognition of the mythical. He argued that historians should not aim to uncover a perfect truth about the past, but instead explore the beliefs of different groups about their histories that they deemed important to safeguard. Historians should not attempt to explain these truths by reducing them to physical causes, biological impulses, economic needs, or social functions. Instead, they should interpret them as the symbolic means by which people react to one another and to the world.

Collingwood's[18] attempt to distinguish between myth and history, where history focuses on human activities situated in specific 'time' and 'place', reveals that:

> Myth [...] is not concerned with human actions at all. The human element has been completely purged away and the characters of the story are simply gods. And the divine actions that are recorded are not dated events in the past: they are conceived of as having occurred in the past, indeed, but in a dateless past which is so remote that nobody knows when it was. It is outside all our time reckoning and called 'the beginning of things'. Hence, when a myth is couched in what seems a temporal shape, because it relates events one of which follows another in a temporal shape, the shape is not strictly speaking temporal, it is quasi-temporal.

Thus, Collingwood maintains that history focuses solely on human activities that are temporally dated, contrasting with myth that involves gods acting in timeless settings. Mythographers find that during the twentieth-century, technological changes have outpaced myth's ability to change with society in ways that function. Joseph Campbell (1991)[19] proclaims that 'our mythology has been wiped out' as a result of modern scientific systems and globalised world. He explains the utilization of myth in the making of history. He has explained four basic functions which all mythological structures serve in any community, in any place, in any time. These are: mystical, which relates to one's sense of wonder about the world, cosmological, by which a culture gives physical shape to its mystical ideas in the form of stories and rituals, sociological which uses mythology as a basis for social order and morality, and psychological through which the individual reaches an understanding of his relationship with his community and the world. With this understanding, 'Kaziranga' has been investigated in relation to Campbell's function of the myth, which originates from Karbi oral traditions, based on the community's myths, legends, and songs.

The book also delves into the relationship between myths and how they influence the course of history. The book suggests that 'myths' have a significant impact on shaping historical events or mystical folklores and therefore, 'mythistory' that are distinct from fables, falsehoods, or fictions. Stories are narratives that we use to define our own 'identities'. They help define our identity, distinguish those outside our group, and provide reasons for our hostility towards them. Myth and its modern form, history, are similar to fiction as they communicate a specific truth that holds significance for a particular group rather than a universal or eternal truth. Considering Mali's argument, there is no distinction between 'history' and 'myth'. The story or oral tradition of Kajir Ronghangpi is now regarded as 'mythistory' of the Karbis. The introduction chapter provides justification with various proposed arguments, which are discussed in the following paragraphs.

Exploring how historical events or mythological narratives are intertwined with the traditions practiced by a community serves to establish a sense of identity in the present day. Historical events or figures frequently experience a metamorphosis into mythical creatures. In *Simulacra and Simulation*, Baudrillard (1981)[20] argues that in the modern era, history has transformed into myth: 'History is our lost referential, that is to say our myth.' Despite being considered as constructed myths, narrated histories continue to hold significance in shaping our future. Both myth and history maintain interconnected relationships with one another. Mythological concepts are often confused and ambiguous and it is precisely because they are historical that history can very easily suppress them.[21] Roland Barthes states:

> It is human history which converts reality into speech, and it alone rules the life and death of mythical language. (...) Ancient or not, mythology can only have an historical foundation, for myth is a type of speech chosen by history: it cannot possibly evolve from the 'nature' of things.

Rudolph Bultman (1961)[22] defines myth as the expression of 'man's understands of himself in the world in which he lives.' Julie Sanders[23] has pointed out that a culture's mythology is its body of traditional narratives appropriated to diverse circumstances. In Mythologies, Roland Barthes (1972)[24] uses appropriate language to illustrate the nature of myth:

> Myth is a system of communication, it is a message. This allows one to perceive that myth cannot possibly be an object, a concept, or an idea; it is a mode of signification, a form. Later, we shall have to assign to this form historical limits, conditions of use, reintroduce society into it: we must nevertheless first describe it as a form.

He argued that myth conveys a message. Myth is not seen as an object, but rather as a form of discourse or language. To effectively analyse myths, it is crucial to grasp the historical and social contexts surrounding them, as well as the individual's capacity to comprehend and interpret the past. However, in *The New Nature of History: Knowledge, Evidence, Language*, Arthur Marwick (2001)[25] defines myth as a version of the past that typically contains some truth but distorts what actually happened to serve a particular interest. This definition effectively considers the impacts of reality. Myths have a hierarchical power structure. Their narrative structure is closed and contains a distinct and well-defined message. In her poem, 'The Past', Oodgeroo (1990)[26] conveys a similar perspective.

> Let no one say the past is dead.

The past is all about us and within.
Haunted by tribal memories, I know
This little now, this accidental present
Is not the all of me, whose long making
Is so much of the past.

Thus, myth is a form of oral expression delivered in an arrangement of language. It converts historical events into natural phenomena, so revealing the underlying myth.

All cultures create and tell stories, and myth-making is an important human creative activity. Myths, stories, legends, folklore, tall tales give valuable insights into how people perceive and think about their world. Ross Murfin and Supryia M. Ray (2003)[27] stated:

> Even when a culture no longer believes that its myths are true explanations, however, these stories often survive as receptacles of important cultural values.

Establishing a single, comprehensive definition of myth has proven impossible. There is no single description that can adequately encompass all of the different types of stories that can validly be classified as myths based on one or more criteria. The endeavor to define myth, however difficult the task, serves to highlight the characteristics of the stories that distinguish them from one another.

In Aotearoa New Zealand literature, the connection between myth and history with current issues like land and the place of the Maori people in the society reflects the idea that myth serves as a form of communication, extending beyond indigenous mythology.[28] These texts highlight Maori myth and show how myth transforms into history, which is crucial for discovering one's place in the modern world. Grace (1987) used the myth of the carver in *Potiki* (1987) to affirm Maori identity by highlighting its significance in comprehending Maori history. As Mali argued, myths shape history. The current book uses the term 'myths' to refer to stories that are not synonymous with fables, falsehoods, or errors. Myths are narratives that we use to describe our own identities. They establish our identity, differentiate others who are not part of our group, and explain the reasons for our distance towards them. Myth and its modern form, history, are akin to fiction since they convey a particular truth that is meaningful to a certain community rather than a universal or eternal truth. Mali's argument is noteworthy because history has been shaped by myths linked with the community's experiences, which cannot be separated from the everyday practice of living with the narrative. Karbis use myths to explain how things came to be through the efforts of a supernatural being or ancestors or mystical figure like Kajir Ronganghpi. The story of Kajir can be explained in the subsequent paragraphs.Michael Carhart (2004)[29] stated in his review article:

> During his 1985 presidential address to the American Historical Association, William McNeill emphasized that facts alone hold little significance. The vast amount of facts faced by historians or scientists lack significance and can only be comprehended by selecting a small percentage of them. To effectively communicate, historians must tailor their narrative, which is constructed from chosen facts they consider important, to meet the expectations of the reader. Thus, the historian is a mythographer.

Donald R. Kelley stated in *The Faces of History* (1998)[30] that history is essentially our myth. Myth and history originate from memory, and historians fulfil a similar role as mythographers. They maintain cultural memory and provide significance to the disorder of previous encounters. Historical truths, like myths, are influenced by symbols that shape human experiences. Enlightenment and Romantic mythistory suggest that primal symbols evolved into rational propositions and axioms of seventeenth-century Natural Law through secular and rational stages. The story of that process represents our myth, namely the myth of Western Civilization, where 'myth' and 'logic' symbolize our legacy and potentially our future. Mythistorians such as Giambattista Vico, J. G. Herder, and Jules Michelet aimed to trace the process of secularization and rationalization back to its primordial, poetic, and preverbal origins in the eighteenth and nineteenth centuries. They tried to reconstruct the life and ideas of the distant past. Many researchers have expanded on Hans Blumenberg's (2023)[31]concept of 'new mythology' from the 1970s, which aimed to demonstrate the enduring impact of myths in the rational, secular modern era, despite being altered by previous generations. Anne Holden Ronning (2009)[32] argued that the transformation of history into myth in our current world without a strong sense of history is likely influenced by the rise of individualism and the spread of global capitalism. Is the history of a nation significant in a globalized world? Is it something we cherish as evidence of our national identity and connection to centuries of history? In 'Writers in the 'New World", Derek Walcott (1974)[33] suggests that we should reconsider the conventional view of history as a linear progression and instead view it as a form of mythology. He argues that history is a fluid and subjective narrative influenced by memory and creativity. Karbis have a rich history of sharing tales about their past and their ideas about the world. These tales were not documented but were transmitted orally from one generation to the next. Many of the narratives revolved around the mysteries of the natural world and the origins of various phenomena. Two long oral narratives (*Mosera Kihir* and *Kacharhe*) play a crucial role in comprehending the natural world of the Karbis. *Mosera Kihir* plays a crucial role in Karbi funeral festival (*Chomangkan*) and the 'collective youth ritual' called *Riso Chojun*. *Kacharhe* or *dirge* singing is a significant genre in the collection of Karbi oral narratives. It portrays the soul's journey into the 'land of eternal happiness' as part of the Karbi funerary ritual. Elderly people persist in singing tales based on traditional legend and myths and female lament singers, known as *Charhepi*, persist in singing for extended periods during funeral ceremonies. Without *Charhepi*'s lament, a Karbi soul is unable to reunite with its ancestors. Without the rendition of *Mosera*, the Karbi funeral festival remains incomplete. However, Karbi oral tradition extends beyond just a *Mosera* or the lament songs of a *Charhepi*. Indeed, the Karbi worldview is evident in their oral performances, chants, sacred prayers, rituals, legends, and myths, which are countless. Typically, myths are symbolic narratives that depict the origin of the world as perceived by a specific group. Subsequently interpretations of the creation myths are influenced by the community's evolving history and needs. Myth is a valued, symbolic tale representing the beliefs and values of a specific community. It conveys the essence of belonging to that particular community. Tales are used to address the loss of traditional narratives and are reshaped to reflect specific cultural identities. It is also true that myths often provide a different viewpoint on the history of communities. Thus, myths are the key motivating factors of the past.

The past of Kaziranga dates back to the seventh century according to historical records and there are several versions of the origin of the name. According to historians the name relates to a Karbi woman named Kajir Ronghangpi who 'ruled the region at one time.'[34] Some historians also believe that the name Kaziranga comes from the Karbi *Kajir-a-rong*, meaning 'the village of *Kajir*' (*Kajir* or *gaon* in Assamese), *Kajir* being a common female name in Karbi.[35] Another legend suggests that the name might have been derived from the 'Land of red goats (Deer)...as the word *Kazi* in the Karbi language means 'goat', and *Rangai* means 'red'...'[36] This version of the myth, in spite of the semantic irregularity wrongly suggesting that *kazi* (actually *karjo* in Karbi, a wild goat) was a red-goat and the absence of the term rangai as red in Karbi, is repeated in various publications.[37] According to the legend the area had an abundant population of wild goats tracking the beels (lakes) in search for water holes which the local Karbi inhabitants very frequently encountered. Karbi name for the wild goats is *Karjo* and rivulets are referred to as *Langso*. In course of time, the *Karjo* and *Langso* (literally, rivulet of red goats) fused together to Kaziranga.[38] A Karbi folklore narrates the descent of a 'unicorn with wings' which could never return as it lost its wings due to disuse and developed an armoured skin for protection and survival.[39]Another story narrates about a certain young man named Kazi from Karbi Anglong who fell in love with a village belle named Ranga from the Assam plains. The lovers however did not find favour with their parents which forced them to occasional rendezvous in the forest. The lovers vanished one day which led to the forest being named Kaziranga in their memory.[40] According to another story, an old childless couple named Kazi and Rangai once approached Sankardev. The couple was blessed with a child who then dug a large pond to mark the occasion as advised by the saint.

In yet another story, once the Ahom king Pratap Singh happened to pass by that area and was offered fish from the pond which he liked immensely, and the name gained popularity since then.[41] Ajit Timung, a Karbi writer asserts that Kaziranga, once part of a Karbi territory, derives its name from a beautiful Karbi damsel named Kajir Ronghangpi, who possessed 'super-natural powers.'[42] It is also asserted that there were 'Fragments of monoliths associated with Karbi rule found scattered in the area seem to bear testimony to that assertion.'[43] Some inquisitive scholars have attempted to trace the linguistic roots of the name and showed that there are 'indelible impression' in the naming and evolution of 'place names' in Assam as reflected in the naming of Kaziranga. It has been argued that 'Kaziranga, Kazironga: A national sanctuary, in Golaghat district (Latitude 26-30 N, Longitude 93-27-12 E.) - 14th century AD, named after the Karbi village. Kazi, personal name of a Karbi lady, + case ending –r, Kazir+ suffix – rang, or rong, Kar. Village, Kazirrang corruption 'Kaziranga''Kazironga' here, case ending 'r' is lost. According to Tai-Ahoms, Kaziranga = a sanctuary for wild Rhinos; Old name:Jatiarong or Jatiarang.'[44]

Maj. John Butler, leading the first British military expedition into the Naga Hills in 1845 who moved through the 'Meekir' land also described the boundary of the Meekir Hills which was bounded 'by the plains of the Meekirpar Mehal, the Mongahs of Rungobegur, Kageerunga, and Bokakhat.'[45] Kageerunga, therefore, was a natural extension of the Karbi settlement even before the colonial subjugation.

The strong presence of a Karbi population of Kaziranga was also asserted in various academic works.[46] The central theme of these stories generally supports the Karbi origin of Kaziranga. This conclusion is logical as the forest that now houses the Kaziranga National Park (KNP) was once one of the last untouched grassy areas in the Brahmaputra valley,[47] where Karbi tribesmen lived in small villages alongside other tribes. Geographical contiguity of the KNP with Karbi Anglong, home to the majority Karbi population in the submontane region, justifies the logic about which Stack wrote that till 1886, very little of the interior of the Mikir Hills was explored and to the north, from Koliabor to Kaziranga, they abut on the Brahmaputra. The geography has not altered much as – 'The present day KNP occupies a vast area which falls under the three contiguous districts of Karbi Anglong, Nagaon, and Golaghat.'[48]

The maps produced by British officials had shown localities

within the KNP with various local names of lakes etc. which were given by erstwhile inhabitants.[49] There are official documents which acknowledge that – '16 acres of annual leased land belonging to the villagers of Harmoti and Bagori within the proposed area. The two villages were ordered to be shifted after payment of compensation @ Rs.25/- per household having land over 20 bighas and @ Rs.15/per household having land under 20 bighas. The annual leases were not renewed. No rights or concessions were admitted. Finally, an area of 56,544 acres of land was declared as a reserve forest vide notification No.37F dated the 3rd January 1908. But subsequently 1441.6 acres of land opposite to Kuthori and Baguri villages was de-reserved vide notification No.2069F dated the 18th April 1911.'[50] Similarly, '...there were four villages within the proposed area consisting of 49 households viz. Lotabari, Bahoni with 13 houses, Latabari, Charighoria with 16 houses, Arimora with 14 houses and Ahom Chapori with 6 houses. All these were temporary villages having annual lease of land and were in existence for about 6 years at that time.'[51]

MYTHISTORY OF KAJIR RONGHANGPI AND HER TRADITION

Some traditions appear to have only been invented in recent times. Traditions are rooted in identity, and identity in tradition. Cultural tradition embodies a blend of continuity and change, serving as a rich source of values and solutions that can be creatively expanded upon and re-imagined or re-invented. Invented traditions are cultural activities that are depicted as traditional, supposed to have originated in the distant past, but are actually relatively recent and purposefully constructed by scholars or authors to capture the conditions of that particular period or society. Eric Hobsbawm and Terence Ranger (1983) edited the book *The Invention of Tradition*, which emphasised on this concept. Eric Hobsbawm defines this term as follows:

> ...'Invented tradition' is taken to mean a set of practices, normally governed by overtly or tacitly accepted rules and of a ritual or symbolic nature, which seek to inculcate certain values and norms of behaviour by repetition, which

automatically implies continuity with the past. In fact, where possible, they normally attempt to establish continuity with a suitable historic past.[52]

Hobsbawm explains on invented traditions as reactions to new circumstances, which 'attempt to structure at least some parts of social life within [the modern world] as unchanging and invariant.'[53]Hobsbawm differentiates between 'tradition,' 'custom,' and 'convention.' Unlike tradition, custom is not regarded to be static and must remain adaptable. It is an established practice that can be quickly modified if necessary. Convention is just a routine, with no ritual or symbolic purpose. Custom and convention are both practices that help with daily routines, but unlike tradition, they lack an ideological foundation.

It is interesting to note that many modern or recent 'traditions' were made up. This creation stands out from establishing a tradition that does not claim to be 'historical'. There is a clear trend in the modern creation of identity through 'fake narratives' crafted by scholars outside the community, resulting in a 'misrepresentation' of the communities' history. The term 'Mikir' has been analysed in etymological framework and discussed by non-Karbi writers. The term 'Mikir' has not been accurately portrayed in the tradition of the Karbis. However, they have continued to use negative connotations when referring to the Karbis. These stories uphold the beliefs of those in power by shaping specific narratives that aim to control the history of communities without writing traditions. For example, since the Karbis resided on hill slopes, they were referred to as 'Arleng' which translates to 'hill men'. Non-Karbi writers (both colonial and post-independence authors) have used various derogatory terms like 'primitive', 'savages', 'timid', 'unwarlike', 'cowards', 'devil worshippers', and 'raw flesh eaters' when referring to the Karbi people. Gunaviram Barua in his book *Asam Buranji* (1875/2003) imported Sanskrit terms such as 'markat' or 'sakhamrig' (both meaning monkey) as the origin of 'Mikir'. The author was aware that the people were known by the ethnonym Karbi (Karbe in the book) who were settled (and still do) in the present Dimoria region of the ancient 'Dumuroya kingdom'. The author argued that the term Karbi was derived from *Kroibad*, another Sanskrit term which meant 'raw flesh-eating savages'.[54]

The book makes a substantial argument that the name 'Kaziranga' derives from the oral tradition of Kajir Ronghangpi. The arguments in this book have been constructed using the 'mythistory' approach. The tourism department of the Karbi Anglong Autonomous Council (KAAC) has installed a statue of Kajir Ronghangpi at the ethnic Village in Kahora, near the Kaziranga National Park. The statue contains a message inscribed on the pedestal, introducing Kajir to the world. It reads, 'Legend has it that Kajir Ronghangpi, daughter of Hok Ronghang, was taken to and brought up in the abode of Gods and Goddesses.' After achieving divine status and receiving special powers, Kajir Ronghangpi descended to earth to find her natural parents and siblings. Kajir Ronghangpi reconstructed the land established by her father in and around the current Kaziranga National Park area. She brought *Kindu* (Rhinoceros) along to help with the tilling. Kajir Ronghangpi returned to the realm of the divine, leaving the Kindu in the territory.

The myth of Kajir only deepens as versions, mostly sketchy and often coloured with local descriptions and discrepancies are in circulation throughout the Karbi inhabited regions. It is now well-nigh impossible to trace the antiquity of the story but it travelled with Karbi ancestors who migrated and settled in various geographical locations in the most volatile and uncertain circumstances – whether in the Khasi and Jaintia Hills and North Cachar Hills in the upland where once they were numerous as in the plains in Nowgong, and in the north of the Brahmaputra in Darrang.[55]

The story of Kajir is in fact the story of the seemingly endless saga of migration of the pre-colonial Karbis to escape[56] the constant slave-taking and head-hunting raids of the neighbouring tribes ascribed to their 'unwarlike'[57]ethos. Ajit Timung's booklet titled 'The Myth behind the Name Kaziranga' (2006)[58], incidentally the first attempt at historicizing the myth, also narrates the migration of Hok Ronghang, the father of Kajir Ronghangpi, from a place named *Bithi Arlok* (cliff of betel leaves) in the vicinity of the Jaintia territory. Similar story of migration of the immediate ancestors of Kajir seems to be very commonly shared by present day Karbis. For instance, Mr. Darsing Hanse (57)[59] of Panbari Karbi village (near Kaziranga), a Sakari Gaonbura (under Golaghat District), narrated a similar story of Kajir's escape from somewhere in the Jaintia territory to Kaziranga. Darsing Hanse's great-grandfather Longkoi Hanse (also a *Sakari Gaonbura*) migrated from a place called Thengklung-Thengrak in the Jaintia Hills and made a settlement in the present Kaziranga forest which his descendants had to abandon due to the Burmese atrocities. Subsequently, a branch of the family came to settle at Arimora between Kahora and Hatikhuli in the vicinity of Kaziranga.[60] William Robinson[61] and Lyall & Stack[62] had also mentioned about Karbi migration from the Jaintia territory. However, the two versions of Ajit Timung (as told him by Sonjoy Ronghang of Tarabasa) and Darsing Hanse differ in identifying Kajir's father. According to Timung, it is Hok Ronghang while according to Hanse (as told him by his grandfather), it is Sai Ronghang, linking Kajir to Ha`imu.[63] Similarly, the two versions also differ in identifying the mother as Bong`e Teronpi and Kache Timungpi. The version of Timung also talks about Kajir having two siblings, namely Khoi and Kading. The version talks about a fabulous journey that Kajir made with seven divine sisters to their heavenly abode who took pity of the seven-year-old girl crying in the wilderness. Kajir returned when she was a grown-up lady of 24, now blessed with divine powers. By then her brother had already got himself a beautiful bride and was installed as the ruler of the territory as Hok Ronghang was too old to handle its affairs. However, in tragic turns of events, her brother was treacherously murdered by his 'close aides' by drowning him in a river. The widow of Khoi and her lover conspired to get rid of the old ruler and his wife and banished them to a place named *Ritlo*. Kajir accompanied with *Chung*, son of Wind God and *Phang`ok*, son of Sun God, saw the dying couple and restored their health. Thus, Kajir was reunited with her parents and returned home where she also met her sister Kading. With her divine powers, Kajir came to know of her brother's tragic death and the river where he was drowned. She found a divine tree named *Alom-Bilom* (Kauri pine) and felled it with her knife. When the tree fell on the river, the water dried up, exposing her brother's lifeless body. Kajir, with her divine powers revived him. After restoring the territory to her brother and father to the utmost joy of the people, Kajir flew back to the heaven, with the promise to return to earth from time to time. One day, Kajir returned to her brother, accompanied with one Sarsomon, who brought a *Kindu* (rhinoceros). Sarsomon tilled the earth with the *Kindu*, turning the wilderness into a rice field, which attracted multitude of birds and animals. The strange markings on the thick hide of the *Kindu* are since then believed to have been caused by the ropes used by Sarsomon to tie the animal with so as to pull the plough to till the land. Karbi belief of the *Kindu* as a sacred animal and the image of the rice spirit began since then. Kajir returned to heaven after ensuring stability of her father's territory. Hanse's version however does not go into any such length.

There is yet another version of the escape of an adolescent Kajir from the enemies who pursued her father Longkidong Ejang and mother Kare Tungjangpi. The story was narrated by Evelin Ingtipi (45) of Sarthe Ingti village of Chokihola, Nilip, who belongs to a vanishing class of the female spirit medium called *Lodeppi.* On a special request, Evelin went on a trance after performing some rituals and started narrating the story of Kajir's torment in verse in the voice of a spirit of an old woman named Lori. According to the verse narrative, invaders named Chongkumbang suddenly attacked the village where Longkidong, Kare and their daughter Kajir lived. The invaders targeted the females forcing the family of three to avoid being killed. There was barely any room for escape as the three were surrounded by the assailants who followed their footprints. The couple had run out of options and decided to give the little Kajir a chance at survival by hiding her in a pit that they found in the deep woodland. Terrified and alone, Kajir began to cry aloud which warned her attackers. Amazingly, hundreds of birds flocked around Kajir's pit and used their loud noises to mask her cries, confusing the adversaries and forcing them to seek other routes. Kajir's parents, meanwhile, started running down a riverine path in a last-ditch effort to elude the enemies. Longkidong persuaded his wife to use an alternate route in order to deceive her pursuers and possibly give her a slight chance of escaping. Unfortunately, the enemies found Longkidong quickly, outran him, and used a creeper to bind him around his stomach. In an attempt to get information regarding the whereabouts of his wife and daughter, his captors started torturing him and tightened the creeper around his stomach for each negative response. Longkidong refused to surrender and was killed mercilessly. The place where Longkidong was tortured to death is today identified as Longso Anglong (near Kat Teron village, Rongongwe). Kare Tungjangpi came to know about her husband's fate and she jumped off a cliff at a place currently identified as Langcharchu (near PaniramTokbi village, Rongmongwe) and gave up her life. Kajir, meantime, cautiously surfaced from the pit and, fearful and uncertain, roamed aimlessly for some time after discovering no indication of her parent's whereabouts. But she was constantly accompanied by a number of birds, including peacocks and peahens, elephants, and rhinoceroses, wherever she went. She grew up into a young damsel in this environment wandering across the length and breadth of the wilderness, in the company of the birds, animals and the rhinos which became her extended family.

She once had a dream in which her parents told her to create a *long-lingpum* (mortar and pestle) as a representation of her earthly sojourn. Her parents made hints that she will shortly ascend to heaven along with them. After a few days, just as predicted, Kajir vanished in a breeze that caused the leaves to drop, leaving the 'long-lingpum' behind. Since then, generations of Karbis have venerated Kajir, the lady with the rhinoceros, with the following hallowed prayers in her honour[64]–

Chong abi Kajir/Song abi Kajir
Chong abi lojir/Song abi lojir
Chong abi kesok/Song abi kesok
Chong abi langhe/Song abi langhe
Chong abi Karong/Song abi Karong
Chong abi aman/Song abi aman
Chong abi kele/Song abi kele
Chong sakhi/Long sakhi
Bang sakhi/Pi longkidong
Po longkidong/Pi songkidong
Po song kidong/Pi kidongpi
Po kidongpi/Chomme kidong
Longme kidong/Dam kidong/Do kidong
Dongpi Kare/Dangpi Kare
Dong Karepi/Dang Karepi
Chong Karepi/Long Karepi

Phang Karepi/Lang Karepi
Chong longripi/Phang longripi
Dak kare/Dok kare...

A version of the story as narrated by former Rongkhang King Harsing Ronghang (75) to Elwin Teron[65] states that the legend of Kajir Ronghangpi is found in the annals of Karbi migration from Tibet to the northern banks of Lut, the Karbi name for the great River Brahmaputra. This batch of Karbi settled in the vicinity of the present Sonitpur district. A group split from the batch and crossed the Lut and settled at Kaziranga on the southern banks, which also included Sereng Ronghang and Kare Ingtipi, the parents of Kajir Ronghangpi. Sereng's brother, Dok Ronghang, also settled with them. Kajir had two siblings, elder sister Kareng Ronghangpi and a brother. As time passed by, once it so happened that an Ahom gentry named Medhibura fell for the charm of Kareng and proposed to marry her which was turned down. Medhibura felt slighted and murdered her. Kareng was cremated at Kuthori. Medhibura later regretted his action and in a way to amend it, he built a Kareng-*ghar* and a *mandir* to perpetuate her memory. But as fate would have it, another Ahom suitor sought for the hands of Kajir, attracted by her beauty and charm. In order to avoid this unwanted overture, the parents of Kajir poured over her a solution of lac, transforming her red from head to toe instantly. The suitor saw her and exclaimed *Kajir-Ronga* (lit. Kajir-red)! Infuriated, frustrated and felt insulted, the suitor killed Kajir as well.

This version of the story does not agree with the other versions which deny that Kajir died in any manner and that she attained divinity. The story asserts that Kajir indeed existed and that the chilli sapling she planted by the bank of Brahmaputra grew into a big tree which is still to be found. The story also narrates about Kajir's only brother being drowned in the great river. Kajir was overwhelmed at her brother's tragic fate and started crying inconsolably by non-stop singing of *kecharhe* (funeral dirge). The power of her song forced the water to part, exposing her brother's body at the river bed.[66] She consoled herself by performing the cremation of her brother as per tradition. Following these series of tragedies, the Ronghangs decided to leave Kaziranga to relocate to nearby Burapahar and then on to the Rongkhang territory.

Another legend told to Elwin Teron by Rupsing Ronghang (81), a resident of Pinpo a`ritlo near Hamren township, narrates that Kajir Ronghangpi's father was Chere Ronghang, the 5th Lindokpo (King) of Rongkhang at Socheng[67], who moved to Rongcheden Kothalguri to establish his new kingdom there. Kajir was immensely beautiful who always wore red garments which earned her the nickname of 'Kajir-Ronga'. Chere Ronghang[68]when he moved, he also carried off with him the 'Golden Seat' of the kingdom. The 'Golden Seat' had some mystic powers which would become extremely hot, making it impossible for persons not fit or destined to sit. However, the Ahom King came to know about it and demanded it to be handed over to him warning of liquidation if Chere failed to do so. Fearing for his life, Chere surrendered the 'Golden Seat' and it is believed, since then, the Rongkhang Kings had to do with a symbolic wooden seat.

Elwin Teron (2023)[69] has attempted to relate the story of Kajir with historical events and offered a suggestion that the episode could have taken place at the early period of the Ahom ascendency in the Assam valley around 1228 AD.

KARBI MIGRATION AND KAJIR'S TERRITORY

The story of Kajir tells an episode of the ordeals of migrations that the Karbi ancestors had faced in the medieval history of pre-Assam period. For a substantially long period of the medieval history, the Karbis were forced to abandon their territories from one end to the other because of the highly volatile environment of the time. Probably for this reason, Edward Gait called the Karbis as 'notoriously migratory.'[70] But the history of a hostile environment that existed throughout medieval history of the region was acknowledged by the colonial government of Assam in its memorandum to the Indian Statutory Commission in 1930 and confessed that '... Historically the hills and the plains have always been hostile.'[71]

Historical accounts reveal that the whole of the Karbi region was under the control of the Varman (350-650 CE), Mleccha (650-900 CE) and Pala (900-1188 CE) dynasties as testified by archaeological remains of Hindu temples and images from Parokhoa to Dighalpani and Numaligarh to Deopani.[72] Following the fall of the Pala dynasty, the Karbis came under Kachari subjugation, which forced them to migrate to the Jaintia territory[73] in the 'pre-Syiemship decades.'[74] It was the period when Thong Nokbe, the famous warrior hero emerged as a military leader to protect his vulnerable tribesmen for some time. Batches of Karbis again migrated to the Ahom territory harassed by warfare between Khasi/Synteng chiefs.[75] According to Ahom Buranji sources, Karbi migration to Ahom territory was due to the imposition of Jaintia matriarchy.[76] The Karbi population faced a precarious existence till the British arrival and by then they were dispersed/settled in at least four different sections and directions. A section of them was under the Ahom Chief at Roha while another was under the Kachari Chief at Moudanga which faced constant attacks from the Nagas. It is interesting to note that there was a section between Dimapur and Golaghat which strongly resisted against the Nagas and maintained its independence.[77] Till the colonial time, an estimated 8800 Karbi population lived within the Naga territory[78] which had migrated to present Karbi Anglong or neighbouring plain districts. Considering these pointers, a scholar claimed that '...the Karbis of Assam had an organized state before the extension of the British rule in the region.'[79]

Karbi presence from Kaliabor to Kaziranga as noted in colonial account[80] is reiterated and acknowledged by the 'large-scale impact of Karbi language elements and its intermixture with the Assamese language' as a result of trade relations and economic exchanges that happened between the hill Karbi population and the plains in Nagaon in the pre-Ahom days.[81] The present day Kaziranga National Park (KNP) itself is surrounded by more than 50 Karbi villages.[82] Of which, Bagori and Kuthori, the two semi-urbanised areas in the periphery with substantial Karbi population, also trace their etymologies from Karbi language. Duar Bagori is a revenue *mouza* under Kalibaor revenue circle, which was a 'door or pass' in medieval Assam which facilitated Karbi tribesmen coming down to the plains for trading purposes. According to a recent scholarship, *Ba* is a Karbi word for five (corrupted from pho) and suggests that the five clans of the Karbis viz. Teron, Terang, Ingti, Inghi and Timung who in course of time settled in the area influenced the naming of the place.[83] Likewise, *Kuthori* derives its name from a Karbi word – *Kunturi* (corrupted from *Kuntiri*) which refers to 'small huts'[84] built to accommodate women in specific ritual occasions like Chojun (ancestor veneration). Rev. James Rae of the Serampore Mission, who was probably the first Baptist missionary to have ever toured the interiors of Karbi Hills in the month of April in 1836 stayed with the Karbis in the present day Kahora and Deithor localities in the neighbourhood of 'Kazi Runga' who narrated his pleasant experiences among them, praising their great kindness who gave food freely to strangers, and whose houses were 'much more comfortable than those belonging to the people in the plains.'[85]

Elders of the Karbi villages under Kaziranga have many interesting stories to tell. According to Rajen Hanse (65) of Panbari Karbi village, within the forest area his ancestors lived in villages named Tiyontuli, Sengbheti (Arimora) and Mikir Tract (marked by British era pillars) now made inaccessible due to the swamp and the conservation restrictions.[86] Another elder – Rengka Teronpi (60) of Mandu Bey village of Kahora, recalls that her forefathers, namely – Chai Teron, Jamin Teron, and Sar Teron and others had inhabited at least for five generations before they were asked to leave the forest. Water bodies namely – Bando, Sanglak, Bilonghong, Daplangso, and Daplangpi were the traditional fishing areas of her ancestors. She informs that *Daplang* is derived from Karbi word *Ingdeiplang* (shallow) which in course of time transformed to *Daplang* as it is presently known. She also narrates a century old story of a famine in the forest villages caused by severe drought which seriously threatened all life forms. *Lekthe Solok* (literally, man with dazzling white teeth), the village chief, tried digging ponds here and there attempting to find water sources that proved futile. A dream revealed to him that unless he sacrificed his wife – Nangpi Timungpi, the drought would continue. Finding no other alternative, he offered his wife to the pond under some pretext. Water immediately gushed out of the pond as the dream had predicted, giving relief to all. The pond transformed into a water body or lake in course of time which became known as *Bi-charhe* (Weeping Lake) which the Assamese renamed as *Deodubi*. It was customary to offer a *banta* (five betel nuts and five betel leaves wrapped in banana leaf in a particular manner) to the spirit of the woman if anyone intended to catch fishes in the lake as a customary form of respect. Another water body or lake which the Karbi villagers named as *Therolangjang* (the water where a monkey was drowned) came to be known as *Bandordubi* in Assamese. Solok Lekthe and other Karbi villages had to leave to various corners of the upland of the present Karbi Anglong after the creation of the sanctuary. Some of them chose to move to Rongmongve area within the present boundary of Karbi Anglong, very close to the KNP.

According to Rengka Teronpi's version, Kajir was born here and did not mention about her migration. Kajir attracted both admiration and awe as she was always seen roaming in the wilderness in the company of animals, birds, and befriending the tigers, the elephants and, particularly – the rhinos. Kajir also walked on the surface of water, as if it was a patch of dry land and she used creepers to move from tree to tree and engaged in farming. There are stories that narrate the discovery of a young calf of rhino by Kajir in her farm land which she befriended. In this version of the story, Kajir did not have any sibling and did not die a physical death either – she simply vanished like a whirlwind.

RHINO, RITUAL, AND FOLKLORE

Rhinoceros (*Kindu*) has been part of Karbi folklore and as already stated, it is given the status of a sacred animal. Rhinoceros appearing in a dream is considered a sign of good luck. A rhino frequented rice fields were believed to lead to good harvest. This belief that holds rhinoceros as the 'spirit of rice' is still in circulation and that the paddy plants consumed by rhinos receive fertilizing effects and helped in better growth and increased yield. The idea that rhinos are the 'spirit of rice' and that the paddy plants they eat have fertilising properties that promote greater growth and higher yields is still widely held. There is also a belief that possession of even a small piece of the rhino hide aided prosperity. In older days, the *sang-rangtik* or rice container/storage, which is held as sacred, was covered with the rhino-horn lid fuelled by the belief that rice spirit (*sang a`minu*) would be contented and would always bless the household with abundance and happiness. A version of the creation myths describes that the rice spirits followed the rhinoceros to earth. Feeding grounds of the animals therefore are believed to produce a good harvest of rice. This belief is connected to the tradition of using a bowl made of rhino-horn to take out rice from the sang rangtik by a housewife or an elderly woman of the household. A sang-rangtik is held sacred in a Karbi household and therefore, rice cannot be taken out of it by any random person. There is a reference to the rhino in the sacred prayer chanted at *Sar Anthok* (ancestor veneration) ritual performed by a household, which is as follows –

Phi langhan taine
Phu langhan taine
Boche aseng`e
Langhan kuntinun
Boche aharlung
Hinpo kindu hindungpo...[87]

Again, the rhino tail (*Kindu arme*) has special ritual significance in the worship of Karbi village spirit deities called Chongkong Rongker. The rhino tail is used to sweep the venue of the Chongkong version of the Rongker as a cleaning ritual, a symbolic act of a spiritual cleansing of the negative vibes of the location and to ensure protection and well-being of all the members of a village, young and old as the following sacred prayer describes –

Oh Ve Chokipi
Oh Dom Chokipi
Oh Ve Narepi
Oh Dom Narepi
Karkok ke nangdei
Karphe ke nangdei
Rongphu ke langkenang
Rongling ke langkenang
So lana ke nang
Su lana ke nang
So paklar ke nang
Su paklar ke nang
Rongphu paklar`et
Rongling paklar`et ...[88]

In the above prayer, *Dom Narepi, Ve Narepi* refer to rhinoceros. As already stated, when ancestor veneration worship (*Sar Anthok*) is performed by a household, a prayer dedicated to the Kindu – *Kindu kuntinun, kuntinun sokvung* – is chanted. Here, the sacred chant referring to sokvung suggests that kindu ensures abundance of paddy.

But there is no such tradition attributing 'magical properties' to rhino-horn among Karbis. In older days, shields (*chong*) made of rhino-hide were used by Karbi villagers, which perhaps indicated that the animal might have been killed for this reason. In this regard, mention may be made of the use of such a weapon by warriors of the neighbouring Khasis as noted in a colonial account which states that 'a large circular shield made mostly out of animal hide, usually buffalo skin or rhino skin...'[89] Some accounts however say that the 'local Mikirs had taken to the profession of killing' the rhinoceros in the early twentieth century when rhino poaching had reached a 'frightening level.'[90] EP Gee, a British a tea-planter and an amateur naturalist in Assam, in his famous book, *The Wild Life of India* (1964) had cited a funny incident of a 'Mikir poacher' evading arrest by the Forest Staff in the following words – 'The Mikirs, the simple, but interesting tribal folk who dwell in the Mikir Hills on the southern boundary of the sanctuary, were among the many poachers. And when they ran away from the Forest Staff their 'tails' (the ends of their embroidered loin-cloths) were caught hold of by the pursuers. The Mikirs would then draw out their sharp chopper knives and cut off their own 'tails' to facilitate their escape.'[91]Longsing Bey (74) of Murap in West Karbi Anglong informed that villagers in earlier days however captured rhinos by a fairly simple technique. Since the animals defecated at the same spot, trapping one in a camouflaged pit strategically dug near the communal dung heap was favoured. He also added that such a trapped rhino was not always killed but released after knocking off (*thengpong*) its horn. Interestingly, between 1871 and 1907, the colonial Assam government paid rewards 'for the destruction of rhinos because of the amount of damage they did to rapidly expanding agriculture. The major pressure on the species, though, came through hunting by Indian royalty and British sportsman.'[92] As a result, the rhino numbers in Kaziranga were reduced to about 200 by 1908 due to overkill via hunting that started in the nineteenth century.

Karbi Anglong forest is home to a variety of wild life, including the rhinoceros.[93] However, the animals today are found only in areas adjacent to the KNP and particularly when the flood waters forced them to seek higher ground in the upland of the nearby Karbi forests. However, rhino sightings in other Karbi forest regions have been reported by elders who would normally point to such a period as 'long ago.' Major John Butler, who travelled to Naga Hills through the Karbi forests between 'Mohung Dehooa and Dheemapoor' through a 'dreary and desolate wilderness' that he had in any part of Assam seen before, around 1854, had stated that rhinoceros was found in every part of Assam.[94] However, the disappearance of the majestic mammal from the Karbi forests leaves no clues.

Being a world heritage site and home to the highly endangered one-horned Indian rhinos, Kaziranga is truly a source of pride for Assam and the entire nation. News that have been shared extensively, both officially and unofficially, as well as by travel writers, commonly agree that the renowned sanctuary's name is linked to the myth of the 'Karbi heroine.' The persistence of the story of Kajir Ronghangpi, spawning its retellings over generations, has given it an aura of an enduring myth. Kaziranga today is synonymous with a *rongman* – literally an 'abandoned village' of Karbi ancestors who once thrived here before the colonial conservation project dispossessed them a century or so ago of their territory, which however continues to stir up a lingering sense of loss, longing and nostalgia to this day.

Considering the 'mythistory' of Kajir Ronghangpi, this book reinforces the argument put forth in the beginning of this chapter. The myth of Kajir Ronghangpi, as told in certain versions, are truly incredible. Could they be history? Or are there any seeds of history? In the words of Karen Armstrong – 'humans have always been mythmakers.'[95] Devdutt Pattanaik, the celebrated Indian author and bestselling mythologist, asserts that '...no society can exist without myths.'[96] Midgely similarly contends that 'Myths are not lies. Nor are they detached stories. They are imaginative patterns, networks of powerful symbols that suggest particular ways of interpreting the world.'[97] Joseph Mali, as already discussed above, emphasizes the persistence of myth in historiography and asserts that '...however modem we might have all become, our life and history are still largely determined by some very ancient myths.'[98] He questions and challenges the antithetical explanation that only the *written* history is 'serious and reliable explanation of what actually happened' with 'empirical sources' and that, myth is 'all fabrication and pure fiction and therefore a spurious description of what merely appears to have happened'.[99] He therefore proposed 'an alternative historiography that recognizes myth for what it is: a story that has passed into and become history[100].' Mali calls this 'mythistory' – 'histories of personal and communal identity'.

In Karbi ontology, ancestors are remembered and deified – praying to them as 'those who have become gods' (*nangtum tirim atum, taram atum/nangtum arni kemantang, arnam kemantang...*), which is an unavoidable ritual of every household, keeping the memories of the ancestors alive. The memory of Kajir Ronghangpi, shaped and reshaped through generations of retellings, she has become as an integral part of the larger Karbi history. Edward Stack and Charles Lyall, author and editor of *The Mikirs* (1908) respectively, described the Karbis as a 'race with short memory'[101] disregarding the fact that such representation only reflected and exposed their own biases against colonized people. And as some of the stories insist, Kajir Ronghangpi only 'vanished', she had never died.

This book argues that it is impossible to create traditions without a tale or myth or legend that reflects the past in our daily cultural life or behaviour. However, certain traditions can be 'created' or 'manufactured' but only continue temporarily. Hobsbawm's (2012)[102] thesis supports the justification of traditions that originated in the past and continue to influence people's lives. He argues that 'traditions' are different from recently created ones. Traditions were well-defined and had a profound impact on cultural behavior, whereas contemporary tradition are frequently unclear and lack explicit values. Also, new traditions are less prominent in people's everyday lives and have less importance in contemporary society compared to old traditions. The non-Karbi writers have been criticised of creating erroneous current narratives, leading in a misrepresentation of the tradition of Kaziranga National Park. This can be observed in the chapter and subsequent chapters of the book. The 'Kajir Ronghangpi tradition', encompassing widely acknowledged 'collective memory' of the past, is being upheld by the Karbis. This book declares that since Kajir Ronghangpi is part and parcel of the Karbi tradition and is at the centre of a worldwide story today, it is essential to reconstruct the history and etymology of 'Kaziranga' based on the 'mythistory' of Kajir Ronghangpi.

THEMATIC FOUNDATION OF THE BOOK

Oral Historians are often seen as reconstructing history with the new sources (oral traditions) of history for present generations, aiming to correct any 'misrepresentations' that may have occurred in the 'written tradition'. William McNeill's argument is pertinent to this book. He stated:

> Historians are always at work reinterpreting the past, asking new questions, searching new sources and finding new meanings in old traditions in order to bring the perspective of new knowledge and experience to bear on the task of understanding the past. This means, of course, that what we know and believe about history is always changing. In other words, our collective, codified memory alters with time just as personal memories do, and for the same reasons.[103]

Thematically this book is divided into two sections. Section-1comprises eight chapters focusing on the importance of the oral history tradition of the Karbis. It also delves into topics addressing the ecological values and traditional knowledge systems of the Karbi people. This section discusses the historical background of the Karbi people and examines the cultural traditions that form the basis for comprehending myths, legends, and other oral narratives that have shaped the history of the Karbis. Section-2 also includes eight chapters. This part focuses on chapters that are dedicated to myth, memory, legend, and narratives and stories related to Kajir Ronghangpi, a mythical figure in the oral tradition of the Karbis. Some chapters discussed the etymological framework of Kaziranga through the stories of Kajir Ronghangpi, providing the basis for explaining the etymological origin of the name Kaziranga. A further significant aspect of this section is that most of the chapters have been developed by Karbi scholars, therefore there is ample room for developing stories about Kajir Ronghangpi from a Karbi perspective.

SECTION I
KARBI ORAL TRADITION

The book series edited by Dharamsing Teron, *Karbi Studies*[104], is a remarkable accomplishment in Karbi historical research. Vulli Dhanaraju, one of the editors of this book, emphasized the importance of this series for scholars who are interested in the study of Karbi oral traditions, comparing it to a philosophical foundation for their research. Teron has developed a unique method for reconstructing the history of the Karbis. The *Karbi Studies* has greatly boosted the interest in Karbi historical research. Any Karbi historical research must recognize, value, and cite the contributions of Teron in this work to be considered valid. He has developed the oral history method to delve into the oral tradition of the Karbis, for instance, *Mosera Kihir*, leading to the method being known as 'recounting the past from memories'. He has been associated with developing various kinds of techniques for gathering oral history material, making him the father of the 'Karbi oral history method'.

Oral tradition emphasises the importance of 'speech' (se) as the basis of human understanding, as exemplified by the well-known phrase 'In the beginning was the word.' Oral traditions offer significant historical insights that might not be present in written records. They provide different viewpoints on events and illuminate often neglected or forgotten aspects of the past. These traditions provide explanations for the current state of affairs and often offer guidance on how things ought to be. Oral traditions, due to their ordered nature and faithful transmission without alteration, can be just as reliable as non-oral methods of recording and transmitting events. Generally, 'Oral Tradition' and 'Oral History' are two recognized concepts that are frequently used interchangeably, despite being different. According to Jan Vansina[105], there is a distinction between the two: Oral historians rely on memories, hearsay, or eyewitness accounts of contemporary events and situations provided by informants who were present during those times. This contrasts with oral traditions, which are no longer considered current. These stories have been shared orally for generations, extending beyond the lifespan of those who originally shared them. He also added that, oral traditions can be communicated through speech, song, or musical instruments. They are transmitted from previous generations but do not always focus on the past or follow a narrative structure. Understanding cultural knowledge and traditions that help bind communities and preserve their history is the essence of oral tradition. Vansina states that oral tradition involves a process of 'intergenerational transmission'. Traditional characteristics involve being part of a living process of transmission, unlike written sources. Thus, he determined that oral traditions serve not only to reconstruct the past but also have their own unique history. It is crucial to thoroughly examine the transmission process to identify any potential alterations and discrepancies from the original historical event. This includes tracing the information from its initial source through each stage of transmission until it is eventually documented and written down. Paul Thompson[106] (1978) defines oral history as 'history built around people'. It imbues history with vitality and broadens its scope. It enables heroes to emerge not only from prominent figures, but also from the lesser-known bulk of the population. It connects history with the community. It assists the underprivileged, particularly the elderly, in achieving dignity and confidence. It facilitates communication and comprehension among different social strata and age groups. For individual historians and others, shared meaning can provide a sense of connection to a specific place or period. It is apparent that oral history presents a challenge to the established notions of history and the authoritative judgment that is inherent in its tradition. It offers a way to radically change the social significance of history. According to David Henige[107] (1982), oral history is viewed as an activity, while oral tradition is considered a genre of historical source. Oral history is studying the recent past through life tales or personal recollections shared by informants about their own experiences. Oral tradition refers to widely recognized memories of the past within a certain culture. Lesser-known versions should be regarded as 'testimony' and, if they pertain to recent events, fall under the category of oral history. Sharon Veale and Kathleen Schilling (2004)[108] made a clear distinction between making use of oral history and oral tradition in recording the history of communities. In their work, it was noted that oral history involves personal stories and memories shared by individuals about the past, as well as the structured collection of these narratives by oral historians and researchers. Stories are frequently passed down through generations within families. Our history is often revisited through our memories, the impressions we hold and can recollect. Exploring memories and the stories we share can provide insight into our sense of 'self' and where we belong. Oral tradition involves a collection of stories transmitted orally from one generation to the next, extending beyond the life time of any single person. It encompasses narratives, music, proverbs, recitations, and historical tales. Studying oral history involves gathering first-hand accounts and memories of past events and experiences from people who have lived through them.

Thus, oral tradition is crucial for the survival of many societies, particularly those lacking a written language. It allows them to save their cultural legacy and transmit it to future generations. Oral tradition is not only concerned with the past but also with the present and future. Our current stories, ritual practices, traditional music and customs will influence the culture of the present and future. This is emphasised by the Karbi idea of time, which is not linear, but the past (*mo*), present (*non*) and future (*aphi*) coexist simultaneously as expressed by the term *mo-non-phi.*

There are a variety of ceremonial rites that are carried out by Karbis on various cultural/religious events. Due to the fact that the Karbis have been forest dwellers, they were raised and brought up in the midst of the natural environment in which they originally resided. The Karbis, like other tribes, have their own deeply held beliefs, which are reflected in the way they interact with one another. There is no disputing that the ceremony is an essential part of Karbi culture. People who practice Karbi beliefs maintain that rituals are an essential component in the process of maintaining their identity. *Chojun* is an important household ritual when ancestor spirits are propitiated. This ritual is held thrice in a row to complete a *Wophong*. (The periodicity of the *wophong* may however vary across various cultural regions.) The other deities propitiated at *Chojun* generally include *Arnam Kethe* (also variously called a *Binong* or *Angsong Asor* or *Barithe*), *Arnam-Kethe a Hi`i* (lesser deity who assists *Arnam Kethe*), *Pampartok* (or *Kampartok*), *Birne*, *Harata*, *Arni* and *Sar*. *Arnam-Kethe* is the Supreme Deity while *Hi`i* and the other deities are subordinate spirit entities entrusted with specific responsibilities which collectively ensure good weather, good health, prosperity etc. The *Sar* is the collective representation of ancestor souls of both male and female lineages which are given the statuses equal to other deities of the Karbi pantheon. The ancestral spirits propitiated must belong to the fourth generation and above thereby maintaining a three-generation gap from the existing one. There are other variations of *Chojun*, but this version is the most common where ancestral spirits are propitiated together with the protective spirit deities who hold the highest place in Karbi pantheon.

Is there any cultural exchange or interaction between the Karbi and neighbouring communities? The Ahoms were among the region's first state to rise to prominence. The state they founded spanned the whole of Brahmaputra valley and lasted approximately 600 years, beginning in the early 13th century. The chapter 'Interface between the Karbis and the Ahoms' by Kadombini Terangpi examines the socio-cultural and political relationship between the Karbis and Ahoms in the precolonial period. The author found that the Karbi culture is distinguished by its distinct nature. According to the author, the previously pervasive lethargy in the society has weakened as a result of external encounters. The Karbis have demonstrated a readiness to participate in cultural exchanges with both the Ahoms and other tribal nations. Simultaneously, they are retaining their culture, which distinguishes them as a unique ethnic group in modern Assam. It is clear that a few issues of related changes in their lifestyle and culture are being noted and communicated among the Karbi and Ahom people nowadays. However, the decline of Ahom kingdom also resulted in the decline of the Ahoms' past grandeur.

Anjana Engtipi's chapter entitled, 'The Significance of Oral Narratives in Karbi Society' describes the role of oral narratives like folktales, folksongs, ballads, myths, and legends in the construction of Karbi identity. This chapter explores Karbi oral narratives to locate their roles in reconstructing Karbi history. Folktales, folksongs, folkdances, ballads, myths, and legends are examples of such oral narratives. In the chapter, the author argues that oral traditions function as a revered conduit for the transmission of ancestral narratives throughout successive generations. Over the course of time, the intricate and significant history of the Karbi people has been carefully crafted and handed down from one generation to the next. The traditional method of storytelling has been manifested via the captivating melodies of narrative songs. The musical chronicles have preserved the spirit of Karbi history by resonating with echoes from the past. The Karbis did not have a written language until the late 20th century. Despite the significant absence, heroic people from the past courageously protected and passed down their valued literary works through the enduring practice of oral tradition, ensuring that these cherished stories endured across countless generations. For example, for any Karbi individual who is truly interested in investigating the migration route/s that their past and unidentified ancestors may have taken to arrive at their current habitat thousands of years ago, it is necessary to study the existing versions of the oral narratives of *Mosera Kihir* and *Kacharhe Alun.*

The chapter titled 'Oral Narratives of Cheleng Athepai and Botor Kikur of the Karbis' by Rashmi Engtipi and Rupali Rongpipi explores the significance of cultural and historical legends in understanding the past of the Karbis, which have not been documented in written form. The authors also collected the oral accounts of *Cheleng Athepai*, which refers to a narrow and steep gorge which was the scene of a tragic event. Annually, the youth of Amri gather to commemorate the *Riso Arnam* (Spirit Deity of Unmarried Youth) by presenting offerings of areca nut and leaves. The *Chengburup*, a small percussion instrument, is prohibited in Amri due to a local taboo. In this discourse, we explore the significance of Jirkedam (youth cooperative) in Karbi society. Karbis have a strong connection to the environment as their livelihood relies on agriculture. The community holds a deep reverence for the weather deity, *Botor Sarpo*, and conducts ceremonies to ensure favorable monsoon rainfall and abundant harvests. Prior to the commencement of *Botor Kikur*, the *Pinpos* (Chiefs), under the guidance of the *Dilli* or *Borpator*, embark on a journey to visit the twelve provinces under traditional governors called *Habes*. During this period, the ceremonies performed were sponsored by the *Habes* of the respective provinces. The ceremonial practice is generally known as *Volo Keter.*

Is there a significant impact that tattoos have on the preservation of cultural traditions? Tattoos have been part of human history for hundreds of years, and tribal tattoos are one of the oldest and most popular types. Tribal tattoos have a long history, dating back to prehistoric times, and have evolved and changed over the years.[109] Indigenous communities initially utilized tattoos to signify their identities, convey their beliefs, and record significant events. Tribal tattoos are still popular and serve as a powerful form of self-expression. In the book titled 'The History of Tattoos and Body Modification,' written by Nicholas Faulkner and Diane Bailey,[110] the writers assert that tattooing is not only an ancient art, but it is also a universal one. It can be found in many cultures that exist all over the world. And while different people may choose to show off their tattoos for a variety of reasons, the common goal is to establish a connection with their communities and the wider world in some specific ways. It is also true that tattoos have a significant cultural significance, especially among Indian tribes. These tattoos are significant in terms of tradition, identity, and spirituality; they are more than just a form of body art or a fashion trend; they represent a way of life. Tattooing is regarded as a highly skilled and revered art form in many tribal groups and hence enjoyed distinct place. Tattooing patterns differ across men and women, cultures, and occupations. Tattoos were viewed as a rite of passage by several communities, marking key turning moments in a person's life. Tattoo art is a form of communication that recounts story and conveys messages. Each tribal tattoo design is extremely symbolic and represents something significant. Tattoo artists are revered in these tribal groups, and their knowledge is passed down from generation to generation. Traditional tattooing techniques usually employ natural colours and hand-carved tools to create distinctive and detailed patterns. Ao Naga and Karbi females were tattooed as part of a rite of passage into adulthood. It represents their individuality, their transition into adulthood, and their readiness for marriage. The chapter 'Making Sense of the Body:

A Comparative Study of Women's Tattooing among the Karbi and the Ao-Naga' by Resenmenla Longchar examines the similarities and differences in tattooing between Ao Naga and Karbi girls, as well as the symbolic value of tattooing. The author observed that in the past, only experienced women were able to excel in the skill of tattooing. Currently, tattoos have gained widespread popularity and are commonly displayed both in public spaces and professional environments. The rising popularity of tattoos, especially among the younger generation, the art form has regained its second life. As the passage of time has occurred, the techniques for administering tattoos have also evolved. In contemporary times, the utilization of advanced tools and high-quality pigments has rendered the process of obtaining a tattoo considerably safer and less agonizing, while also yielding more enduring outcomes. Tattoos serve as a potent medium for conveying and showcasing one's unique identity and uniqueness. It holds various connotations for each individual and serves as a platform for self-expression through the art form of body modification. Likewise, several individuals opt to acquire tattoos as a method of articulating their emotions and views. Occasionally, the emphasis is placed on asserting one's autonomy or cherishing a deep bond. Tattoos and other forms of body art have played a significant and lasting role throughout human history, and they will likely continue to do so in the future. The author provided an analogy by stating that the tattoo designs of the Karbis and Ao Nagas are drastically different. When compared to the complex Ao tattoos, the Karbi tattoo is clearly more modest in style and will undoubtedly endure in the future.

Rites of passage are a type of ritual that are generated by individuals or civilizations to commemorate the development and various stages of their existence, both biologically and socially[111]. A rite of passage is a type of ritual that is performed by individuals or cultures. According to Bowie (2006)[112], rites of passage are a transition from one stage of an individual's or group's life to another stage, events, and seasons, all of which are typically connected with status adjustments. Arnold van Gennep was the one who first proposed the idea of rites of passage. He viewed them as a universal method for organizing human communities through life cycle rituals such as birth, marriage, and death. It has been suggested by Bowie (2006)[113] that the essential structure of rites of passage can be explained using a model that is composed of three distinct components. The transition from one situation to another is represented in a manner that is both obvious and simple by these models, which are referred to as separation, transition, and incorporation/re-aggregation. Between the two stages, the transition stage is referred to as the liminal state, while the separation stage is also referred to as the preliminal state. 'People can change and renew through this process,' says Van Gennep[114]. He continues by providing an example of how elderly persons die to make room for their successors. Van Gennep's statement can be found in Marranci (2008). As a means of elucidating the sequential nature of the three phases, Van Gennep employs the metaphor of a home, in which individuals ascend and descend through the levels to reach their respective rooms. In his argument, Van Gennep contends that the rites of passage have an impact not only on the individual who participates in a particular ritual, but also on the community that he belongs to. As an illustration, in the event of a marriage, for instance, the change in status of the bride or groom is accompanied by a change in the status of their respective families. When it comes to rites of passage, this is the conventional and original perspective. In the context of *Chomangkan*, a secondary cremation ritual of the Karbi people, Amphu Terangpi's chapter, 'The Concept of the Liminal Soul in Karbi Culture,' draws a parallel between the ideas of the Karbis in *Chomangkan* festival and the concepts of liminal soul and its incorporation as discussed by Arnold van Gennep in his work 'The Rites of Passage' and Victor Turner's concept of the 'betwixt and between.' The Karbi people believe in the concept of *angthek*, which refers to indicators of their prior existence. This belief in rebirth allows them to establish a logical connection between the past, present, and future. This is related to the concept of life cycle. The cyclical process of life, death, and rebirth is not only recognized among Karbis, but also in religions such as Buddhism and Hinduism. It is a universal belief system of the humankind. Example of the idea of 'separation' is 'death'. In Karbi culture, after the physical body dies, the soul, which is intangible and undying, travels to a place called *phu-phi arong* or 'ancestors' village' which is the afterlife. For the Karbis, death is a moment of transition during which the soul returns to earth in the same clan in another body in a phenomenon known as *menchi-menvang* (literally – name dead, name return). *Chomangkan* or the funeral festival is an extensive socio-religious and cultural event when the souls of the deceased are reunited with their ancestors', and for the living – it is the strengthening of the kinship network. Turner's concept of 'betwixt and between' can be seen in the Karbi concept of ritlo-pharla which is neither the world of the living nor the world of the dead (*phu-phi arong*), but the soul exists in a liminal place (ritlo-pharla). The soul is in a transitional state, existing on the border between the ancestral village (world of the dead) and the world of the living. This allows us to realize that the soul is in the 'stuck' or 'trapped' phase, and hence, it is a 'liminal soul'. That is why, in the Karbi worldview, if *Chomangkan* is not yet performed for the departed, the souls are stuck in a 'liminal space'.

The indigenous Karbis have long upheld a body of customary laws that form the basis of their social structure. The strong culture and traditions of the community are intended to be preserved and passed down to future generations through the implementation of these laws. In this framework, how can we understand the concepts of women empowerment and economic self-reliance? Assam has a considerable tribal population, with the Karbis being one of the most prominent tribal residents in the two districts of Karbi Anglong (East) and Karbi Anglong (West). Women play a vital role, particularly in terms of societal and familial economic progress. Gender empowerment can be apparent in local markets, where Karbi women predominate. Indigenous knowledge of the environment, participation in rituals, and expertise in traditional crafts have all been important factors in becoming economically self-sufficient, making Karbi women the backbone of their families and a potential contributor to the development of the society. However, nowadays women face many challenges, pointing out that the neoliberal economy has created disparities in the society. Barnali Sarmah's chapter 'Gender Empowerment and Economic Self-Reliance among Karbi Women: An In-Depth Analysis' made a fascinating observation about gender equality in Karbi society. As the author mentioned in this chapter, the local markets are a thriving hub where various women sellers actively sell their locally manufactured items and crafts as stated by a Karbi man. This insight reflects women's societal status. According to man's claim, women actively participated in a variety of economic pursuits. These operations included a variety of tasks such as cultivation, pruning, weeding, and the difficult process of clearing the forest for *jhum* cultivation. Women were also involved in the collection of fruits, tubers, and other useful resources. Their enormous contributions to these economic undertakings were crucial to the survival and development of their community. According to the author, this contribution is particularly important because these women participate in public activities, such as selling items at the local weekly market. This phenomenon distinguishes the Karbi women, emphasizing their uniqueness and demonstrating their empowerment in terms of gaining economic independence. The evidence presented gives a clear picture of Karbi women's tenacity, as they take on a wide range of responsibilities, from household maintenance to actively contributing to their families' financial growth. The author also identified three key characteristics as fundamental indicators of economic self-reliance among Karbi women, and based on these, the author argued that Karbi women embody the spirit of women's empowerment, confronting challenges with unwavering confidence and asserting their influence as the foundation of their families. Karbi women, with their wealth of traditional knowledge, skills, and ability in agriculture, medicinal herbs, and weaving, have enormous potential as entrepreneurs. With suitable training in entrepreneurship skills, these women would definitely make major contributions to the growth of their families and society as a whole.

Tribes and their societies typically attribute great spiritual and cultural importance to forests, considering them as sacred spaces for conducting rituals, sharing narratives and establishing a link with their ancestors. Vulli Dhanaraju and Dawatshogmo Lama's chapter, 'Ecological Values of the Karbi Belief System,' tries to look into the cultural practices of the Karbis that relate to nature and ecology, highlighting their importance in ensuring the preservation of the natural environment. The Karbis exhibit a plethora of distinct cultures that are deeply ingrained in a strong spiritual bond with their land and its abundant natural resources. They do not see themselves as separate from nature, but rather as an essential component of it. The Karbis regard Karjong (soul) as sacred, believing it to be a manifestation of the creator that exists in all of his creations. This respect applies to all living creatures and supernatural entities. The author noted that the indigenous belief systems surrounding sacred groves (*arnam keso*, literally *angry gods* in Karbi) significantly influence the understanding and development of sustainable conservation strategies among the Karbis. The sacred groves of the Karbis play a crucial role in conserving and safeguarding ecological diversity. Hence, it is imperative to protect and enhance the traditional values and systems that uphold biodiversity preservation, alongside mainstream conservation endeavors.

Ethnic communities around the world experience and interact with environment in unique ways depending on their traditional knowledge and belief systems. With a long history of attachment to the relevant ecological surroundings, they have developed specific ecological knowledge and abilities to support their lives and livelihoods. Similarly, the ethnic people of Assam have created the current cultural landscapes using their traditional ecological knowledge and abilities. The state's rural inhabitants have maintained a cordial relationship with the environment through an intimate engagement with natural landscapes and the prudent use of ecological resources. However, the introduction of modern socioeconomic activities has altered the traditional ecological knowledge and skills (TEKS) held by various ethnic groups. The TEKS, which have been passed down through generations and cultural transmission, have only recently been recognized as having tremendous cultural and ecological benefits, which are important for ecology conservation and sustainable management as well in the current context of environmental degradation. Many experts believe that the TEKS have become increasingly significant as the majority of them have been recognized as supplementary and equivalent to scientific knowledge. Furthermore, the TEKS have the ability to help mitigate the climate change challenges. The last chapter of this section, 'Traditional Ecological Knowledge and Skills (TEKS) of the

Karbis: The Case of Magursila Village of Kamrup Metro District, Assam,' by Barasha Rani Das and Nityananda Deka, explores and documents the Karbi traditional ecological knowledge and skills. This study is considered significant because it has the potential to explore traditional nature conservation measures and sustainable livelihood practices of an ethnic community, which may encourage researchers, environmentalists, ecologists, and policymakers to investigate such practices and manage natural resources in a sustainable manner by incorporating TEKS. The writers noted in the chapter that traditional ecological knowledge and abilities are firmly ingrained in the folk life and culture of the Karbi people who live in Magursila village in the Kamrup plains. Their daily lives and traditional activities rely heavily on the natural resources available in their environment. They strive to maintain an intimate and harmonious relationship with environment because they recognize that nature continues to sustain their lives and cultures on its own. As a result, nature is strongly represented in their folk culture. During the course of the study, the authors also made observations regarding current shifts in the traditional ecological knowledge and skills. Ethnic life in this community has also begun to change as a result of modern material culture. The rise of sub-urban transportation and communication development has already reduced the temporal distance between cities and villages. Interestingly, changes in traditional farming practices, green cover, and housing in the village have begun to have an impact on the area's ecological system. As a result, the looming shifts in cultural landscapes will undoubtedly overwhelm the village's generally rich natural environment. They also suggested some strategies to preserve traditional ecological knowledge. The authors believe that maintaining a sustainable relationship with nature necessitates the preservation of traditional ecological knowledge and skills for a sustainable socio-cultural existence. In addition, there is an urgent need for well-documented instances of such TEKS that are utilized by villagers. If these examples were to be transmitted to other locations that are comparable, they would surely be of help in the management of natural settings on the one hand, and in the maintenance of rural livelihoods on the other.

SECTION II
ORAL TRADITION OF KAJIRRONGHANGPI

Many articles and books have investigated into the Kaziranga National Park from different perspectives. No article has delved into the oral tradition of 'Kaziranaga'. This book revolves around the 'mythistory' of Kajir Ronghangpi, who inspired the naming of Kaziranga. Kajir Ronghangpi is not just known for her inspiration in the etymological framework of 'Kaziranga', but also for being a 'living oral tradition' of the Karbis in the surrounding areas of the Kaziranga National Park, which has become the flagship conservation effort of the state today. This tradition probes into identity, culture, ritual performances, man-animal relationship, eco-philosophy, indigenous knowledge systems, 'space and time', gender equality, and more. However, some traditions of the Karbis have been altered because of external influences and the state's institutional claims over the land of 'Kaziranga.' This book explores the historical factors leading to the deterioration of the oral tradition of Kajir Ronghangpi, the appearance of new traditions, and the persistence of the existing ones. When examining the idea of 'the invention of tradition' as presented in this book, it is crucial to appraise the Karbi perspective on the reinvention of the Kaziranga National Park, which has been transmitted through the oral tradition of Kajir Ronghangpi. A total of 8 chapters have been included in this section. Each chapter explores the oral tradition of Kajir Ronghangpi in relation to the argument presented in the introduction chapter.

Elwin Teron's chapter 'Kajir Ronghangpi: The Legends in Rongkhang' attempts to provide an academic foundation for the narrative pertaining to Kajir Ranghangpi. This chapter declares Rongkhang to be the cultural 'epicentre' of the Karbi people. According to the author, the Karbi Anglong Autonomous Council's (KAAC) decision to hold an elaborate celebration of the legend of Kajir Ronghangpi has sparked renewed academic interest in the life and times of the Karbi legendary lady after whom the Kaziranga National Park is thought to have been named. However, other from brief write-ups on the subject by Ajit Timung and Dhaneswar Engti, there are limited materials available for studying the mythical person.

In this context, it is critical to search the huge expanse of public memory for any information that could be used to reconstruct a plausible historical, mythical, or legendary story about the subject, particularly on her familial ancestry, works, exploits, or myths. After interpreting the oral interviews, the author argued that any noteworthy events, accomplishments, or tragedies that have an enduring influence on the Karbi people would be recollected and deliberated in Rongkhang. The analysis has serendipitously revealed new facets of the narrative, and further investigation may unveil other insights into the life and era of Kajir Ronghangpi. This chapter offers fresh insights on the oral tradition of Kajir Ronghangpi.

Serdihun Teronpi, Beena Rongpipi, Rengka Timungpi, and Maggie Katharpi's chapter, 'The Legend of Kajir Ronghangpi through the Lens of the Collective Memory of the Karbis,' explores the significance of myths and folktales in relocating the 'distorted history' of the 'self' while contesting viewpoints are perpetuated through the lens of the 'other.' Rhino Lady Kajir Ronghangpi is one of those individuals who the Karbis remember in everyday activities. Since language and migration are dynamic agents of change, the culture, and history of the community also change with time, which often distorts 'collective memories'. Many oral narratives glorify Kajir Ronghangpi, giving us different shades and tones of the Rhinoceros Lady's life and lore. But the colonial and post-colonial State of Assam has largely used this term to refer to the Kaziranga sanctuary. As a result, many of us are completely unaware of her identity, history, or anything else connected to her. However, her name is a living memory for the Karbi reflected in socio-cultural practices and traditions. In this context, this chapter attempts to investigate how the community's 'collective memories' were represented through folktales and myths, and how such elements have represented Kajir Ronghangpi's persona, and vice versa, as well as what made and transformed her into the person we know her as today. According to the authors, Kajir Ronghangpi's life narratives serve to provide a historical perspective on past events and occurrences, with the goal of revitalizing historical narratives, deeply engraving and cementing Karbi history in our collective memory. The historical and mythological traditions surrounding

Kajir Ronghangpi prove that such a person existed. The authors are deeply influenced by the memories of Kajir Ronghangpi and her wonderful traits. According to the version the authors could gather – Kajir Ronghangpi was beautiful, fluent in Assamese, competent, and intelligent in commercial dealings. This observation emphasizes the importance and position of women among Karbis. Rarely is a village named after a woman. However, Kajir Ronghangpi has effectively challenged her opponents, as the very mention of Kaziranga serves as a reminder of her stature. The fact that a specific site has been named after her demonstrates that women can achieve significant position. This speaks well of the Karbis, a society traditionally prioritizing women, which is commendable. Kajir Ronghangpi is a character of historic proportion. The recurrent elaborations depict Karbi history via the life of Kajir Ronghangpi.

Perspective is a key concept in academic discipline and plays a vital role in the comprehension of epistemologies of phenomena. At the same time, there are two premises in history writing. The first premise is that history that is written based on empirical sources is called 'scientific history, and the other is that 'histories' are a sort of history told from the perspective of groups that are marginalized in history writing. Keeping these two premises in mind, the argument presented by Junmoni Hansepi and Sumi Daa-dhora in the chapter titled 'Exploring the Multiple Narratives of Kajir Ronghangpi' is based on oral narratives that are still being told by the local people living in and around Kaziranga. This chapter presents a detailed analysis of the oral history discourse. This discourse frequently functions to magnify the voices of disadvantaged or disregarded individuals or communities, offering them a forum to share their narratives and articulate their viewpoints. The primary focus of this chapter is to understand the stories of Kajir Ronghangpi and how these stories help in reconstructing the history of the Karbi people. This reconstruction can potentially lead to an accurate portrayal of the Karbis in the present historical discourse. This chapter concludes by stating that historians, while conducting study on historical events or persons, present unique perspectives that are shaped by factors such as their cultural background, personal experiences, ideological beliefs, or the specific research questions they want to answer.

These perspectives exert a significant impact on historians' choices and analysis of evidence, focus on certain events or individuals, and creation of narratives. This chapter explores the concept of multiple narratives that are connected to the mythical legend of Kajir Ronghangpi. By examining these narratives from a different perspective, it offers a new insight into the historical understanding of the origin of 'Kaziranga'. The only way to accomplish this is by reconstructing the event or individual through the use of oral history discourse. This discourse helps us in reconstructing the history of marginalized or overlooked members of society. Reconstruction is crucial for the proper representation. The process of reconstructing history often gives rise to various interpretations of a particular historical event or historical figures. Gaining insights from several viewpoints is beneficial when examining a past experience.

The historian's viewpoint of myth as a matter of interest has changed over the course of time. At first, there was an inclination to disregard myth as an undeserving field of inquiry. Nevertheless, it is evident that the belief in myth is a widespread and significant component of human nature that cannot be disregarded by those responsible for understanding the complexities of the human story. When examining the historical event, it is crucial to carefully assess the accuracy of the many viewpoints expressed by the people involved. To differentiate between genuine and false accounts, it is necessary to thoroughly analyze the available information. By carefully examining the consistency between oral stories and the existing data, we can identify those that are in agreement with the historical facts, as well as those that show inconsistency and should thus be classified as mythical. In their chapter titled 'Kajir Ronghangpi: What Makes her a Mythological Figure in Karbi History,' Langmili Terangpi, Mirbin Katharpi, and Arnika Terangpi discuss the myths and folktales associated with Kajir Ronghangpi, as well as the connection between Kajir Ronghangpi and Kaziranga. Myths that revolve on Kajir Ronghangpi are told in the Kaziranga National Park, which contains numerous such tales. This location has been generously provided by nature with a wide variety of plants and wildlife. The authors presented their argument by stating that the accounts surrounding the well-known figure of Kajir Ronghangpi, as recounted in folk narratives and mythologies, show some consistency, despite the fact that there are notable variations due to the diverse recollections, regional perspectives, belief systems, cultural practices, and traditional customs of the people present. The tales of her extraordinary feats have endured beyond the passage of time and have been passed down from generation to generation without fail. Throughout the years, succeeding generations have found that it is elusive and unfamiliar due to a lack of documentation and sources. The position of Kaziranga in Karbi history is a contentious issue, and this is something that must be acknowledged. Kajir Ronghangpi is a figure of immense significance, yet our renowned folklorists and mythographers have been unable to figure out the particular origins and historical trajectory of this character. This is the main reason for this variation. The stories that Kajir tells continue to serve as a source of motivation, creating in us a profound sense of connectedness to our fellow humans and the greater community. She occupies a crucial position within the illustrious Karbi Cultural Heritage, and she plays an important part in educating the future generation about the Karbi past that is so rich.

Ramesh Kathar and Sangita Das' chapter 'The Story of Kajir Ronghangpi via the Memories of the Local People' attempts to provide insight into Karbi's legendary figure, Kajir Ronghangpi, who is portrayed as a nature lover who achieved divinity after her earthly voyage. This chapter began the discussion by claiming that the origin of the mythic legend Kajir Ronghangpi is not only related to the location of Kaziranga National Park, but also to the oral tradition, culture, and ritual of the people who have lived there for centuries. Existing myths and folktales, folklore, and narratives about Kajir Ronghangpi that are widely held by locals may open the way for greater scientific and methodical inquiry into the subject. Until now, little research has been undertaken on the famous lady Kajir Ronghangpi, and textual sources are insufficient for future studies. The chapter is based on three oral narratives that the authors gathered from oralists. The authors rightly noted that 'since Kajir introduced the Rhinos to earth at Kajir-Arong (also known as Kajir-Village), these majestic creatures have made it their permanent home.' The Assamese people altered the name from Kajir-Arong to Kaziranga due to a lack of understanding of the Karbi language. Kaziranga National Park is well-known for its one-horned rhinoceros. There are various reasons for such misrepresentations, such as a lack of documented proof and a failure to understand the semantics[115] of specific meanings. This chapter justifies the argument by providing semantics for the numerous words used in the Kajir Ronghangpi narrative.

Places and spaces are fundamental concepts that relate to both the tangible and intangible parts of human existence. Although they have some overlap in their overall meanings, there are significant differences between them. Locations are identified by their distinctive physical qualities. They are associated with geographic locations, landmarks, and tangible things. Locations may include both natural components such as mountains, forests, or rivers, as well as man-made constructions such as cities, buildings, or parks. They have a distinct presence in space and can be observed and experienced using our senses. Locations frequently hold cultural, historical, or personal significance, impacting our interactions, memories, and sense of 'self'. Locations can generate strong feelings of significance, connection, and separation, leading to a location being perceived as sacred, familiar, repulsive, or even strange. Spaces, on the other hand, are more conceptual and include a broader awareness of the environment. They expand beyond physical bounds to include philosophical, social, and symbolic domains as well. Spaces are dynamic and can be shaped and altered by human actions, viewpoints, and interactions. They are influenced by different cultural, social, and psychological factors. The Karbi worldview incorporates the idea of humans and non-humans coexisting in the same space, and the concept of space/place is deeply embedded in their traditional rituals and storytelling. As a result, if the place's agency is valued, it can be used for settlement, farming, and other human activity. There are distinctions amongst entities such as the ancestor's spirit, wild spirit, and territory spirit, but most of them are collectively propitiated annually or after a period of time after establishing or organizing a mutual agreement with the entities, and these pacts are narrated. These pacts are made in the presence of a 'witness', which is typically a natural resource such as plants, metals, trees, and so on. The Karbi initiates this contract by verbal communication. Sometimes the entities of location express their interest by upsetting individuals through disease, possession, or dreams. In this context, Kareng Ronghangpi's chapter 'The Role of Narratives in Transmitting Traditional Knowledge: Exploring Anomalous Places and Spaces in Karbi Worldview in Context with Kaziranga and Other Places' shedding light on the importance of narrative in transmitting traditional knowledge and shaping our understanding and connection to various spaces and places. The Karbi worldview provides unique insights into how stories are used to promote community, maintain cultural history, and cultivate a harmonious relationship with nature. Looking into strange locales such as Kaziranga, Rongbin, Phi-Phu Arong, and Ritlopharla gives fascinating tales that challenge our knowledge and inspire us to explore undiscovered territory. Understanding the power of storytelling enables us to better understand how established knowledge shapes our views and interactions with the environment. The chapter investigates the concept of uncommon locales and areas in Karbi Anglong, with a focus on Kaziranga National Park. The term Kaziranga is synonymous with the Karbi people's narratives and local traditions, dating back to the story of Kajir Ronghangpi, a mythical character associated with the park's founding. Kaziranga is regarded as a sacred site due to its relationship with Kajir Ronghangpi and its critical role in the conservation of a diverse range of plant and animal species, as well as unique geographical features. The chapter also looks into additional concepts of space and place found in Karbi cosmology, such as Rongbin, Phi-phuarong, and Ritlopharla. Kareng argued in the chapter that shared experiences and stories give communities a strong sense of purpose and emotional connection to certain locales. The inherent value of a location is only completely realized when its significance is recognized by the people who live there. Places are extremely important to the Karbi people and feature strongly in their belief systems and storytelling. Take, for example, the village of the dead, Phu-phi arong, which is close to the village of the living but has its own character. Rongbin, on the other hand, is a living village that exists independently of the greater Karbi community yet coexists with it. Kaziranga is an important part of the community's shared memory, as evidenced by stories and oral traditions passed down over centuries. It is a great source of information, providing insights into the past and challenging us to reevaluate our understanding of certain cultural values.

Bandita Teronpi's chapter 'Kajir Ronghangpi: A Living Myth and Folklore of Other Communities/Regions from Northeast India' aims to support the argument for arguing a claim to the Kaziranga National Park by examining the colonial and oral traditions of the Karbis. This chapter also draws an analogy between The Legend of Ka Likai (Meghalaya), The Myth of Tsomgo (Sikkim), The Myth of Unakoti (Tripura), The Legend of Kamakhya Temple (Assam), and the myth of Kaziranga. In this chapter, Teronpi argues that Kaziranga does not necessarily trace its roots to the Assamese narratives from nearby Golaghat and Nogaon areas. Karbi Folklore offers insights into the mythological figure of 'Kajir Ronghangpi', a legendary woman in Karbi history. There is a scarcity of study on the Karbi inhabitants in the region. Oral tradition or narratives are utilized by most tribes as a cultural method to educate and socialize successive generations. In this chapter, Teronpi highlights the Karbi ancestors' migration narratives as they relocated and settled in various regions. Their journey began in North Cachar, Khasi and Jaintia hills and continued to Kamrup and eventually to the plains of Nowgong in various historical periods. In course of their migration, batches of Karbis settled in Kaliabor extending to the Kaziranga region. These movements were recorded in colonial accounts indicating Karbi settlements in Sibsagar, Nogaon, Karbi Anglong, Naga Hills, Kamrup, Sylhet, and even in Goalpara.

Each culture has its own unique traditions and rituals that are firmly embedded in its everyday existence. Occasionally, these narratives or behaviours may seem irrational or difficult to explain to persons from diverse external groups or identities. These narratives or ceremonies serve as a manifestation of human encounters and are passed down from one generation to the succeeding one. The Karbis have an abundance of cultural myths, although the accuracy of some of them may be sceptical due to the absence of historical documents. Due to the lack of adequate documentation, preserving the valuable cultural traditions of Karbi culture, which heavily relies on oral tradition, has become a difficult task. An interesting myth that requires a thorough analysis is the myth of Kajir Ronghangpi, which calls for a new viewpoint. Myths have significantly influenced the formation of individual and societal identities throughout the course of history. They provide narratives that provide individuals and communities with a sense of significance, intention, and inclusion. The last chapter of the book Mongolsing Rongphar and Thejani-iPohena titled 'Myth and Identity Formation: Revisiting the Oral Tradition of Kajir Ronghangpi' seeks to investigate the relationship between myth and the construction of identity. This chapter examines the process of creating, transmitting, and interpreting myths, and investigates how they affect individuals and societies. The primary emphasis is on the extant accounts of the myth of Kajir Ronghangpi, which have predominantly been transmitted through oral traditions. This chapter also seeks to investigate the impact of myths on the formation of a community's identity by examining how myths shape the collective consciousness, worldview, and historical understanding of the community. The authors of this chapter argued that Kajir Ronghangpi's story might be viewed as a rebellious response to external forces. It allows the Karbi community to regain indigenous knowledge, find ancestral territory, and challenge the dominant narratives placed on them. Although the tale has several variants, all agree that there was a woman named Kajir Ronghangpi and that the Karbis settled in the Kaziranga region. The myth also emphasizes and encourages the battle against gender inequality and injustice. It investigates the potential for dramatic change within the Karbi community. It gives information on gender dynamics in the Karbi community. Kajir Ronghangpi is a young girl who challenges conventional expectations and established conventions. The myth empowers Karbi women and helps them establish gendered identities that contradict societal conventions. Thus, the legend of Kajir Ronghangpi serves as a cultural repository, preserving and transmitting shared memories. The Karbi community maintains a strong connection to their history through oral tradition, ensuring the preservation of their cultural norms, principles, and convictions. This active process of cultural transmission fosters a sense of connectedness, common history, and intergenerational togetherness within the Karbi community. The Karbi community's oral tradition emphasizes the importance of myth as an alternative storytelling style, a tool of defiance, and a repository of shared memories. Through a comprehensive inspection and thoughtful analysis of myths, we can get significant insights into the complex processes of identity formation, cultural preservation, and societal transformation. The narrative of Kajir Ronghangpi provides as a compelling example of how myths may form and maintain identities in the midst of external obstacles and the changing dynamics of the modern period.

NOTES AND REFERENCES

1. Edward Stack, *The Mikirs*, David Nutt, London, 1908 (This book had been edited, arranged and supplemented by Charles Lyall), p. 2.
2. Ibid., pp. 2-3.
3. Himangsu Samah, *Toponomy of Nagaon District*, Partridge, 2017, p. 21.
4. See the coverage of the book, Joseph Mali, *Mythistory: The Making of a Modern Historiography*, Chicago / London: University of Chicago Press, 2003, Available at https://press.uchicago.edu/ucp/books/book/chicago/M/bo3616512.html (Accessed on 02/02/2024)
5. See the arguments of these historians: William H. McNeill, 'Mythistory, or Truth, Myth, History and Historians,' in *American Historical Review*,Vol.91 (1), 1986; Peter Heehs, 'Myth, History, and Theory' in *History and Theory*, Vol. 33, No. 1, February, 1994, pp. 1-19; Joseph Mali, *Mythistory: The Making of a Modern Historiography*, University of Chicago Press, Chicago/London, 2003.
6. Ibid.
7. Theodore Reik, *Myth and Guilt: The Crime and Punishment of Mankind*, University of California, 1957.
8. Dharamsing Teron, 'Memories of Migration in Karbi Oral Tradition' in Dharamsing Teron (Ed), *Karbi Studies*, Vol.1, Assam Book Hive, Guwahati, 2008, pp. 175-221.
9. Scott E. Robinson, *Dichotomy in American Western Mythology*, Master of Science (Interdisciplinary Studies), May, 1991 (Thesis Presented to the Graduate Council of the University of North Texas in Partial Fulfilment of the Requirements, Texas).
10. Ibid.
11. Harold M. Foster, 'The New Literacy: Television, Purveyor of Modern Myth,' *The English Journal*, 73, February, 1984. (Cited in Scott E. Robinson, 1991).

12. William McNeill, op. cit.,1986,p. 1.
13. Peter Heehs, op. cit., pp. 1994, 1-19.
14. Joseph Mali, op. cit., 2003.
15. J. Habermas, quoted in John Foster's Review Article on Joseph Mali's *Mythistory: The Making of a Modern Historiography*, University of Chicago Press, Chicago/London, 2003, *Journal of the Philosophy of History,* 2, 2008, pp. 105-118.
16. William H. McNeill, *Mythistory and Other Essays*, University of Chicago Press, Chicago, 1986.
17. Joseph Mali, op. cit., 2003, p. 27.
18. R.G. Collingwood, *The Idea of History*, Oxford, 1976, p. 15 (cited in C.F.G. Lorenz, 'Drawing the line: 'Scientific' History between Myth-making and Myth-breaking' in S. Berger, L. Eriksonas, and A. Mycock (Eds.,), *Narrating The Nation: Representations in History, Media and the Arts*, Berghahn, 2008, pp. 35-55.
19. Joseph Campbell, *The Power of Myth*, Anchor Books, New York, 1991.
20. Jean Baudrillard, *Simulacra and Simulation* (Translated by Sheila Faria-Glaser and Ann Arbor), University of Michigan Press, Michigan, 1981, p. 43.
21. Roland Barthes, *Mythologies*(Selected and translated from French Annette Lavers), The Noonday Press, New York,1972.
22. Rudolph Bultman, 'New Testament Mythology' in Werner Bartsch (Ed,.), *Kerygma and Myth*, 1961 (Cited in Eliot Deutsch in 'Truth and Mythology' in Shlomo Biderman and Ben-Ami Scharfstein, (Eds.,) *Myths and Fictions*, New York, 1993.
23. Julie Sanders, *Adaptation and Appropriation*, New Critical Idiom Series, Routledge, London, 2008. (Cited in J Anne Holden Ronning, 'Some Reflections on Myth, History and Memory as Determinants of Narrative', in *Coolabah*, Vol.3, 2009, Observatori, Centre d'Estudis Australians, Australian Studies Centre, Universitat de Barcelona, pp. 143-151).
24. Roland Barthes, op. cit.,1972, p. 109.
25. Arthur Marwick, *The New Nature of History: Knowledge, Evidence, Language*, Palgrave, Hampshire, 2001, p. 292.
26. Oodgeroo, *My People*, Jacaranda Wiley, Milton, Queensland, 1990 (Cited in Anne Holden Ronning, 'Some Reflections on Myth, History and Memory: As Determinants of Narrative' in *Coolabah*, Vol.3, 2009, pp. 143-151), p. 86.
27. Ross Murfin and Supryia M. Ray, 'Myth' in Ross Murfin and Supryia

M. Ray (Ed.,), *The Bedford Glossary of Critical and Literary Terms,* Bedford, Boston, 2003, p. 284.

28. Barthes, Roland, op. cit., 1972. (Cited in Anne Holden Ronning, op. cit., 2009).
29. Michael Carhart, Book Review on *Mythistory: The Making of a Modern Historiography* in *CLIO*, Vol. 34, No. 1-2, Fall 2004, pp. 1-184, Gale Academic OneFile,link.gale.com/apps/doc/A131937398/AONE?u=anon~2072b5a2&sid=googleScholar&xid=90714cfb. (Accessed on 26/2/2024).
30. Donald R. Kelley, *Faces of History: Historical Inquiry from Herodotus to Herder*, Yale University Press, New Haven, 1998.
31. Pini Ifergan. 'Blumenberg: on bringing myth to an end' in *History of European Ideas*, Vol. 49 (8), 2023, pp. 1236-1251.
32. Anne Holden Ronning, op. cit., 2009, p. 86.
33. Derek Walcott, 'The Muse of History' in Orde Coombes (Ed.,), *Is Massa Dead? Black Moods in the Caribbean*, Doubleday, New York, 1974(Cited in Justin E. Edwards,*Postcolonial Literature: A Reader's Guide to Essential Criticism*, Routledge, London, 2008, p. 64).
34. See *Karbis of Assam*, Available at https://karbi.wordpress.com/ (Accessed on 25/7/2023).
35. 'Did you know – The Possible Love Story behind the name Kaziranga?: in *The Migrator*, December 3, 2016; Available athttps://thenortheasttoday.com/states/assam/did-you-know-the-proba-ble-love-story-behind-the-name/cid2552060.htm(Accessed on 25/7/2023).
36. Karbi name for wild goat is Karjo, which could have degenerated to Kazi in non-native tongues; however, *rangai* is probably an Assamese addition as Karbi word for red is 'ke`er'.Available at https://www.newworldencyclopedia.org/entry/Kaziranga_National_Park (Accessed on 25/7/2023).
37. Ranjt Barthakur and Bittu Sahgal, *The Kaziranga Inheritance, Sanctuary Asia*, Mumbai 2007, p. 29.
38. 'The Brief History of Kaziranga National Park', Available at http://assamforest.in/knp-osc/linkpages.php?u=hr (Accessed on 27/7/2023).
39. Gautam Prasad Baroowah, *Where Wise Owls Dare: The Life of the Rhinoceros in Kaziranga*, Notion Press, Chennai, 2017.
40. C.P. Oberai and B.S. Bonal, *Kaziranga: The Rhino Land*, B.R. Publishing Corporation, Delhi, 2002, p. 28.
41. V.B. Mathur and P.R. Sinha, *UNESCO-IUCN Enhancing our Heritage Project: Monitoring and Managing for Success in Natural World Heritage*

Sites (Technical Report 7), (Opportunities and Limitations for benefit sharing in selected world heritage sites), UN Foundation. (Year and Place of Publication Not Available), p. 14 available at https://web.archive.org/web/20080530041002/http://www.enhancingheritage.net/docs/UNESCOEoH_Project_South_Asia_Technical_Report_07_v1.pdf (Accessed on 12/7/2023).

42. Aji Timung, *The Myth behind the name Kaziranga* , a booklet published by Bhuban Chandra Terang, Integrated Tribal Development Project, Rongmongve Block, Karbi Anglong Autonomous Council, Diphu, 2006, p. 4.
43. 'Kaziranga National Park', Available at https://www.newworldencyclopedia.org/entry/Kaziranga_National_Park#cite_note-history-1(Accessed on 25/7/2023).
44. Sarat Kumar Phukan, *A Linguistic Study of 24 Place Names of Assam*, Available at http://sealang.net/sala/archives/pdf8/phukan2000linguistic.pdf (Accessed on 13/7/2023).
45. John Butler, *Travels and Adventures in the Province of Assam*, Smith, Elder & Co., London,1855, p. 138
46. Medhi Shapna, 'Conservation Induced Marginalization: The Case of Two Tribal Communities of Assam, India' in *International Review of Social Research,* 9(2), 2019, pp. 200-212.
47. E.P Gee, *The Wild Life of India*, Collins, United Kingdom, 1964, p. 143.
48. Sanjay Barbora, 'Riding the Rhino: Conservation, Conflicts, and Militarisation of Kaziranga National Park in Assam', in *Antipode,* Vol. 00 ,No. 0, 2017, pp 1–19.
49. ArupjyotiSaikia, 'Rhinoceros in Kaziranga National Park – Nature and Politics in Modern Assam in Reframing the Environment' in Manisha Rao (Ed,.)*Resources, Risk and Resistance in Neoliberal India* Routledge, Lonodon, 2021, p. 172.
50. 'The Brief History of Kaziranga National Park', Available at http://assamforest.in/knp-osc/linkpages.php?u=hr (Accessed on 27/7/2023).
51. Ibid.
52. Eric Hobsbawm and Terence Ranger (Ed,.), *The Invention of Tradition*, Cambridge University Press (Canto Classics), Cambridge, 1983 (Reprint 2012), p. 1.
53. Ibid., p. 2.
54. Gunaviram Barua, *AsamBuranji* (in Assamese), Publication Board Assam, Guwahati, 2003,pp. 13-14.
55. Edward Stack and Charles Lyall, op. cit., 1908, p. 2.

56. James C. Scott, *The Art of Not Being Governed: An Anarchist History of Upland Southeast Asia*, Yale University Press, New Haven, 2009, p. 22.
57. DharamsingTeron, 'The Colonial Karbis and the making of an Unwarlike People in U. Goswami and A. Dutta (Ed,.),*Making Peace Mutually-Perspectives from Assam*, Bhabani Books, Guwahati, 2021, pp. 137-158.
58. Ajit Timung, op. cit., 2006.
59. Interview with Mr. Darsing Hanse (60), Sarkari Gaonbura, Golaghat District, and resident of Panbari Karbi village, Kaziranga, on March 29, 2023.
60. RengmiliIngtipi conducted an interview with Mr. Darsing Hanse, Mauzadar of Golaghat District and a resident of Panbari Karbi village near Kaziranga, on May 21, 2023.
61. William Robinson, *A Descriptive Account of Assam*, Ostell and Lepage, London,1841, p. 308.
62. Edward Stack and Charles Lyall, op. cit., 1908, p. 5.
63. Ha`imu is a tragic legend who had to embrace death at the hands of a certain Dilli, a powerful traditional elder of the Rongkhang Kingdom who forcibly married her disregarding the fact that she already had a husband and a child. When she died, refusing to eat or drink, her story could not be suppressed, forcing even the Rongkhang Kingdom to deify her, paying annual tribute to her on the occasion of the ritual worship of the spirits of weather, identifying her as a 'Rain Goddess'. To this day, singing verses of Ha`imu is believed to bring rain and good harvest.
64. Bilison Terang of Dholalangso, Chokihola, collected the story from Lodeppi Evelin Ingtipi (July, 2023).
65. Elwin Teron, 'KajirRonghangpi: Legends of Rongkhang', Unpublished paper presented on May 1, 2023 at the Centre for Karbi Studies Lecture Series, Farmers' Growth Centre, Diphu, 2023.
66. A legendary dirge singer known as 'Kare Langlile' who could evaporate river water by the power of her singing is regarded as the dirge-maestro by generations of dirge singers who still has many followers.
67. Ronghang Keplanglapen Ser AnghoiKelongaPhurkimo (January 2023). Published by Ronghang Nok`humChingrum Amei (Estd 2012). Pp. 13 as appearing in Elwin Teron's KajirRonghangpi – The Legends in Rongkhang (paper presented in CKS Lecture Series, held 1st May, 2023 at Farmers' Growth Centre, Diphu).
68. This personality is also referred to as Titua Mikir or Chet Lindok in some accounts, who fled to the plains of Dimoria as a consequence

of conflict among the ruling elders. (For further information, readers may refer to DharamsingTeron and Manas Jyoti Bordoloi, 'Migration Narratives and Ritual Regeneration Among the Karbi and Tiwa of Highland Assam' in J.J.P Wouters and MichaelHeneise (Ed,.),*Routledge Handbook of Highland Asia*, Routledge, London, 2022, p. 291).

69. Elwin Teron, op. cit., 2023.
70. E.A Gait, *Census of India, 1891 (Assam),* Vol. 1, Report, Shillong, 1892, p. 75.
71. See Memorandum Submitted by the Government of Assam to the Indian Statutory Commission, 1930, London, p. 112.
72. E.H Pakyntein, Census *of India, 1961, Assam District Hand Book – United Mikir Hills and N.C Hills*, 1965,p. 11.
73. Ibid.
74. Hamlet Bareh,*History and Culture of the Khasi People*, Published by the Author, Shillong, 1964,p. 55.
75. Edward Stack and Charles Lyall, op. cit., 1908, p. 5.
76. S.K Bhuyan, *Deodhai Asam Buranji*, Department of Historical and Antiquarian Studies, Guwahati, Assam, 1962, p. 98.
77. E.H Pakyntein, op. cit., 1965, p. 11.
78. W.W Hunter, *The Imperial Gazetteer of India,* Vol. X,Trubner& Co., London, (2nd Ed.), 1886 ,p. 151.
79. K.S Singh, *Tribal Ethnography, Customary Law and Change*, Concept Publishing, New Delhi, 1993, p. 26.
80. Edward Stack and Charles Lyall, op. cit., 1908, pp. 2-3.
81. Himangsu Samah, *Op. cit* , 2017, p. 21.
82. Sarar Sarma, 'Glimpses of Kajir's Realm – Karbi Village inside Kaziranga to Showcase way of Life' Published 24.09.07, Availbaleathttps://www.telegraphindia.com/north-east/glimpses-of-kajir-s-realm-karbi-village-inside-kaziranga-to-showcase-way-of-life/cid/684839 (Accessed on 21/7/2023)
83. Himangsu Samah, *Op. cit* , 2017, p. 41.
84. Ibid., p. 42.
85. See *Calcutta Christian Observer, Vol. 5 (January to December, 1836)*; Edited by Christian Ministers of Various Denominations & Printed at the Baptist Mission Press, Circular Road, Calcutta, p. 171.
86. Interview with Rajen Hanse (67) of Panbari Karbi village, near Kaziranga National Park, on July 18, 2023.
87. Narrated by Longsing Bey (74), Murap, Karbi Anglong West on July 21, 2023.
88. The sacred prayer is shared by knowledge keeper and ritual practi-

tioner Adv. Dhoni Son Lekthe, Diphu Judicial Court and Headman of Monsing Lekthe village, Volongkom Aji. Only a relevant stanza has been quoted here.

89. Valentine B. Sohtun, 'Anglo-Khasi War: Tribal Warriors and their Weapons' in *Migrator*, September 19, 2019. Available athttps://thenortheasttoday.com/states/meghalaya/the-khasis-of-meghalaya/cid2532764.htm (Accessed on 20/7/2023).
90. Arupjyoti Saikia, *Forests and Ecological History of Assam, 1826-2000*, Oxford University Press, New Delhi, 2011, p. 270.
91 E.P Gee, op. cit.,1964, p. 144.
92. E.Rashkow, *The Nature of Endangerment in India: Tigers, 'Tribes', Extermination and Conservation, 1818-2020*, Oxford University Press, London, 2023, p. 115.
93. See https://karbianglong.gov.in/departments/forestry
94. John Butler, *Travels and Adventures in the Province of Assam*, Elder Smith, United Kingdom,1855, p. 219.
95. Karen Armstrong, *A Short History of Myth*, Canongate Books, United Kingdom, 2008, p. 1.
96. Devdutt Pattanaik, 'No society can exist without myths'in *Hindustan Times*, July 4, 2016, Available at https://www.hindustantimes.com/books/no-society-can-exist-without-myth-says-devdutt-pattanaik/story-PG1v4iB17j07dV5Vyv86QN.html (Accessed on November, 16, 2023).
97. Mary Midgley, *The Myths We Live By*, Routledge, London and New York, 2003, p. 1.
98. Joseph Mali, op. cit., 2003, p. xii.
99. Ibid.
100. Ibid.
101. Edward Stack and Charles Lyall, op. cit., 1908, p. 5.
102. Eri Hobsbawmand Terence Ranger, op. cit., 2012, p. 10.
103. William H. McNeill, 'Why Study History?'(1985) Available at https://www.historians.org/about-aha-and-membership/aha-history-and-archives/historical-archives/why-study-history-(1985) Accessed on (12/3/2024).
104. Dharamsing Teron, *Karbi Studies*, Vol. I-IV, Assam Book Hive, Guwahati, 2008, 2011 and 2012.
105. Jan Vansina, Oral Tradition As History, University of Wisconsin Press, Madison, 1985, pp. 12-13.
106. Paul Thompson, *The Voice of the Past – Oral History*, Oxford University Press, Oxford, 1978 (Reprint 2000), p. 18.

107. David Henige, *Oral Historiography*, Longman, London and New York, 1982, p. 2.
108. Sharon Veale and Kathleen Schilling, *Talking History: Oral History Guidelines*, Department of Environment & Conservation, New South Wales, Cultural Heritage Division, 2004, p. 2.
109. Editor, 'The Cultural Significance of Tribal Tattoos: A Journey Through Time' in *Funhouse Tattoo*, Available at https://funhousetattoosd.com/2024/03/11/the-cultural-significance-of-tribal-tattoos-a-journey-through-time/ (Accessed on 15/03/2024).
110. Nicholas Faulkner and Diane Bailey, *The History of Tattoos and Body Modification*, Rosen Young, New York, 2018.
111 Gabrielle Marranci, The *Anthropology of Islam,* Oxford University Press, New York, 2008.
112. F. Bowie, *The Anthropology of Religion: An Introduction*, Blackwell Publishing, Australia, 2006.
113. Ibid.
114. Gabrielle Marranci, 2008, Op. cit. Also see in Najah Nadiah Amran and Rozita Ibrahim, 'Academic rites of passage: reflection on a PhD journey', in *Procedia-Social and Behavioral Sciences*, 59, 2012, pp. 528-534.
115. Semantics is a systematic study of 'meaning'. This has been employed in Semantics philosophy, which is the study of word and sentence meanings. It describes how native speakers interpret sentences by examining the links between linguistic structures, non-linguistic concepts, and mental representations.

SECTION I

KARBI ORAL TRADITION

CHAPTER 1

Interface between the Karbis and the Ahoms

KADOMBINI TERANGPI

INTRODUCTION

The Karbis are a major ethnic tribe of Assam living in the district of Karbi Anglong. Known for their policy of non-interference and self-sufficiency, the Karbis are considered to be one of Assam's first tribes to inhabit the present region by Bishnu Prasad Rabha, a doyen of Assamese culture and nationalism.[1] Due to the minimal written records, it is very challenging to trace the age-old history of the Karbis. However, they have a rich repository of resources found in their legends, myths, songs, socio-religious practices, and other cultural aspects of their society. The oral narratives like *Kathi keplang*, *Mosera kehir*, *Thap keplang*, *Kecharhe*, and *Pirthe keplang* have significantly contributed to the construction of their history. Although we have some written records about the Mikirs, such as the works of Edward Stack and Charles Lyall, there remains a significant gap in research regarding a comprehensive examination of Karbi society as a whole. This is primarily due to the lack of comprehensive and systematic research conducted on the various aspects of Karbi society. This is mostly due to the lack of comprehensive and systematic research conducted on the different facets of the Karbi society. One of the objectives of this paper is to examine the interactions and cultural exchanges between the Karbis and the Ahoms. This study focuses on examining the socio-cultural and political relationship between the Karbi and the Ahom communities. It is based on a thorough investigation and interpretation of diverse sources pertaining to the Karbi-Ahom kingdom. Both primary and secondary sources were utilized in this study.

HISTORIOGRAPHICAL OUTLINE

Only a limited number of researchers have undertaken research and authored publications on the Karbi people. Edward Stack, with the assistance of Sardoka Perrin Key, successfully documented their observations on the "Mikirs" in a written publication. Charles Lyall, after editing, arranging, and supplementing Edward Stack's work, produced a book titled *The Mikirs*[2]. In this book, Lyall extensively discusses the 'Mikirs' (now Karbis), making it a significant and primary source for understanding the Karbis. Lakshmi Devi's book, *Ahom-Tribal Relation: A Political Study*, provides additional insights about the relationship between the Karbis and the Ahoms[3]. Dharamsing Teron's book also discusses the relationship between the Karbis and the Ahoms.[4] Phukan Chandra Phangcho, another Karbi writer, also emphasizes the Ahom-Karbi relationship in his work[5].

AHOMS AND THE KARBIS

The Ahom reign in Assam was the first ruling dynasty to attain eminence in the history of India's northeast region. Beginning in the early 13th century, they ruled for 600 years, forming an extensive empire that encompassed the entire Brahmaputra valley. The Ahoms belong to the Shan branch of the larger Tai or Thai family.[6] Sukapha widely recognized as the first Ahom ruler is also the founder of the Ahom dynasty. An important contribution of Sukapha was his meticulous record-keeping[7], which later came to be known as Buranji. The Ahom Buranji is highly regarded as a significant historical source. The Ahoms consistently maintained cordial relations with the tribal communities, characterized by a fundamental approach of conciliation.

The Karbis, who identified themselves as *Arleng*, meaning men, were an ethnically uniform group among the Tibeto-Burman ethnicities of the region.[8] Their primary habitat was the densely forested hills, known by their name, located inside the triangular region formed by the Brahmaputra River to the north, the Dhansiri valley to the east, and the Kopili and Jamuna valleys to the west and south. The tale of the early history of the Karbis was undoubtedly a blend of reality and legend as mentioned by Basanta Das[9]. Based on these accounts, they were once formidable rulers in their own way. *Sot Richo* (Raja), the final ruler of his kingdom, faced mistreatment from his people.[10] In response, he placed a curse upon them, condemning them to endure countless years without the guidance and protection of a sovereign. The Karbis are still believed to be anticipating the cessation of this curse. Exploiting the lack of a leader among the Karbis, a king from the lowlands conquered their land. The Ahoms were able to achieve the subjugation of the Karbi area. Thereafter they dispersed in various directions, and a portion of the Karbis established themselves in the regions of Kamrup and Nowgong.[11]

According to Colonel Dalton[12], the Mikirs were originally settled in the North Cachar Hills but were driven westward into Jaintia territory by the Kacharis. Dissatisfied with the reception they received, they sent an embassy to the Ahom Governor at Raha, offering to place themselves under his protection. However, since the unfortunate delegates were unable to make themselves understood, they were forthwith buried alive in a tank that the officer was excavating. Hostilities ensued, but the Mikirs were soon suppressed and were settled in the hills that bear their name, though a considerable colony are still to be found in south Kamrup and the northern slopes of the Khasi Hills. They are divided into four tribes or region, Chinthong, Rongkhang, Amri and Dumrali, and these tribes are again subdivided into various exogamous groups. In the hills, the 'Mikirs' practiced jhum or shifting cultivation growing crops such as cotton, chilies, rice and vegetables. All the members of a family lived in one house, which was thus of considerable size.

Among the 'Mikir' tribes, *Chinthong* and *Ronghang* rank higher than Amri because it is said that Amri declined to send a representative on dangerous missions to the Ahom king in Sibsagar when a delegate was required from each tribe. Hence Amri is excluded from sharing the liquor at a sacrifice and rather looked down upon by the western

Mikirs in particular. Dumrali acted as interpreters to the embassy at the Ahom kings. Hence, we may presume that the 'Mikirs' had been settled in the Assam Valley for some time.

MIGRATION STORIES OF THE KARBIS AND CULTURAL INTERFACE

According to the Karbi oral traditions, the Karbis migrated from the Khasi and Jaintia Hills, located near the Kopili river. A significant number of Karbis still reside in this area. This region is referred to as Nihang, in contrast to Nilip, the Duar Baguri region where they previously lived. They were eventually forced out of this area by the Kacharis. Displeased with their new living arrangements, they ultimately sought refuge under the patronage of the Ahom king. However, there were two traditions that provided insight into the migration and settlement of the Karbis in the past.

Both traditions corroborate and elucidate the Chinthong migration towards the eastern region from the Rongkhang hills. Their establishment in the Diphu-Lumbajong region and the Dimapur-Dhansiri valley appears to have taken place subsequent to the complete abandonment of Dimapur by the Kacharis[13]. Consequently, these areas experienced a decline in population, and the Chinthong community found it favorable to settle there around the 16th century.

Consequently, these individuals acquired the appellation Dumrali or Thoi aso or Thoi asor, which denotes a resident of the plains according to their counterparts residing in the highlands. The areas of Sonapur, Khetri, and Jagiroad, located between the East Khasi Hills to the south and the Kalang River to the north, are collectively referred to as Dimoria (possibly derived from the term Dimarua, which may have originated from Dumura). According to the story or legend, once king Dumura received a golden banana flower as present from the Syiem of Khyrim. Upon receiving news of these costly gifts, an individual named Titua or Situa Rongpi felt jealous. He plotted and successfully assassinated Dumura, acquiring not only the coveted golden banana flower from him but also Dumura's reign. The younger brother of the King, Noongphalang, managed to flee and sought sanctuary in Jamunamukh. Titua was ultimately vanquished by Noongphalang in a confrontation, although he successfully evaded capture and fled with the important item to Baropujia, located near Raha. Noongphalang successfully regained control of the Dumura throne and subsequently maintained his dynastic reign. Titua reassumed leadership over a group of Karbis in Baropujia during the time when Srimanta Sankardev, the Vaishnavite leader of Assam, passed away. Upon learning of Sankardev's demise, a group of Brahmins from Kanauj traveled to Bardua, his birthplace, and encountered Titua Rongpi during their journey. Titua assisted the Brahmins from Kanauj in locating the route to Bardua by dispatching a group of Karbi individuals to accompany them. Subsequently, these Brahmins facilitated the conversion of some of them and some of his followers in Baropujia to Vaishnavism, resulting in their transformation into Koch.

The narrative suggests that Dumura and Syiem of Khyrim maintained amicable relations. The arrival of the Brahmins following the demise of Srimanta Sankardev and their encounter with the Titua, also involved the fact that Karbi settlements had already commenced at Baropujia/Raha, around the mid-16th century or somewhat beyond, as Srimanta Sankardev passed away in 1569 A.D. Also, it was reported that Srimanta Sankardev appointed one of his Karbi disciples to propagate the teachings of Vaishnavism among the Karbis. Thus, the evidence suggests that the Karbis resided in the plains of Raha throughout the 15th century, and a significant number of them embraced Vaishnavism in the early 16th century. The above narrative also demonstrates that the kingdom of Dumura was founded in the early years of the sixteenth century, if not prior to that. Further, it could be determined that the Dumralis were in fact the Amris. The Karbis of Raha-Baropujia were in close proximity to the Amris as the areas were geographically adjacent. It is also highly likely that these individuals came to be known as *Dumuralis*, similar to their neighbours..

The migration of the Karbis from the Khasi and Jayantia Hills to the Duar Baguri in the 17th century is documented in a single Buranji. Under the rule of King Jayadhvaj Singha (1648-1663 A.D.), the Ahom kingdom erected outposts at Raha and Jagiroad to prevent the Kacharis from invading their territory. Teleka Sandikai, the king's father-in-law, was appointed as the Rohial Barua or the Ahom Governor in Raha. He was accompanied by four loyal lords and a large number of people. Eventually, *Teleka Sandikai* observed a blaze atop the adjacent hills.[14] He sent his officers to examine those locations. They encountered villages inhabited by industrious settlers. Such settlers scattered to several locations upon witnessing the Ahom army. The Ahom warriors appropriated the sustenance that they were able to save from the abandoned residences. The elderly and frail hill men who remained at home due to their physical weakness were very delighted to observe that the Ahom warriors had consumed their meal. Based on that, they deduced that they belonged to the same social class as themselves. These individuals, confident in their security, arranged for the repatriation of the escaped individuals. The Karbis presented an annual tribute. The tribute was presented in the form of various items such as cotton and mats, with a total value of Rs. 300 every year. The Karbis were granted authorization by the Ahom monarch to farm a designated area of land adjacent to the hills. Moreover, they were allowed to utilize specific fisheries and river ferries, in exchange for an annual payment consisting of rice and dried fish.

In her book 'Ahom-Tribal Relations'[15], Laxmi Devi stated that the Karbis breached the conditions of their agreement with the Ahoms by refusing to fulfil their obligation of paying the yearly tribute. In July, 1765 A.D., King Rajeswar Singha led an expedition as a consequence of these events. The Ahom soldiers progressed along the Kopili River and annihilated the Karbi dwellings situated in the hills. The Karbis subsequently reached an agreement once more. They were resettled in their villages. This marked the only uprising of the Karbi people against the Ahom dynasty. There is no documented evidence of the Karbis engaging in raids in the Ahom region nor were engage in any raids in other areas as well.

ECONOMIC INTERFACE

The Revenue was collected annually from the common households, either in the form of cash or in kind. A predetermined quantity of tribute was regularly dispatched to the Ahom monarch, and occasionally a small portion of revenue was also transferred to the Karbi King, although it was not obligatory. The revenue collection was facilitated by the *Achom–Asar*, and the gathered funds were thereafter paid to the representative *Wofong–Asar* on a specific date in January. The *Wofong-Asars* were then responsible for depositing the equal amount to the Karbi King[16]. One of the Karbi King namely *Waisong* had the power to allocate the portion to the king on a specific day determined by him. He enforced the social and traditional customary laws with great strength and impartiality throughout the society. Refers to as a great Karbi warrior known as Waisong who took revenge by attacking the Khasia villages one after another and established a liberal state for the Karbis.[17]

The first encounter between the Ahoms and the Karbis occurred around the mid-17th century, during the reign of King Jayadhvaj Singha (1648-63 A.D.). This initial meeting was marked by friendly relations rather than hostility. The Ahom king graciously welcomed the Karbi envoy, assuring them of the privileges granted by his realm and allowing them to establish a settlement within Ahom territory. The condition was that they pay an annual tribute to the Ahom ruler, whom they were obliged to acknowledge as their superior. The Ahoms' generous treatment helped establish amicable relations between the Karbis and the Ahoms. The Karbis consistently adhered to their agreements with the Ahoms[18], except for one instance during the rule of Rajeswar Singha (1751-69 A.D.) when they temporarily postponed the payment of their yearly tribute. Despite this lapse, the Karbis quickly reestablished contact with the Ahoms. Known for their gentle nature and aversion to war, the Karbis even abandoned their weapons when seeking the safety of the Ahom king. This action was necessitated by the Karbis' breach of the agreement, specifically their refusal to pay the annual tribute. In response to which, the Ahom king dispatched two forces to confront them: one led by Nyaisodha Phukan of the Jalambata family, advancing from Chapanala, and the other commanded by Dayangia Rajkhowa of the Sandikai family, approaching via the Kopili River. The outcome of this confrontation was highly significant. Two opposing groups converged at a juncture in the hills and proceeded to ignite the homes and storage facilities of the Karbis. They acquired a substantial quantity of daggers, caps, hoes, spears, goats, and various other items as plunder. Subsequently, they returned and stopped at Raha. Subsequently, the Karbis descended upon Raha collectively, bearing several tributes, and expressed their desire for peace. Nyaisodha Phukan and Dayangia Rajkhowa conferred with each other before conveying the information to the King. The King commanded them to bestow gifts upon the Karbis and resettled them in their own settlement. Consequently, they bestowed gifts to the Karbis and reinstated them in their original positions. This was the first and last expedition sent by the Ahom dynasty against the Karbis.

SOME GENERAL OBSERVATIONS

Several observations have been made regarding the socio-cultural connections between the Karbi and the Ahom communities:

i) The Karbis acquired knowledge of wet farming from the Ahoms.
ii) The Karbis were also incorporated into the *paik* system of the Ahom Administration.
iii) Undoubtedly, there must have been a mutual exchange of cultural influences among the tribes. Consumption patterns, such as the preparation of rice and vegetables through steaming, as well as the inclusion of fish and meat in the diet. Cooking with Soda (Alkane) was exclusively derived from the Ahoms.
iv) The Karbis engage in ceremonies to pacify their forebears. The Ahoms also engage in comparable ceremonies and pay homage to their ancestors.
v) The Ahom rulers granted the Karbi community permission to cultivate a designated area of land situated beneath the hills[19]. They also provided them with fishing resources and transportation services using boats. For countless generations, the Karbis have maintained close connections with fish. The Karbi people paid a tax to the Ahom ruler in the form of Toman, which is dried fish. Since that period, fish has been regarded as a symbol of social prestige in the Karbi society.[20] Individuals who were bestowed with Toman (dried fish) were regarded as having elevated social standing. The tradition of cooperative fishing

among the Karbi tribe began after receiving permission from the Ahom monarch 'Ok-Kipru'. The Karbis' traditional institution and life cycle are depicted, therefore highlighting their cultural history.

vi) Both Karbi and Ahom women possess exceptional weaving skills. Karbi women adopted the practice of using Seleng Chadar from the Ahom people. Conversely, the Ahoms learned to use piba, a type of fabric for carrying infants, from the Karbis. Currently, the use of piba by Ahom women is rare.

CONCLUSION

So far, the study has examined diverse socio-cultural facets of the Karbis and the changes observed throughout the period as a result of the cultural exchange with the Ahoms. Karbi culture is characterized by its unique and distinct nature. However, the previously prevalent state of isolation has weakened. The Karbis have shown a willingness to engage in cultural exchanges, not only with the Ahoms but also with other tribes. At the same time, they are preserving their own culture, which sets them apart as a distinct ethnic group in present-day Assam. During the fieldwork, various issues about the transformations in their lifestyle and culture were observed and expressed. However, on the other side, the Ahom kingdom experienced a decline in both its stature and its distinctiveness. Today, the distinctive culture of the Ahoms has diminished from its former grandeur, and it is now the responsibility of the new generation to retain its magnificence.

NOTES

1. Suren Baishya, *Bishnu Rabha Rachanavali,* Published by Suren Baishya on behalf of Bishnu Rabha Sunwarani Gobeshona Samity, Nalbari, 1982, p. 59.
2. Edward Stack, *The Mikirs*, David Nutt, London, 1908 (This book had been edited, arranged and supplemented by Charles Lyall, (1908).
3. Lakshmi Devi, *Ahom Tribal Relations:A Political Study*, Lawyers Book Stall, Assam, 1968.

4. Dharamsing (Ed), *Karbi Studies: Memories, Myths and Metaphors*, Vol. 1, Assam Book Hive, Guwahati, 2008.
5. Phukan Chandra Phangcho, *The Karbis of North-East India*, Angik Prakshan, Guwahati, 2003.
6. S.K. Bhuyan, *Deodhai Assam Buranji*, Department of Historical Antiquarian Studies, Guwahati, 1962, pp. 101-102.
7. H.K. Barpujari, 'Preface', in Barpujari, H K (Ed.), *The Comprehensive History of Assam*, Vol. I, Publication Board, Guwahati, Assam, 1990, pp. ix–xii.
8. Basanta Das, *Karbi Sanskritir Dhara (A study of the Karbi Culture)*, Karbi Lammet Asong, North Eastern Printer, Guwahati, 2000, p. 1.
9. Ibid., p. 3.
10. Ibid., p. 4.
11. Ibid., p. 4.
12. *Census 1951*, Edited by R. B. Vaghaiwalla. ICS, Superintendent, Census Operations, Assam. Manipur and Tripura, p. vi.
13. Op. cit., p. 5.
14. Gohain B.K., *The Hill Lalung*, Anandaram Barua Institute of Language, Art and Culture, 1993, p. 17.
15. Lakshmi Devi, *Ahom Tribal Relations:A Political Study*, Lawyers Book Stall, Assam, 1968.
16. Mondol Sing Bey, *A Glimpse of the Socio-Political Evolution of the Karbi of Karbi Anglong*, Monjir Press, Diphu, January 2005.
17. Longkam Teron and Deben Gogoi, *Karbi Ratnamala*, Karbi Anglong Zila Sahitya Sabha, Diphu, 2004, pp. 67-68.
18. Mondol Sing Bey, *A Glimpse of the Socio-Political Evolution of the Karbi of Karbi Anglong*, Monjir Press, Diphu, January 2005, p. 15.
19. U.N. Gohain, *Assam under the Ahoms*, Spectrum Publications, Guwahati, 1994, p. 139.
20. Robindra Teron, "Use of Fish in Socio Religious Life of the Karbis" in *Souvenir of Lokimo*, Karbi Cultural Society, 2011, p. 94.

CHAPTER 2

The Significance of Oral Narratives in Karbi Society

ANJANA ENGTIPI

INTRODUCTION

The genre of oral narratives encompasses both fictional and non-fictional accounts, extending beyond mere humorous anecdotes and historical chronicles. Oral narratives, characterized by their intricate nature, have been transmitted across generations, conveyed by fervent orators to fascinated listeners. The historical records indicate that these forms of communication were skillfully tailored to suit the intended audience, displaying a penchant for dramatic flair. The oral narrative, in its essence, bears a closer kinship to the dramatic arts rather than prose. It is noted that the visual aspects of a theatrical performances are captivating and exciting for the audience, but it is important to note that the oral storytelling mostly focuses on the act of attentive listening[1]. In Vansina's seminal work, *Oral Tradition as History* (1985)[2], he highlights the significance of reported statements from the present generation. These statements, as Vansina elucidates, must adhere to certain criteria. Firstly, the message must be conveyed through oral means, encompassing spoken, sung, or called out expressions, often accompanied by musical instruments. Additionally, Vansina emphasizes the crucial element of transmission, whereby the information is passed down through word of mouth. He pointed out that the definition being presented is one that has been crafted specifically for the purpose of aiding historians in their scholarly pursuits. Various scholars from disciplines such as sociology, linguistics, and the verbal arts have put forth their own theories and perspectives. In the field of sociology, for instance, there is an emphasis on the significance of shared knowledge. Within the realm of linguistics, scholars have long been preoccupied with identifying the distinctive features that set a particular language apart from ordinary conversational speech. These language experts, commonly referred to as linguists, have dedicated their efforts to discerning the unique characteristics that differentiate a language as a whole. Similarly, in the domain of the verbal arts, scholars known as folklorists have focused their attention on the intricate elements of form and content that serve to define and distinguish various forms of artistic expression. These dedicated individuals have diligently examined the nuanced features that imbue a piece of art with its distinctive identity. Both linguists and folklorists, through their respective areas of study, have attempted to unravel the intricate tapestry of human communication and artistic creation, shedding light on the distinguishing features that shape and define these realms of human expression.

The practice of oral history entails the meticulous process of conducting interviews with individuals or collectives, with the aim of gaining valuable insights into the lived experiences of a specific era or the unique perspectives of being a member of a particular societal group. The act of conducting interviews with a collective of individuals serves as a means to construct a comprehensive depiction of a particular occurrence, thereby facilitating the preservation of a fragment of the past. This endeavor, often undertaken on a grand scale, assumes the role of safeguarding a significant historical narrative for posterity. When engaging in an interview with an individual, we acquire insights into their personal experiences, which may or may not reflect the prevailing norms and values of their respective era and society. In the pursuit of historical knowledge, it is imperative to expand our understanding of various societal factions, particularly those whose experiences have often been overlooked or inadequately recorded. This includes but is not limited to the working class, ethnic or religious minorities, and women. By delving into the narratives of these marginalized groups, we can gain valuable insights into their lived realities and contribute to a more comprehensive historical account.

ORIGIN OF THE KARBIS

The Karbis, a prominent ethnic group in North East India, have long established themselves as one of the major tribes in the region. Their presence is particularly notable in the hilly regions of Karbi Anglong, Assam, where they have resided in communal settlements for countless centuries. Throughout the vast expanse of the North East, Karbi people have been dispersed, their influence spanning across the entire region. The oral traditions of the Karbis suggest that in the past, they resided along the shores of the Kalang and Kopili rivers. It is worth noting that the present-day Kajiranga area, renowned for its status as a National Park in Assam, was encompassed within their inhabited territory. During the period of Kachari ascendancy, the rulers were compelled to seek refuge in the hilly regions. As a result, a portion of the Kachari population migrated to the Jaintia hills, which were previously governed by the Jaintia kingdom. These Kachari people chose to live under the suzerainty of the Jaintia rulers.[3] During the period under consideration, a significant divide within the Karbi community became apparent.One faction decided to stay in the Jaintia kingdom, while another group set off on an adventure to the northeastern region. This migration was facilitated by crossing the formidable river Barapani, a tributary of the Kopili River. After that, the Karbis explored the Rongkhang Ranges, which was a key event in their historical trajectory. The migration of the Karbis to the Ahom kingdom was marked by the formidable challenge posed by the Burmese invasion.[4]

The Karbi population is predominantly situated in Assam, specifically in the districts of Karbi Anglong, Dima Hasao, and the surrounding plain districts of Kamrup, Nagaon, Sonitpur, and Golaghat, which has been historically documented.

There are different opinions about the term Karbi.[5] According to Barua, the term 'Karbi' might have originated from the Sanskrit words *Kroibya* (flesh) or *Kroibad* (flesh eater). He also stated that the Karbis were an aboriginal community under the rule of the Kachari king. But it is also mentioned that there is no historical evidence to support the above line.[6]

Historically, the Karbis were known as 'Mikir'[7]. The etymology of the term 'Karbi' continues unknown, but it is firmly embedded within the history of the legendary songs pertaining to this particular group of people.[8] The exact roots of this phenomenon are still shrouded in obscurity and have yet to be clearly determined. One school of thought posits that it was bestowed upon the race by American missionaries, while another school argues that it was gifted by the Assamese. The self-proclaimed title of 'Arleng' has been embraced by the Karbi themselves, representing a collective reference to the human species as a whole. This term, derived from the language of their culture, carries the connotation of 'man' in its broadest sense, encompassing both genders within the human population. According to Lyall's description (1908)[9], the term *Arleng* has historically been used to refer to a member of the *Mikir* community rather than a man in general. The Karbi community, known for its rich cultural legacy, is delicately interwoven with a tapestry of folklore, folksongs, and folktales.

IMPORTANCE OF ORAL NARRATIVE IN KARBI SOCIETY

Making use of oral narratives holds significant prominence within the Karbi society, serving as a crucial source for the recollection of past events and the subsequent reconstruction of historical accounts. The Karbi people, historically, have not developed a system of written language or have produced very limited written records. Instead, their cultural heritage has been primarily preserved and transmitted through oral traditions, which hold significant importance within their society. The Karbi people possess a wealth of oral narratives, encompassing various forms such as folktales, folksongs, folk dances, ballads, myths, and legends. Within the Karbi society, the significance of folklore and folktale cannot be overstated, as it serves as a vital component in the preservation of social customs, historical recollections. The Karbis are very rich in oral narratives, which they have passed down from generation to generation.

FOLKTALES

Folktales, an enduring form of oral narrative, have managed to persist within the Karbi Society. A folktale, a recognized genre of narrative, encompasses a fictitious account that has been transmitted orally across numerous generations, spanning several centuries, and occasionally even millennia. The etymology of the term 'folk' can be traced back to its Germanic origins, specifically the German word 'volk.' In the German language, 'volk' denotes the collective concept of 'people.' Folktales, being narratives intended for a wide audience, cater to the collective human experience. Typically, these narratives are characterized by their simplicity, employing easily comprehensible plots conveyed through direct and uncomplicated language.[10] According to Edward Stack's observations, the 'Mikirs', also known as Karbi people, have a history of telling stories or narratives.[11] Folktales, a genre of narrative that has endured the test of time, are stories that have been transmitted orally from one generation to the next. In the realm of folklore, it is widely acknowledged that true folktales lack a singular authorship. As the passage of time ensues, these narratives undergo a process of evolution, transforming into distinct entities as they are recounted by various individuals. These entities, known as 'the folk' or the common people, can be regarded as their creators. The antiquity of numerous folktales is readily apparent. Throughout countless generations, the narratives were transmitted orally, their words resonating through the ages without ever being committed to written form. In ancient times, it was customary for individuals known as storytellers to commit various narratives to memory, thus ensuring their preservation and perpetuation throughout generations. These dedicated individuals would diligently memorize these tales, effectively safeguarding them from the ravages of time and ensuring their continued existence. By undertaking this noble task, storytellers played a crucial role in the preservation and dissemination of cultural knowledge and traditions. The folktales of Karbi include:

1. A Hen and her Lazy friends (*Vopi Ejon Lapen Asangho Atum*)
2. How the Drongo Got its Racket Tail (*Voraju Ani*)
3. The Hog Deer of Pantisang (*Pantisang Aoqhinuqrang*)

4. A lazy spider (*Ijon Kaselet Asangman*)
5. Sita Kamar (*Sita Kamar*)
6. The Legend of Binongvopo (*Binongvopo*)
7. The origin of two-shore (*Kengphi Keplang*)
8. The 'winter-summar way' (*Chung-Phang:okAtovar*)
9. How the Hornbills originated (*Vo:ingkeklapen Voterang*)
10. A Frog and a Tiger (*Teke Lapen Chongho*)
11. The Tigers' Rongker (*Teke Rongker*)
12. Songsar Recho (*Songsar Recho*)
13. The Hingchong Twins (*Hingchong Musoso*)
14. A Black ant and a Frog (*Misorongpo Lapen Chonghokaloso*)
15. The Legend of All Women Village (*Arloso Arong Alamo*)
16. The orphan and the Vulture's feather (*Takun Arveng*)
17. Two Orphan Brothers (*Jangreso Kortete*)
18. The Sunbird and His Wife (*Voso Lindok*)
19. The Sun and the Moon (*Chiklolapen Arni*)
20. The Tiger's Revenge (*Teke Aseme*)
21. The Legend of Baby Hill (*Osothi:I Anglong*)
22. The Tiger and His Human Twin (*Teke Recho*)
23. Mangbon the Brute (*Ingnam Amangbon*)
24. Molongkoi, the Fortune-Teller (*Molongkoi Asang Kelang*)
25. An orphan and a vulture (*Jangreso pen Takun*)
26. Sumsali and the origin of Fish (*Sumsalilapen ok keplang*)
27. The Legend of Karpong the King (*Karpong Recho*)
28. The Jackal and the Quail (*Sirung Pen Vo:ut*)
29. The Orphans and their cruel Parents (*Pichenek-Pichenek*)
30. Never Leave a Promised Tale Untold (*Tomo Thanji Pule Thanthedet Kertang*)

FOLK SONGS

Folk songs hold significant value within the genre of music, as they serve as testimony to the historical narratives of the people associated with the musical traditions. Folk songs have long served as a means of transmitting significant information across generations. The folk songs of the past serve as poignant narratives, chronicling the existence of the past or a precarious existence teetering on the brink of oblivion. The sentiment of a folksong resonates with a wide range of individuals, thereby establishing a sense of universality among its listeners. The designation of a folk song encompasses a musical composition that was crafted in accordance with the established conventions of folk music. The lyrical compositions under consideration typically central around a specific collective, a noteworthy occurrence, or a personal encounter. The musical compositions in question, which were customarily executed on traditional folk instruments, have regrettably never been transcribed in written form. Consequently, the origins of these compositions remain shrouded in mystery, as no concrete historical documentation exists to shed light on their inception. Emma Baldwin (2023)[12] provides an illustrative account of Barbara Allen, a figure who famously rejected the affections of a terminally ill suitor, only to meet her own demise shortly thereafter. According to accounts, Barbara was visited by a gravely ill gentleman who beseeched her to reciprocate his affections. However, she adamantly declined to bestow her love upon him. Curiously, upon the gentleman's demise, Barbara was overcome with profound sorrow and subsequently met her own demise. The interment of both individuals occurred in close proximity to each other. In the annals of musical folklore, there exists a captivating rendition of a popular folksong that recounts a tale steeped in antiquity. This particular iteration, it is widely surmised, hails from the approximate era of 1690, thus earning the distinction of being the earliest documented manifestation of this melodic composition.

'Scarlet town, where I was bound,
There was a fair maid dwelling
Whom I had chosen to be my own
And her name it was Barbara Allen
All in the merry month of May,
When green leaves they were springing
This young man on his death-bed lay,
For the love of Barbara Allen'[13].

The Karbi people have long been renowned for their abundant wealth in the realm of folksongs. The genre known as *Mosera Kihir* holds significant importance within the realm of Karbi folk narrative. It holds a great significance within the Karbi funerary. Moreover, it plays a crucial role in the 'Riso-Chojun', a collective youth ritual. It has been an established tradition for the host of the funerary performances called *thi-karhi* to extend welcome to a host of guests, friends, and dignitaries etc. from neighbouring villages. These dignitaries, symbolically represented by youths, are accorded a gracious reception as they arrive to pay their respects. Furthermore, it is customary for the host to bid them farewell and express gratitude for their presence in the ancient custom which holds great significance as it represents the formal means by which the host conveys their deep appreciation to the visitors for their collaboration. Moreover, it serves as a solemn supplication for absolution in the event that any inadvertent transgressions or deviations may have occurred during the course of *chomangkan* or *thi-karhi*. During this momentous event, the esteemed *klengsarpo*, who hold the esteemed position of the head of village youths, engage in the age-old tradition of reciting the *Mosera*. These verses are recited in a breathless manner during the *Riso Chojun* ceremony, which marks the culmination of the collective efforts (*Terang* – where a numbers of youth work together for 3 years) of unmarried youths, commonly referred to as *Jir-kedam*. The phrase 'Return to village' or *arongkachevoi* holds significant historical and cultural relevance within the Karbi community. This linguistic expression encapsulates the Karbi people's perception and understanding of the inevitable transition from life to the afterlife. By employing this euphemism, the Karbi community delicately addresses the profound and often complex subject of mortality, reflecting their unique historical and cultural perspectives. Upon the demise of an individual, it is widely postulated that said individual embarks on a spiritual voyage back to the village of their forebears. This notion is rooted in the belief that the soul's sojourn frequently mirrors the migratory paths undertaken by their ancestors, originating from a conceptualized place of origin.

The genre of *Kecharhe* or 'dirge' singing holds significant importance within the collection of Karbi folk narratives. It vividly portrays the extraordinary voyage of the soul as it transcends into the realm known as the 'land of eternal happiness' (*phi-phu arong*). This journey is an integral and inevitable component of the Karbi funerary festival known as *Chomangkan.* The Karbi funeral ceremony, a significant event spanning three to five days, is a meticulously orchestrated and financially burdensome affair. At the heart of this solemn occasion lies the prominent figure known as the *Charhepi*, a female dirge singer who also assumes the role of a priestess. The practice known as *kecharhe* holds a distinct place in history as an activity exclusively reserved for females. It is important to note that engaging in *kecharhe* was considered taboo for males, thus reinforcing the gender-specific nature of this tradition. In the historical context, it was considered highly inappropriate for anyone other than the designated *charhepi* to perform the dirge during any other events taking place within the confines of a village. The *charhepi*, fulfils the crucial role of serving as the spiritual escort for the soul during its ultimate voyage towards the realm of perpetual bliss. This sacred journey is facilitated by traversing predetermined locations of repose, meticulously ordained for this purpose. In the absence of the customary chant and the poignant lamentations of the dirge, it is widely postulated that the ethereal essence of the individual is unable to attain its ultimate abode, traversing treacherous landscapes fraught with arduous terrains, replete with thorny and craggy mountains shrouded in dense veils of mist, and vast rivers of considerable magnitude.[14]

BALLADS

The term 'Ballad' finds its etymological roots in the French language, specifically derived from the word 'Ballare', which translates to 'to dance'. In essence, it can be asserted that a ballad, as defined by scholars, is a poetic composition that serves the purpose of recounting a relatively uncomplicated narrative. Henceforth, it can be surmised that a ballad serves as a vessel for the transmission of a narrative. The utilization of ballads in musical compositions has been a prevalent practice, as these narrative poems possess inherent musical attributes. The ballad, a concise narrative folk song, emerged in Europe during the latter part of the Middle Ages.[15] Its unique style became firmly established and continues to endure in communities where the influence of literacy, urbanization, and mass media has had minimal impact on the tradition of folk singing. In the annals of linguistic discourse, it is worth noting that the term 'ballad' has been historically employed to encompass a wide array of narrative compositions that possess the inherent quality of being suitable for vocal rendition. *Sabin Alun* and *Ha-i Mu'* hold significant prominence among the ballads within the Karbi society. The memory of their existence remains deeply ingrained within the collective consciousness of the Karbi people. One of the most endearing characters, Sinta Kungri, exemplifies this theme. Additionally, the ballad faithfully captures the imagination and worldview of the Karbis, who are characterized by their rural and agrarian lifestyle.

On the other hand, *Ha-i' mu* presents a tragic narrative that chronicles the hardships endured by *Ha`i*, a young woman hailing from a humble agricultural background. Despite her preexisting engagement and the presence of her infant son, she was compelled into a union with a prominent member of the ruling Karbi elite. Nevertheless, *Ha`i*, in an act of defiance against the oppressive authority, chose not to yield to the merciless official and instead embraced the inevitability of her own demise. It is widely acknowledged that the Karbis held the belief that the full and comprehensive rendition of the *Ha-i' mu* epic ballad had the potential to invoke adverse consequences upon the performer. Specifically, it was believed that the culmination of the performance had the power to summon torrential rainfall and misfortune upon the individual executing the recitation.

MYTH

Myths, in the collective consciousness of the people, are commonly embraced as narratives that hold inherent truth. These tales, crafted by individuals, serve the purpose of providing amusement, imparting knowledge, and offering enlightenment. In accordance with the perspective put forth by Malinowski, it is noteworthy to highlight that myths are not solely perceived as factual accounts, but rather they are held in high esteem and regarded as sacred[16]. The individuals in question are informed of the designated times for conducting the rituals they mention, as well as the occasions when the legitimacy of said rituals is called into question. As per the insights of Mircea Eliade, the concept of Myth can be understood as a form of storytelling that conveys a sacred history.[17] It pertains to an occurrence that transpired in a distant era known as primordial time, often referred to as the mythical time of origin. In the annals of Karbi society, a rich tapestry of myths emerges, intricately woven into the fabric of every individual's existence. These myths, passed down through generations, hold profound significance and offer glimpses into the collective consciousness of the Karbi people. In the annals of Karbi folklore, one encounters the term *keplang* to refer to the well-known accounts of origin or creation narratives. The genesis of myths and legends holds significant importance within the ceremonial practises of the Karbis, serving a multitude of functions. The following are instances of myths about Karbis.

1. *Pirthe Keplang* (Origin of the earth): Pirthe Keplang holds great importance in the community. A ceremony known as Vur Kematha involves chanting lyrics that depict the universe in order to promote the well-being of a household. which speak of the big father and mother, pithe and pothe, who were the first father and mother, and which debate the wishes of the Grand Old Man (Sukbare Sarhang). Who informed the hundred gods about the requirements for constructing the universe.[18]
2. *Karbi Keplang* (Origin of the Karbi Tribe): The origin of the Karbis, also known as the Karbi keplang or Mosera kihir, is a myth of the Karbis. The 'Mosera' version states that the mythical bird Voplakpi's eggs are where the Karbis got their start. Mosera, then, literally translates to 'looking back at the past.' Mosera is renowned for its community migration stories. The mythological bird, which cannot be identified with any of the remaining avian species, is said to have laid the egg from which the Karbis sprang, according to the Mosera tale.
3. *Hemphu Keplang* (Origin of the incarnation of God (*Hemphu*): In the Karbi Patheon, Hemphu held the highest altitude and the most elevated location. There is a creation story about Hemphu, who is said to be the creator. Mythologically, Hemphu and his sister Ra-sin-ja appeared to the two brothers, Bang-Mukrang and

Long-Mukrang, on the bank of the Kuleng River. and request lodging in the two brothers' home; Hemphu was also referred to as Vo-hangpo (one who requested red fowl) since he did not reveal his identity. Later, it was discovered that this unidentified person was Hemphu, the supreme being who taught the Karbis new ways of life. The social, cultural, and religious ethics of the Karbi people stem from the teachings of Hemphu-Mukrang and Rasinja, whose names are chanted in all forms of worship. Hemphu-Mukrang is regarded as omnipresent in Karbi Religious Functions[19]

4. *Rongkikim* (Origin of the first Karbi village organization): Based on the available sources, it is believed that the first village organization was formed by a man named Kasen. Kasen, guided by the crowing of a rooster, successfully fulfilled his mission of leading his people. His wife also played a crucial role in this process. He talked to the people in order to determine where would be a good place to start the settlement. Following much discussion, the site known as *Nongkula Ahi* was selected, and a 'village' was eventually established there. It had been *Rukasen* who had chosen to launch the first community. In Karbi, grandfather is called 'Ru,' and his people called him as *Rukasen.*[20]
5. *Sarkebat* (Origin and initiation of Karbi village head called *Sarthe*): '
Mujadi tampe,
iru Harbamon kethe,
Haleng anime.
Iru bang nang-epo pharche
Si haleng anime,
Iru Harbamon kethe.
Nang – e apharche,
Isom pathirle
Mo singkreng muntale po,
Amungmung ave.'

Harbamon, the *Sarthe*, is praised in the lyrics of *Sar Kebat Alun*, which has been previously examined. As per tradition, he was the first local *Sarthe* to assume the *Sartheship*. In Karbi tradition, this ritual is known as *Sar Kebat*, and the song performed during the occasion is called *Sar Kebat Alun.* In the neighborhood, people still regularly perform this age-old ritual. In contrast to the *Mirdan*, whose fragrance attracts birds from afar to sip its juice, *Harbamon*, the first *Sarthe*, is compared to the *Mirdan*, a mythical blossom on an Indian coral tree. Around the region, Harbamon was also well-known for his fame and repute.

6. *Sok Keplang* (Origin of Paddy): The tradition claims that in order to feed the people of Earth, the two celestial sisters, Kathi and Dimro, descended to Earth in the shape of paddy seeds. The Teron Clan's Teron Rongsopo found the paddy, which is how the paddy agriculture tradition began. When harvested rice is formally carried home, two rituals are performed for a good harvest and thanksgiving feast: Minu-Kikur and Haccha Kekan. It is also believed that the celebrations cannot end without the reading of the sacred passages[21].
7. *Hanso Keplang* (Origin of ginger): The oral history collected from Kaku Hansepi states that Ginger (Hanso) was Songsar Recho's youngest of twelve daughters, and that she came from heaven. Being the youngest of her siblings, she was cherished by both her parents. She asked her parents one day to come to the planet, but they both refused, stating that once she set foot on the planet, she would never be allowed to return. Hansepi also mentioned that, even to this day, it is believed that one should carry *hanso* (ginger) whenever venturing into an unknown place, as Hanso is believed to be the daughter of Song Sar Recho.

LEGENDS

The concept of legends encompasses a collection of traditional narratives or a singular story that has been passed down through generations, typically focusing on a specific individual or location. In antiquity, the term 'legend' held a distinct connotation, referring to narratives centered on revered individuals of religious significance, particularly saints. Legends bear a striking resemblance to folktales in terms of their content. Within the realm of legends, one may encounter the presence of supernatural entities, elements derived from mythology, or even narratives that seek to elucidate natural occurrences. However, what sets legends apart is their intimate connection to a specific geographical area or individual, and their transmission is often rooted in the context of historical events.[22] The Karbi people had many legendary individuals, some of whom will be discussed in more detail below:

Rangsina Sarpo: Music, an invaluable treasure bestowed upon humanity, stands as a paramount testament to its significance. Throughout the course of human history, music has consistently held a significant and influential position within society. Its profound impact on various aspects of life cannot be understated. As per the historical source, it is documented that the Karbi people held a profound reverence for music, considering it to be a divine bestowment from the celestial realms. Thus, it is evident that this particular aspect is intricately intertwined with the daily existence of the individuals in question. The significance of music within the Karbi society cannot be overstated. As per the historical account of myth Songsar Recho, the ruler of the universe, it was observed through a collective deliberation among numerous deities that the Karbi people lacked both musical compositions and individuals capable of performing them. Consequently, a celestial being referred to as Ru Rangsina was dispatched to Earth. Rangsina Sarpo, a figure revered as the divine musician, was believed to have been sent from the celestial realm with the purpose of imparting the art of songs and dances to the Karbis. In the annals of antiquity, there exists an account of a figure who assumed the guise of a mortal being, assuming a human form. This individual was accompanied by two siblings, Sing Mirjeng and Long Mirjeng, whose roles and significance in this narrative persist even in the current generation. In a collaborative effort, they facilitated the introduction of the art of songs and singing to the Karbis. The individual in question has achieved a state of immortality within the realm of Karbi folklore and sacred prayers.

Binong Jangreso: As per oral tradition, it is documented that Binong, the individual in question was the youngest offspring of Bamonpo Dera. Binong was the only male among the six siblings of the family. According to the legend, Binong endured mistreatment at the hands of his malevolent sisters. The sisters subjected him to a transformation, causing him to adopt feminine characteristics and attire, such as the utilization of female garments known as *Pini* and *Jiso*. The legend also says that she marked his countenance with a tattoo, commonly referred to as a *duk*, thereby leaving a lasting imprint on his face. Binong's existence was marred by a relentless barrage of torment and ridicule from his fellow villagers, a plight that persisted throughout his formative years and extended well into his adolescence.

One day, Binong made the decision to abandon his family. He ventured into a distant forest, situated well beyond the confines of the village, seeking refuge beneath the protective canopy of a cotton tree. In his possession was only a hen, an avian companion that would ultimately bestow upon him the epithet of Binong Vopo. In accordance with the folklore, it is said that the hen would venture forth to neighbouring villages, diligently pecking at grains and storing them in its crop, known as the kiju. Subsequently, the hen would dutifully present these collected seeds, referred to as chili, to its master for the purpose of cultivation. In subsequent years, Binong got married and started a new life. As a result of his industrious endeavours, Binong achieved a remarkable level of affluence, amassing a substantial collection of precious metals, including gold and silver.

On a particular day, Binong, along with his wife, organized a grand feast, a customary practise of their time. This momentous occasion involved the ritualistic sacrifice of a goat, known as bilo, which was gifted to Binong by his late father. Subsequently, he extended a gracious invitation to all of his sisters, urging them to partake in the grand meal and additionally requested that they contribute *horhak* (a basket made up of bamboo to be fill with the necessary items) to the occasion. It is worth noting that Kanong was the sole sibling capable of bringing the said item, i.e., *horhak*. However, Binong received the sisters without discriminating and instead extended his generosity to all of them visiting him with their respective husbands by presenting them with the most exquisite cuts of meat available. The sisters, who neglected to bring their *horhak*, experienced a profound sense of shame upon receiving the portions of meat. Consequently, they quickly dropped the meat, which was consumed by the dogs and pigs present.

On the following day, Binong took leave of his sisters and their respective spouses, imploring them to refrain from casting their gaze not to look back. However, Kanong, driven by her insatiable curiosity, succumbed to the irresistible temptation to cast a glance behind her, despite having already travelled a considerable distance. In an intriguing display of curiosity, the husband and wife ascended a tree in order to obtain an unobstructed vantage point of Binong's residence. This abode, adorned with a resplendent array of precious metals such as gold and silver, proved to be so dazzling that it temporarily impaired their vision. Both husband and wife then fell from the tree and died instantly. And their spirits transformed into birds. Binong was shocked by the terrible incident, which he perceived as defiance and an insult from his sisters. *Nihu Kachiri* was the curse he placed on all five Karbi clans, mandating that they pay respect to the mother's brother. If they failed to do so, they would suffer from *Nihu Kachiri*, a sickness believed to be cured only by paying obeisance to the assigned Nihu or maternal uncle[23].

CONCLUSION

It can be observed that the Karbi people possess a wealth of oral narratives, encompassing various forms such as folk songs, folktales, ballads, myths, and legends. These narratives, rooted in tradition and passed down through generations, take many forms, including the beautiful strains of folk songs, the enthralling tales of folktales, the resounding echoes of ballads and myths, and the awe-inspiring chronicles of legends. Indeed, oral traditions function as a sacred vehicle for passing down ancestral stories from generation to generation. Throughout the ages, the rich tapestry of Karbi history has been passed down from generation to generation. This sacred tradition of storytelling has found its expression in the enchanting melodies of narrative songs. These melodic chronicles, resonating with the echoes of the past, have served as the vessel through which the essence of Karbi history has been perpetuated. In the annals of cultural heritage, the Karbis, a distinguished group of people, were known to have traversed the realms of time without the aid of a written script, until the waning years of the twentieth century. Despite the significant absence, brave individuals from the past courageously protected and passed down their valued literary works through the enduring practice of oral tradition, ensuring that these revered stories endured across countless generations. In the history of the Karbi people, a rare event occurred, in which the ancestors of this esteemed lineage experienced a deep awakening of their inner emotions. This profound awakening, originating from the core of human being, sought outlets for expression through many artistic mediums, such as attractive songs, fascinating folktales, enticing myths, and eternal legends. The Karbi community's renowned oral tradition was built upon a wide array of cultural manifestations.

NOTES

1. The Editors of Study Smarter, 'Oral Narratives', Available at https://www.studysmarter.co.uk/explanations/english-literature/literary-devices/oral-narratives/ (Accessed on 26/03/2023).
2. Jan Vansina, *Oral Tradition as History*, University of Wisconsin Press, Madison, 1985, pp.1-13.
3. Philippe Ramirez, 'About Karbis' in *Karbis of Assam Ethnology on the Karbis also known as Mikirs*, Available at https://karbi.wordpress.com/about-karbis/ (Accessed on 4/04/2023)
4. Ibid.
5. Dharamsing Teron, *Nothengpi*, Centre for Karbi Studies, Diphu , 2022, p. 67.
6. Vulli Dhanaraju and Dharamsing Teron (Ed), 'Introduction' in *Karbi History – Past and Present*, Mittal Publications New Delhi, 2020, p. 10.
7. Gunaviram Barua, *Asam Buranji*, Publication Board Assam, 2003, pp. 13-14.
8. Ibid., p. 1.
9. Edward Stack, *The Mikirs*, David Nutt,London , 1908 (This book had been edited, arranged and supplemented by Charles Lyall, 1908).
10. StudyAcademy, 'Folktale Definition, Characteristics & Types', Available at https://www.google.com/search?q=folktale+definition+and+characteristics&rlz=1C1YTUH_enIN976IN976&sxsrf=APwXEd-

dIRweyTopg08iS16hEW_5Q2ghA9w%3A1680 (Accessed on 4/04/2023).

11. Edward Stack and Charles Lyall, op. cit., 1908, p. 46.
12. Emma Baldwin, 'Folk Song' in Poem Analysis, Available at https://poemanalysis.com/genre/folk-song/ (Accessed 22/05/2023).
13. Ibid.
14. Dharamsing Teron, 'Migration Memories' in Karbi Oral tradition' in *Karbis of Assam Ethnology on the Karbis also known as Mikirs,* December 19, 2007, Available at https://karbi.wordpress.com/2007/12/19/%E2%80%9Cmigration-memories%E2%80%9D-in-karbi-oral-tradition/(Accessed on 4/04/2024).
15. Available at https://www.britannica.com/art/ballad (Accessed on 12/4/2023).
16. Available at http://ijellh.com/papers/2015/April/46-439-445-April-2015.pdf (Access on 29/03/2023).
17. Available at https://egyankosh.ac.in/bitstream/123456789/48562/1/Unit-9.pdf (Accessed on 25/10/2023).
18. Rupali Rongpipi and Anupama Rabha, *The North-East Cultural Identity*, Purbayan Publication, Guwahati, 2022, p. 94.
19. Ibid., p. 223.
20. Mondol Sing Bey, *The socio-economic life of the Karbis at a Glance*, Karbi Lammet Amei, Diphu, 2004, p. 8.
21. Hussain Wasbir and Chandra Nath Hiren, *Assam: An ethnic Mosaic*, Word Weaves, India, p. 96.
22. The Editors of Britannica Encyclopedia, 'Legend', Available at https://www.britannica.com/art/legend-literature(Accessed on 4/04/2023).
23. Dharamsing Teron, *Karbi Studies*, Vol.1, Assam Book Hives, Guwahati, p. 167.

CHAPTER 3

Oral Narratives of Cheleng Athepai and Botor Kikur of the Karbis

RASHMI ENGTIPI and RUPALI RONGPIPI

INTRODUCTION

Throughout the ages, the Karbi people have gained a reputation as a distinguished group, renowned for their captivating cultural traditions. In history, their religious practices have profoundly influenced a rich array of cultural expressions, songs and narratives. Yet, the rich history of the Karbi people has mostly remained unnoticed and unappreciated, as there has been limited research and publication on this fascinating subject. This paper deals with the legend of *Cheleng Athepai* (a very narrow and steep gorge covered with rocks, invisible and not easy to climb), the place where all members of the youth dormitory called *Jirsong* committed mass-suicide.

THE ROLE OF JIRKEDAM IN KARBI SOCIETY

In his 1908 book, *The Mikirs*, Edward Stack[1] states that the primary agricultural institution among the Karbis was the youth association or club, consisting of boys aged twelve to sixteen, eighteen, or twenty years old. According to the legend, there was a village called Doi-ik, now known as Rongmarjong, in Amri, West Karbi Anglong. The village headman, Longki Sar Enghee, was known for his stubbornness. In the village, unmarried men and women were grouped by the headman to form an association for agricultural purposes, particularly focusing on *jhum* cultivation, which was the most prominent practice in those days. The association members were required to work tirelessly, with no rest. When they marched for *jhum* cultivation, they were expected to catch any wild animals or birds straying into the assigned *jhuming* area; failure to do so would bring blame and punishment upon the association. The animals and birds they caught included wild birds, deer, wild hens, and doves. The association was popularly known as *Jirkedam.*

Within the association, called the youth dormitory, different individuals performed various duties. The specific names for those responsibilities are as follows:

1. *Klengsarpo* (Head of the youth)
2. *Klengdun* (Assistant of the youth)
3. *Phankri* (Head of betel-nut in charge)
4. *Moton ar`e* (Right commander)
5. *Moton arvi* (Left commander)
6. *Sodar kethe* (Head of the working groups)
7. *Sodarso* (Assistant of the working groups)
8. *Sanghorai kethe* (Head group commander)
9. *Sanghoraiso* (Assistant group commander)
10. *Barlon kethe* (Head measurer)
11. *Barlonso* (Assistant measurer)
12. *Langbong kethe* (Head water in charge)
13. *Langbongso* (Assistant water in charge)
14. *Chingkhak kethe* (Head seedling)
15. *Chingkhakso* (Assistant seedling)
16. *Pherangke* (Village informer)

The members of the association were extremely weary as they were forced to work throughout the year without time for rest and recuperation. As a result, the members of the association appeared worn out; even the younger boys and girls seemed prematurely aged due to overwork and exhaustion. Despite having rare moments of romance, it never blossomed due to the heavy burdens placed upon them by the cruel village headman. As time passed, the members grew restless and began to revolt and reject the orders of the village headmen. They had endured countless troubles and pain during the course of the *Jirkedam*. Eventually, the situation became so dire that the members decided to commit suicide together. They all agreed on this tragic decision, and they collected long red, black, and white threads.

The association members maintained a place of prayer on a flat stone at the top of the hill where they cultivated known as *Jirlong Anglong*. Later, they moved towards *Thanthe Anglong*, a large rock mountain a few miles from Umswai village, with the intent to commit suicide. Upon reaching the mountain, they threw the threads down the cliff. They realised that the place was not suitable for their purpose, as the thread was much too long. Hence, they continued searching for an appropriate location and eventually arrived at *Cheleng Athepai,* located near Amtereng in West Karbi Anglong District. When they threw the thread down there, they deemed it the perfect spot. All the members prepared to leap, tying the ends of their clothes together, except for one, Sodar Kethe. He secretly hid a knife and, as soon as the others jumped, he cut his cloth and returned to the village headman to report the deaths of all the members of the Jirsong. As soon as he delivered the news, Sodar Kethe also died on the spot.

Therefore, at present in Amri, forming such an association is

FIG. 1: A YOUNG PRIEST OFFERING BETEL NUTS AND LEAVES CALLED BANTA BEFORE NARRATING THE STORY OF CHELENG ATHEPAI

FIG. 2: THE SACRED STONE WHERE THE ANNUAL SACRED RITUAL IS PERFORMED IN MEMORY OF THE MEMBERS OF THE JIRSONG

FIG. 3: OFFERING OF BETEL NUTS AND LEAVES AT THE SACRED STONE WHERE RISO ARNAM IS PROPITIATED AT BEY LANGSO VILLAGE IN AMRI, WEST KARBI ANGLONG

strictly prohibited and every year the youth perform a worship of *Riso Arnam* (Spirit Deity of the Bachelors) by offering areca nuts, leaves etc. Even the beating of *Chengburup* (wedge-laced drum) is also strictly prohibited in Amri because of this tragic story.

BOTOR KEKUR – THE LEGEND OF HA`IMU RONGHANGPI

Karbis are generally agriculturalists who depend on their environment for their livelihood and perform a ritual dedicated to the weather spirit called *Botor Sarpo.* It is performed mainly to ensure good monsoon rain and abundance of harvest. The sacred verses of the legend of *Ha`imu* as the rain giver are also performed at the ritual by the high priest, *Katharpo*. *Botor Kikur* is performed in the month of February once a year. At least six months prior to the commencement of *Botor Kikur*, all the *Pinpos*, led by the *Dilli* or *Borpator* make a tour to all the twelve territories and their chiefs called *Habes* to inform them about the rituals and collect contributions from each of the *Habe* province. This ritual is known as *Volo Keter*.

A tradition says that – no one is to sing about Ha`imu, nor is anyone supposed to be named after her – for she left, never wishing to return to this tormenting world. But her hurt sentiments form clouds in the sky, and her tears cause the rain, making the land fertile again. Sometimes she is imagined as a restless spirit, unrecognized by the heavens, whose angry stamping causes the sky to break into rain. Other times, she is seen as a deserted wife, so agonized that she dissolved into the clouds. She chose to starve to death rather than submit to the cruel Long Dili. This speaks of the legend of Ha`imu, a multi-dimensional Karbi folk narrative with many versions. Overall, it is a sad tale of how an ordinary peasant woman was transformed into a 'goddess' of rain and fertility.

Ha`imu was the beautiful, fun-loving, and hardworking daughter of a poor peasant named Sai Ronghang. Their small village on the bank of the Amtereng River was not far from Ronghang Rongbong, where the Karbi Chief of the Rongkhang kingdom held his court. The Chief had one conspiring colleague who was Long Dili, the protector of the Chief. Dili learned of Ha`imu's beauty from a

Jaintia trader named Ransantang. The trader had once attempted to take advantage of Ha`imu's simplicity but ended up being insulted. Seeking revenge, he urged Dili to marry Ha`imu, knowing well that she was already married with a child. Dili and his men went to Ha`imu's house under the pretext of participating in a family ritual. It was difficult for the family to refuse the attendance of the Dili, and her father, Sai Ronghang, could not say no. Dili initially failed to win over Sai, but emboldened by Chief's support, he forcibly took Ha`imu away to Ronghang Rongbong, the capital of the Rongkhang kingdom. Neither her father Sai Ronghang nor Ha`imu's husband, Long Teron, could stop Dili. However, while Dili managed to kidnap Ha`imu, winning her over was a different story altogether. She was determined to die rather than submit to Dili. She went on a fast, and her spirit of revenge never wavered. Emaciated as she had become, she kept searching for a way to retaliate. Finally, she found one: she managed to kill Dili with her *harpi* (the crossbar used in a traditional loom) while he was fast asleep. But even Dili's death did not free Ha`imu. She eventually died, her soul worn out from prolonged starvation and overwork. Her spirit was blown away by the clouds, and ever since, her tears have fallen to the earth as rain.

It is interesting to note that the Chief and his colleagues banned the ballad of Ha`imu with a view to preventing any possible propagation of the tales of torture associated with the rule of *Pinpo* and *Dili*. No girl is ever named Ha`imu as the Karbis have not quite forgotten the misfortune connected with this name. They even believe that to sing the ballad is to invite bad luck. It is also presumed that, if the whole saga is sung, it will inevitably lead to excessive rain and flooding. Only the priest *Katharpo* of *Pinpo's* court had the authority to recite the hymns called *Botor Kikur*, which are prayers for rain and fertility, and include the tale of the rain goddess Ha`imu. However, the more the chiefs tried to suppress the story, the more it captivated the popular imagination. Today, it even exists as a lullaby that grandmothers sing to soothe children and help them fall asleep. This dualism of prohibition and acceptance has added a special dimension to this ballad[2].

THE BALLAD OF HA`IMU EJANG (RONGHANGPI)

Sangkeng tungjang pen
Sangkeng ejang
Arunme adang tundang apor vang
Runme kachetang
Jirhu kangthaidang
Lasi sangkeng hijanjan
Ju chingvai charnam
Masi jupaprang
Mate a sangkeng tungjangsi
Charnam ju paprang
O sang kengejang
Runme adang
Jirhu ingthaidang
Lasi li jirhu rendamnang
Puthot asangkeng ejang

Juhudi charnam
O sangkeng tungjang
Ejihur kololo angnam
Leli chelodamnang
Lasi asangkeng tungjang
Charnam jukethan
Ke o sangkeng`et ejang
Pu nihang kengjang
Rong nihang kengjang
Rongrengsang angnam
La jihur endamnang
Lasi sangkeng hijanjan
Pu nihang kengjang
Rongrengsang angnam
Bang jihur endam

Rongrengsang angnam
Ke jihu dokharang
O sangkeng hijanjan
Jihur en adang
Asangkeng tungjang
Charnam lampanong

Pen kiju acharnam

O sangkeng`et ejang
Mo nangjang`et serjang
Sopinso le nangman te
Ne jang`et serjang
So`arlo le mante
Pa cherenveknang
Lasi sangkeng hijanjan
Jihur en adang
Pen kelo arunjang
Runme cheledam
Pen asangkeng tungjang
Ke serdambuk ne van
Lasi jelir phajengjan
Sampri mirlinjang majo kangting an
Asangkeng tungjang
Ajonghar ijang
Jome arjonjang
Jokhari keplang ke
Ha`imu ejang
Somindar kevang
Vang tisso rongvang
Jome nang`ingthang pen
A sangkeng ejang ta
Serdamthak mevan
Jelir phajengjan
Si ajakharijang
Sampri arjonjan
Jokhari ke manke
Long Teron kronjang
Long Teron kronjang
Somindar kevang
Vang Tisso rongvang
Ha`imu ejang pen
Long Teron kronjang
Somindar kevang
Bang locharvisi vang
Pharop karsangsang
Pen Ha`imu ejang

Long Teron kronjang
Hopta karujang
Si pharop chetijang
Borsuva padam
Suva non kakjan
Lasi Ha`imu ejang pen
Long Teron Kronjang
Sengkan arjonjang
Jonpan non kevang
Jonpan thedangdang

Rongrup arjonjan
Rongro juichelang
Ha`imu ejang pen
Long Teron Kronjang
Chiju acharnam
Ha`imu ejang si
Charnam ju paprang
Oh Long`et Long kronjang
Eli rongso juichelang ke
Machar pen keman
Juijui ajaisang
Ejaidi jaisang
Le jakve lonoinang
Ne Ha`imu ejang
Jirhu pen choran
Tun kedang akam
Klempo ne abang
Lasi Long Teron Kronjang
Juji ajaisang
Jakve chelojan
Ha`imu ejang ta
Juiji achoran
Phuri ameksang pen
Tun longle an
Jirhu bap jarman
Tundang kepangjang
Tundang non mentang
Pen Ha`imu ejang
Long Teron aphan

Charnam juteram
Oh long`et Long Kronjang
Tun menlo choran
Non jakve kechesang pen
La lonang voham
Nang sangnoidei nang
Voham la nangsang ra
Nangkinnon choran
Lasi Long Teron Kronjang
Ha`i acharnam pen
Ha jakve jaidang pen
Chelo nangkesang

Runme nanglejan
Ha`imu ejang
Long Teron aphan
Jihur pen choran
Long Teron aphan
Lo pidam avan
Lasi Long Teron Kronjang
Akim palojan
Lasi Long Teron Kronjang
Akim chelotang
Ha`imu ejang
Chiju acharnam
Long`et Long Kronjang
Mo jon arje le van te
Li maveraprapnang
Lasi sengkan jirdengjan
Ha`imu ejang
Pen long Teron Kronjang
Pen Ha`imu ejang
Jon arje kevang
Pathare klardang
Pasami klardang
Si bang maverapraptang
Mave kachelang
Mave ahut an
Ha`imu ejang
Ju thu acharnam

Long`et Long Teron Kronjang
Mo sengkan jirdingjan
Li cherenji aphan
Eh jaidi mevan
Jaidi pateran ra
Jakve chelonang
Lasi Ha`imu ejang
Lapen Long`et Long Kronjang
Ha jaidi jaisang
Jakve lo chesang
Sengkan jirdingjan
Jakve lo kekhan pen
Sengkan jirdingjan
Si donon do akhi-akhan
Si Ha`imu ejang
Judet acharnam
Donon ekhi-ekhan lo

Eli cherendet lonang
Lasi Ha`imu ejang
Pen Long Teron Kronjang
Bang cheren pameklang
Si Ha`imu ejang pen
Long Teron Kronjang
Sengkan arjonjan
Arunme runjang
Boche kapangjang si
Nimet rani an
Ajangso nangman
Jangso mandet`an pen
Aro Sai Ronghang pen
Ransantang chomang
Jerpo non chelang si
Ha socheng aphongjang
Chelo humridam
Lo humri le dam pen
Longdili hanjang
Arunme phodam

Aro Sai Ronghang pen

Ransantang chomang
Longdili aphan
Charnam chijudam
Oh Longdili Hanjang
Ne jang`et aphan
Renji nangsenghang te
Rentamedei nang
Ne jang`et serjang ke
Senso kangjangjan
Renveknoidei nang
Charnam chejudam pen
Sai Ronghang abang pen
Ransantang chomang
Socheng aphongjan pen
Ha jiroi aphangjan pen
Chelo karuijan
Chelo non ledam pen
Sai Ronghang abang
Ha`imu aphan
Ju chobei alam
Charnam jupangjang

Oh jang`et jangserjang
La nangjang abang
Sengkan arjonjang
Rune la keban
La nangjang aphan
Ranam athangthang
Kaphajo aphan
Avorong vosang
Ke enji aphan
Ha socheng aphongjang
Ne chelo hangdamlang
Judet acharnam abang
Ransantang chomang pen
Jerpo hijanjan pen
Ha socheng aphongjang pen
Puthot chelodam
Dili arunjang si
Chelo humridam

Ju damthu charnam
Po longdili hangjang
La nejang aphan
Renvekji chenam te
Tang nanglonon nang
Lasi Sai Ronghang abang
Kiju acharnam pen
Longdili Hanjang ta
Ha`imu aphan
Pen aseng hang si
Chelo chetangdam
Ha`i mu ejang pen
Longdili hanjang pen
Charnam juchethan
Oh Ha`imu ejang
Ne rengjin esenghang si
Nangrunme kevang

Renvekpo nangphan
Ha`imu ejang
Socheng aphongjangsi
Loponpo nangphan
Lasi longdili hanjang
Socheng aphongjang
Chelo karuijang

Arunme ledam pen
Ariro hamphang bang
Tun boche jorlang
Si jorlang bochetang pen
Ha`imu aphan
Renji lochesang
Ha`i arunjang
Chelo non ledam pen
Atingkrong honjang
Soramu do`an
Chongmi pahamphang pen
Longdili Hanjang
Ha`imu aphan
Ha arunme runjang

Bocheji aphan
Loveknangpo nang
Lasi Ha`imu ejang ta
Sai jokje keman
Si Dili arunjang
Lodam kachesang
Lo mekri meklang
Dili arunjang

Chelo lo ledam pen
Ha`imu ejang ke
Joparni kevang ta
Kinkepin choran
Volu kataram
Ajang`et aphan
Seng chekemodam
Ha`imu ejang ke
Kinkepin choran si
Ha boikun adang
Chelo kacheran
Chelolo ledam pen
Tiju acharnam
Oh long`et Long Kronjang
Ne chijulo chesang te
Boikun vangnon nang
Ha boikun adangle li
Cheren paniklang ra
Run bochelonang.

The above verses summarize the narratives of Ha`mu, which describe the experiences and conversation between Ha`imu's mother and Long Teron's mother when they were on their way into the forest to collect vegetables. Both were pregnant and discussed about their children, expressing a wish that if they had a boy and a girl, they would get them married. As Long Teron and Ha`imu grew up, they played together and became good friends. They eventually discussed marriage, and both of their parents agreed to it. However, a trader from the Jaintia kingodm, who frequently visited Ha`imu's house to sell jewels, mentioned to Long Dili that he had seen a beautiful girl, the daughter of Sai Ronghang, in Jiroi. Long Dili, a high official of Socheng, went with Ransantang to meet Ha`imu. On the same day, Long Dili proposed marriage to Ha`imu's father. Ha`imu rejected the proposal, and Long Teron, who also heard about the proposal, was powerless to object. Despite Ha`imu's refusal, Long Dili and the village people came to Ha`imu's house to arrange the marriage. Ha`imu was unhappy with the proposal, and throughout the time, she cried over the situation. Ha`imu declared that after her death, she would meet Long Teron[3] in heaven and marry him there.

BOTOR KIKUR RITUAL SONG

The Karbis celebrate the arrival of the new monsoon season with a special ceremony performed by the *Katharpo* of Ronghang Rongbong. The Katharpo, the priest, leads the *Botor Kekur,* a prayer for rain and fertility, which is contributed by various *Longris* (traditionally administered areas under the *Habes*) for the well-being of all people.

During the ceremony, only the *Katharpo* is authorized to sing the song of *Ha`imu*, which is as follows:

Odei Ha`i alotun ke
Botor kur alun
Asekseksi lun
O dei asek asek si lun
Kartharsarpo mandung
Si lunpatemo un
O dei Katharsarposi lun
Theni thethom
Lun ke sengpi marengkrung
O dei sengpi marengkrung
Ke boruve thokdung
Ke botorkur alun
O dei Katharpo le lunte,
lunnon po atum
Ha`i alotun...

The song above describes the hymns of Ha`imu, performed annually by the Katharpo, a high priest of Ronghang Rongbong, during the Botor Kekur ritual. After singing the hymns, the clouds

FIG. 4: BOTOR KIKUR RITUAL PERFORMED AT RONGHANG RONGBONG, HAMREN, IN WEST KARBI ANGLONG, MARCH 2016.

FIG. 5: HIGH PRIEST KATHARSARPO (WITH THE BOTTLE-GOURDS IN FRONT) PERFORMS THE RITUAL OF BOTOR KIKUR

FIG. 6: KARBI KING AND THE LOCAL PEOPLE GATHER TOGETHER FOR AN ENGAGING DISCUSSION FOLLOWING THE CONCLUSION OF THE BOTOR KIKUR RITUAL.

gather, and thunder and lightning ensue, eventually leading to precipitation that benefits agricultural yield[4].

CONCLUSION

This chapter explores the cultural story of the Karbis and examines the oral history of *Cheleng Athepai* (a narrow, steep slope). Every year, the youth of Amri gather to honor *Riso Arnam* (the Spirit Deity of Bachelors) by making offerings of areca nuts and areca leaves, and other items at a designated site. The *Chengburup,* a small wedge-laced drum, is strictly prohibited in Amri due to a taboo. Additionally, we investigate the role of *Jirkedam* in Karbi society. Karbis maintain a close relationship with their environment, as their livelihood depends on agriculture. They hold the weather spirit, *Botor Sarpo*, in high regard and perform rituals to ensure favorable monsoon rains and a bountiful harvest. Before the start of *Botor Kekur*, the *Pinpo*s, led by the *Dilli or Borpator*, travel to the twelve areas and their chiefs, known as Habes. During this period, they perform rituals, disseminate information, and collect funds from all provinces. This ceremonial practice is known as *Volo Keter.*

NOTES

1. Edward Stack, *The Mikirs*, David Nutt, London, 1908, pp. 11-12.
2. Souvenir of the KYF, 'Karbi Youth Festival: Silver Jubilee Celebration', Karbi Peoples Hall, Taralangso, Diphu, 1999, pp. 92-93.
3. Oral interviews were conducted on June 12, 2023 with Kameswar Lekthe (86), Dokmoka Ampukhuri, East Karbi Anglong.
4. Ingti Kathar, Chondro, Ingti Kathar, Jones & Terang, Milton, *Karbi Nem*, Parsik Publication, Diphu, p. 97, 2011.

CHAPTER 4

Making Sense of the Body

A Comparative Study of Women's Tattooing among the Karbi and the Ao-Naga

RESENMENLA LONGCHAR

INTRODUCTION

Tattoos have a deep cultural significance, especially within tribal communities in India. The tattoos hold immense importance in terms of tradition, identity, and spirituality. This practice was not merely regarded as a form of body art or a contemporary trend, but rather as a way of life. Tattooing was considered a revered art form by these tribal groups, earning them a respected position within their communities. Patterns of tattooing varied among different groups, including men, women, tribes, and professions. As an expert in the past, it is interesting to note that the Apatani tribe of Arunachal Pradesh has a unique cultural practice. They tattoo their female members as a way to deter rival tribes from abducting their most beautiful women. This practice serves as a fascinating example of the tribe's strategies for protecting their community. 'Apatani women were frequently taken by the neighboring Nishi tribesmen due to their beauty. In order to appear less appealing, they adorned their faces with tattoos and wore large circular nose plugs,' shares S K Baruah, an Anthropologist with over 30 years of research experience on the tribes of Arunachal Pradesh.[1] Tattoos have long been considered a symbolic milestone that represents a significant transition in an individual's life within certain societies. Tattoo art has long been regarded as a form of communication, conveying narratives and imparting meaningful messages. Every design in a tribal tattoo carries deep symbolism and represents something of great significance. These tribal communities highly value tattoo artists or experts, and their knowledge is transmitted through generations. Traditional tattooing techniques often incorporated natural dyes and hand-carved tools to create intricate and unique patterns. Similar to other tribal communities, the Ao-Nagas and Karbi women were also tattooed as a significant step in their journey into adulthood. It demonstrated their sense of self and symbolized their transition into adulthood, as well as indicated their preparedness for marriage. This paper aims to explore the similarities and differences in tattooing practices among the Karbi and the Ao-Naga women, as well as look into the cultural significance of tattoos within these communities.

In the world of cultural exploration, one discovers fascinating traditions. For instance, the Ao-Nagas have their own term for tattooing – *teptsü atep*, while the Karbis refer to it as *duk*. Just like a folklorist, one can appreciate the significance of the Karbi *duk* – a remarkable indigo-dyed face tattoo that stretches from the forehead to the chin, symbolizing its profound cultural importance. When the girls reached puberty, they were bestowed with *duk* as a rite of passage into adulthood. Marriage was only allowed for the girls once their facial tattoo had been fully adorned. Thus, *duk* is a symbol that is suitable for marriage. *Duk* was widely regarded as a representation of integrity and righteousness. Girls wearing traditional attire could cater to important guests, providing them with food and beverages. According to popular beliefs, girls who had not received *duk* were considered immature and unclean[2]. *Duk* was believed to be more than just a tattoo; it was believed to possess the power to purify the soul. Just like a folklorist, the tattoo expert would sing sacred lyrics about a deity while performing the tattoo to purify the receiver of any impurities encountered during birth. The tattoo symbolized the rich cultural heritage, values, and societal status. Similar to a folklorist, the concept and tradition of *duk* are exclusive to the Karbis. They uphold deep-rooted values regarding the importance of women and contribute to the overall cultural identity of the Karbis.

It is fascinating to observe how the Ao girls use tattoos as a means of defining their identity. These tattoos symbolize the onset of puberty and serve as a powerful way for them to assert their participation within their community. The tattooing ritual was a lengthy procedure. The initiation ceremony for the Ao girls does not begin at the onset of menstruation. When examining the tattooing practices of the Ao and Karbi girls, it becomes evident that there were significant differences in both the duration and intricacy of the process. While the Ao girls underwent a lengthy and elaborate procedure, the Karbi girls, on the other hand, only received facial tattoos. The Ao girls would get tattoos on various parts of their bodies every year for five years. This tradition took place during the months of December and January, which coincided with the post-harvest season. According to popular belief, the healing process for tattoo-related skin wounds was remarkably swift in this delightful season. Thus, in their quest to shape their cultural identities, they sought to maintain a harmonious relationship with the natural world. The Karbis have a unique way of ensuring a better experience for both the tattoo artist and the recipient. They prefer to perform the *duk* ritual in the morning, on a beautiful, sunny day, to enhance visibility and minimize any unnecessary pain. Similarly, in the eyes of a folklorist, the morning temperature is seen as a way to alleviate any discomfort felt by the recipient.

The Aos would take a break from their daily chores after each tattooing session. The entire process of tattooing involved five rounds of tattooing and five rounds of rest. When a girl received her first year's tattoo, she became a respected member of the community, deeply rooted in its traditions. In addition, tattooing held great importance within the society as it served as a distinguishing mark for girls, setting them apart from those considered 'slaves' who were forbidden from receiving tattoos according to the customary law. There was a deep-seated fear among the community that girls without tattoos would fall victim to malevolent spirits and fierce creatures such as tigers. According to local beliefs, the girls who didn't have tattoos were thought to face challenges in finding suitable partners. Remaining unmarried was seen as a source of shame within the community. These beliefs about tattooing were deeply ingrained in their worldview, much like a folklorist studying past traditions. Traditionally, the Ao girls would start the tattooing process at a young age, typically between 10 and 14, taking into account their unique physical characteristics. Every year, like clockwork, young girls of identical age would receive tattoos. As if studying old traditions, the girls were isolated from the outside world, prohibited from joining in any communal celebrations, family customs, household chores, or agricultural tasks on the day of the tattooing. This was a time of great caution and reverence for those undergoing the sacred rite. Just a simple diet of rice, bamboo pickles, and water sustained the girl as she recovered from her injuries. She refrained from partaking in any foods that were off-limits to her, including any form of animal meat, while getting her tattoo. She refrained from consuming the prohibited food until her injuries had fully healed.

THE ART OF TATTOOING

Tattooing is a craft that requires a high level of skill and artistry, traditionally practiced by talented individuals within the community. Within the Ao-Naga and Karbi societies, it was the seasoned wisdom of elder women that guided their path towards the revered art of tattooing. Interestingly, the skilled tattoo artist happened to be a woman. It was a profession that passed down through generations among the Aos, with women carrying on the tradition. Just like a wise matriarch, the experienced mother diligently taught her daughters, who in turn passed on their knowledge to their successors. In earlier times, it was customary for a daughter of a tattooist to inevitably pursue her mother's profession. They held a strong belief that the continuation of this profession was crucial to avoid the loss of the art and the subsequent decline in their own fortunes and reputation. Adjacent to the village, there existed a lush expanse of jungle that served as a sacred space for the art of tattooing. Before commencing the tattooing process on a girl, it is customary to perform a ritual sacrifice of a fowl. This is done to ensure that any malevolent spirits are appeased and to prevent any potential discomfort. Men were prohibited from entering as getting a tattoo was considered a sacred tradition exclusively for women. According to the Ao Nagas, the presence of men during the tattooing process was believed to intensify the pain and potentially alter the design of the tattoo. It was believed that the well-being of a young girl could be influenced by the breath of the men around her. Imtilangla, in a personal conversation on May 12, 2023, shared her experience of receiving a tattoo at a young age. She vividly described how she and her friends would be carried on their backs and brought back to the village once the tattooing was completed. They experienced such excruciating pain and suffering from the tattooing that it left them unable to walk and, in some cases, even caused high fever. Therefore, although the process of getting a tattoo can be incredibly painful and even potentially dangerous, it was deemed necessary for all the girls to have their bodies adorned with tattoos[3]. Among the Karbi community, it was a tradition for the recipient of a high-quality tattoo to present the tattoo artist with a bottle of *hor* (distilled alcohol) and *horlang* (rice beer). These offerings were then reverently dedicated to the recipient's *kuru*, or ancestors. With precision and care, she delicately pricked the recipient's skin, moving from the forehead down to the chin, using spines of rattan palm. With one spine in each hand, she skillfully avoided any damage to the inner tissues as she gently pricked the skin, following the contours of the nose[4]. Following a successful tattoo, the recipient was expected to offer the skilled artist a pair of *pini*, a traditional women's lower garment dyed/colored with *sibu*, along with a *pekok*, a higher garment. In accordance with tradition, no payment has been made for the tattoo.

TOOLS AND COLOUR FOR TATTOOING

In the traditional Ao-Naga society, the colours utilized for tattooing were derived from the juice of the bark of a tree called *Ngupti* or *Naptti*. Similarly, the Karbis relied on *sibu*, a traditional source of indigo dye, for their *duk* tattoos. The *sibu* plant, scientifically named *marsdenia tinctoria*, is a member of the *Apocynaceae* family. They possess an inherent inclination towards climbing. The leaves are simple and wide. An individual's maximum height is 5 meters. *Sibu* can be easily propagated through seeds, and its management doesn't demand extensive expertise or expense. Women are the ones who cultivate and care for this indigo plant. The technology used by the Aos was quite basic. The tree's bark was gently caressed by a rough, uneven stone slab. The bark juice was carefully collected into a pot and gently boiled over a crackling wood fire. Once the juice had reached its halfway point of boiling, a delightful addition of rice beer was made. The design on the skin was adorned with vibrant hues, delicately applied using sharp cane thorns affixed to a wooden holder. The girl's skin became a canvas for the elderly woman, who skillfully used a piece of wood dipped in color to create a beautiful tattoo design. The instrument was delicately pressed into the skin to finalize the piercing. The root of the *kamri* tree functioned as a needle, piercing through. Once the initial piercing was complete, the color (*Nap*) was carefully reapplied after the blood had been gently washed away. In a similar fashion to the Aos, the Karbis also utilized the delicate, young leaves of *sibu* and ground them in a wooden mortar. Next, the *sibu* juice is delicately applied to the girl's pricked skin, using a feather or a soft puff of cotton. After a few days, the skin that was pricked would heal. However, if the tattoo did not turn out to be of the desired colour and intensity, the process had to be repeated. Typically, there were no more than three rounds of pricking. A truly captivating tattoo showcases a mesmerizing blend of black and deep blue hues, gracefully stretching from the forehead to the chin, elegantly crossing the nose[5].

TATTOOING DESIGNS

The tattoo designs of the Karbis and the Ao-Nagas exhibit distinct variations. When comparing the intricate Ao tattoos to the Karbi tattoos, one can observe that the latter is more modest in design. The following song presents the story of two Karbi girls, Hanri and Harvi, who were the first to receive facial tattoos.

Original song titled – Duk Kacheduk Alun[6]	*Translation*
Oh...oh...oh...Bang Hanri pen Harvi	Hanri and Harvi

Ke Duksangso kar`i
Lo thengri o phi
Nangju athengri o phi
Ke Duksang le nangji…
E… Duksang le nangji te honmi
phir nangji
Bang Hanri pen Harvi ke
Duksang si kar`i
An honmi phir tangri te Murong
rongsopi
An Murong rongsopi ke oh
Hanri pen Harvi ke chilolo ra`i
An loti mabeng`ri ke prisek ta
nangji
Oh…oh…oh… Murong
rongsopi
An Murong rongsopi mumang
bang lengri
An jengkeng bang puri ra kam
parvi damri
An kam par`e choksi bang
jenghong kupmeri
An mumang bang chongni
An Kami pen Kaphi ke pi
kevang mati
An kei vangve vangpli ke aron
do boti
Ne Hanri pen Harvi ke
charnam thakdunri
Ne Duksang si kar`i…
An bang Duksang le ar`i te
kangkong hong masi…
Eh…eh…eh Bang Duksang
kedukji (ke)
An Kami pen Kaphi

Desired for duksangso (facial tattoo)
So they went to their grandmother
Their grandmother said
If you want duksangso
You make new thread
Hanri and Harvi really desired for duksangso
They made new thread and are ready to go
Thus Hanri and Harvi goes to Murong village
On their way, they also collected prisek (cane having thorns)
They reached Murong village
And seeing the bamboo stairs began the climb with left foot
Climbing a step after another they ascended to the courtyard
And sat down to rest
Kami and Kaphi asked the purpose of their visit
For they are not usual visitors
So Hanri and Harvi give the reply
We want Duksangso
If you want duksangso, you'll have to wait
They want to make tattoo
So Kami and Kaphi were ready

Hanri pen Harvi ke Duksanglok kar`i	To fulfill the desire for Hanri
Ili soKarbi ke Duksang do	and Harvi's for Duksangso
nangji	All Karbi women must have Duksangso
Si bang Duksangso dukkri…	So they made the duksang so on
Hanri pen Harvi	
An Hanri pen Harvi ke	Hanri and Harvi
Duksangso jangkri	Now Hanri and Harvi has
An Duksangso jangkri…	Duksangso
Loti mabengri vur ajat vurri	Do not stop by anywhere on
An jipu chikurki ra chevang arindi	your way back home
	Covering faces with cloth they come home
Oh thengri o phi ne Duksang do loti	They tell the grandmother
An phi ne Duksang do loti	about the Duksang
An athengri aphi ta charnam nangron ri	The grandmother is happy
	And she said
An ili soKarbi ke duksang do nangji	All Karbi women must have Duksang
An jothom pen joni ke mumang ingmur ri	For two-three nights do not wash face
Duksang dakpetji	Or else the Duksang might be erased

Various patterns of tattooing adorned different areas of the bodies of the Ao girls. According to the traditional account, a mother from Chungli was responsible for creating various designs to distinguish the different groups in the village. 'In past, the young girls would sleep in the *tsüki*, dormitory at night. Girls from both rich and poor families would meet each other and they spent time singing and narrating stories. Amongst the group there were two girls. One girl belonged to a wealthy family from the Chungli clan, while the other came from a poor family of the Mongsen clan. The latter was intelligent, beautiful, and popular among many of the other girls. This made the wealthy girl jealous leading her to develop a dislike for the other girl. The rich girl started to make fun of the poor girl in front of the other girls. Since Mongsen girl was very beautiful so out of jealousy the mother of the rich girl put a criss-cross tattoo on the Mongsen girl and a parallel tattoo on her daughter. However, once the wound on the leg of the Mongsen girl healed, it was greatly admired. From that day on, the villagers started tattooing and different patterns of tattoos were applied for the two groups. The patterns of their tattoos gave identity and even the boys found it helpful in distinguishing the girls they admired[7].'

The Ao girls adorned their bodies with various tattoo designs, each carefully placed on specific parts. According to the local lore, it is said that a mother from Chungli was responsible for creating various designs to distinguish the different groups in the village. Observing the tattooing process among the Ao girls, during the initial year, only the lower legs were tattooed, as it was customary to wait until they reached puberty before tattooing other parts of their bodies. During the second year, tattoos were applied to the chest, chin, and shoulder. By the third year, the previously unfinished patterns on the calves had been fully realized, and by the fourth year, intricate tattoos adorned the knees. Finally, in the fifth year, the tattooing process is finished, covering the wrists and stomach. The pattern exhibited some slight variations within the Mongsen and Chungli group of the Ao-Naga. Typically, the chin is adorned

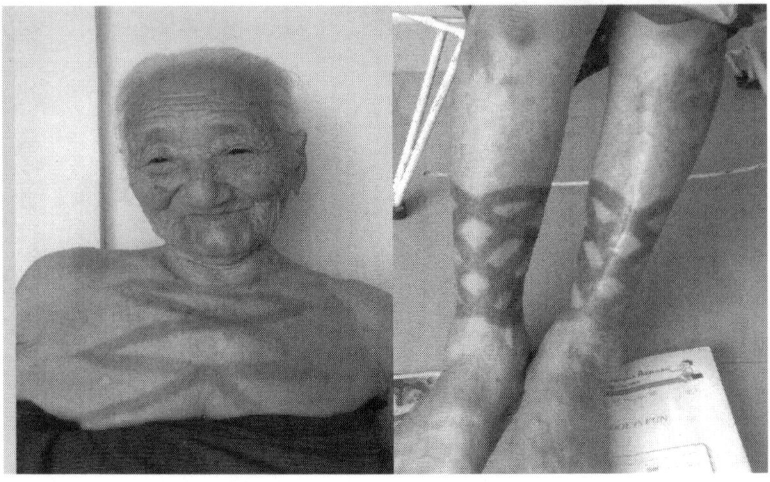

PICTURE 1: IMTILANGLA IS AN AO NAGA FROM MERANGKONG VILLAGE, 100 YEARS (PICTURE TAKEN ON MAY 12, 2023)

with four vertical lines, forming a pattern of lozenges that extends from the throat down to the bottom of the breastbone. The front of the shoulders and stomach display an inverted letter 'V' shape, while the wrists feature lozenges and square patterns on the sides. Moving down to the lower part of the leg, one can observe lozenges, and the knee proudly displays an arrow pattern[8]. Once the tattooed wounds have fully healed and the dry skin has been shed, the true beauty of the intricate designs is revealed. These pictures showcase the intricate tattooing designs of the Ao-Naga people:

The people of Merangkong village had a rich history of tattooing that spanned many generations, long before they embraced Christianity. Based on information from an informant (personal interactions on May 12, 2023), it is observed that girls from affluent backgrounds are more inclined to ink tattoos after reaching puberty compared to their peers. Imtilangla and Jungzungtula are the only two survivors from Merangkong village who bear tattoos on their bodies. When Godhula and Longjunglepzuk arrived in the village, they shared their beliefs and encouraged the community to reconsider their tattooing practices in light of their Christian faith. As a result, the village eventually stopped tattooing altogether.

PICTURE 2: KASANG TERONPI[9]

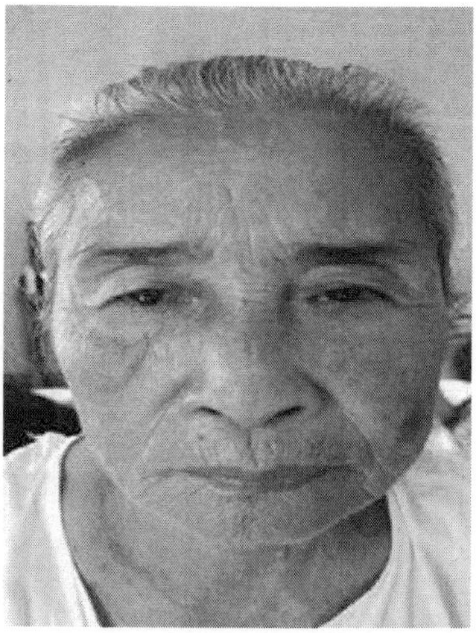

PICTURE 3: OMPHU SINGNARPI[10]

KARBI WOMEN FACIAL TATTOO DESIGN

Similar to the decline of tattooing among the Aos, the tradition of *duk* among the Karbi is rapidly fading. According to Robindra Teron and SK Borthakur, modern Karbi girls no longer see the value in *duk*, considering it outdated and ineffective in enhancing one's appearance[11]. Finding skilled *duk* dyers can be quite a challenge in today's times. It suggests that *duk* is presently a 'dying art,' and there is a concern that the accompanying traditional knowledge may soon vanish from the community.

CONCLUSION

Based on my research, it can be concluded that in earlier times, tattooing served as a significant symbol of culture, morality, and one's position in society. In this context, one can recognize the uniqueness of tattooing among the Karbis and the Ao-Nagas, as it is closely connected to their beliefs in the empowerment of women and the safeguarding of their cultural heritage. Basically, these tattoos hold great importance in terms of tradition, identity, and spirituality. It played a crucial role in shaping their sense of self as it symbolized the onset of adolescence, a time when they could actively engage in their community. It was regarded as a symbol of honor and purity, signifying eligibility for marriage. However, in today's world, tattooing has evolved into a captivating art form, a means of personal expression, and a fashion trend. In the past, only experienced women were able to excel in the skill of tattooing. Currently, tattoos have gained widespread popularity and are commonly observed both in public spaces and professional environments. The rising popularity of tattoos, especially among the younger demographic, is a captivating phenomenon to see. With the passage of time, the techniques for administering tattoos have also evolved. In contemporary times, the utilization of advanced tools and high-quality pigments has rendered the process of obtaining a tattoo considerably safer and less agonizing, while also yielding more enduring outcomes. Tattoos are a powerful form of self-expression, allowing individuals to showcase their unique identity and personal style. They serve as a means of conveying individuality and uniqueness. It holds various connotations for each individual and serves as a platform for self-expression through the art form of body modification. Likewise, several individuals opt to acquire tattoos as a method of articulating their emotions and views. Occasionally, the emphasis is placed on asserting one's autonomy or cherishing a deep bond. Tattoos and other forms of body art have played a significant and lasting role throughout human history, and they will likely continue to do so in the future.

NOTES

1. Sanghamitra Baruah, 'Tattoos-a tribal heritage', February 19, 2011, Available at https://timesofindia.indiatimes.com/life-style/fashion/buzz/Tattoos-a-tribal-heritage/articleshow/6040717.cms (Accessed on 2/3/2023)
2. Robindra Teron and S K Borthakur, 'A History of Duk Facial tattooing with indigo dye of the Karbi women of Northeast India', in *Turkey Red Journal*, 18(1), Winter, 2014, pp. 1-5.
3. W.C Smith, *The Ao-Naga Tribes of Assam,* New Delhi, Mittal Publications (1925), 2002 (Reprint), p. 22.
4. Robindra Teron and S K Borthakur, 'A History of Duk Facial tattooing with indigo dye of the Karbi women of Northeast India', in *Turkey Red Journal*, 18(1), Winter, 2014, pp. 1-5.
5. Ibid.
6. Research and transcription works done by Dilip Kathar, Principal KTMCRI, Art & Culture Department, Karbi Anglong Autonomous Council, Diphu on 13/03/2017. The main song sung by Mrs. Kachai Ronghongpi, wife of Kro Miji, Ronghang Rongbong Rongcheicho Artu, West Karbi Anglong. All translation done by Welsing Hanse, Teacher by profession and Chairman of Jambili Literary Foundation.
7. The oral interview was conducted on December 20, 2007 with Longrichila Longchar (78 years), Longkhum village, Nagaland. For further reading on the story of how tattooing came about (Ao Folktales), refer to https://nagajournal.com/the-story-of-how-tattooing-came-about-ao-folktales/
8. J.P. Mills, *The Ao Nagas*, Director of the Government of Assam, Guwahati, 1926, p. 30.
9. She is a Karbi woman from Diphu, Karbi Anglong, who is 104 years old as of 2023. Photo courtesy: Longbir Engti.

10. She is a Karbi woman from Vothatlangso, Dera Arong who is 87 years old. The picture was taken on July 28, 2023.
11. A History of Duk Facial tattooing with indigo dye of the Karbi women of Northeast India. Ibid. Retrieved June 7, 2023, from https://tattooschool.com/how-technology-is-changing-the-world-of-tattoos/; https://www.tattoodo.com/articles/smart-tattoo-technology-the-future-within-skin-14567.

CHAPTER 5

The Concept of the Liminal Soul in Karbi Culture

AMPHU TERANGPI

INTRODUCTION

The Karbis are an indigenous ethnic group predominantly residing in the hilly area of Karbi Anglong, located in the state of Assam within Northeast India. Karbi Anglong, founded in 1951, the biggest district in the Northeast, in geographical term, has since been partitioned into two districts for administrative purpose, namely Karbi Anglong and West Karbi Anglong in 2015. The Karbi language is classified as a member of the Tibeto-Burman language group, which is a subcategory of the larger Sino-Tibetan language family. The Karbis are postulated to be among the various tribes that have migrated from the region of Central Asia.[1] The Karbis prefer to live in the foothills and has a tranquil nature. Identifying this community involves highlighting their agrarian lifestyle, which includes both *jhum* cultivation and wetland cultivation. Based on the data from the 2011 census, it is evident that a significant portion of the rural population, approximately 81.1%, relied heavily on agriculture as their primary occupation. It is worth noting that the cultivation in these areas chiefly depended on rain water as the sole source of irrigation.[2] The cultivation method known as *jhum* has been observed to be traditionally practiced during the spring season, while wetland cultivation, on the other hand, has been historically documented to be carried out during the autumn season.

In accordance with their intricate social framework, it is observed that the Karbis possess a system of five exogamous clans known as *'nok'hum.'* These entities, namely *Lijang, Hanjang, Ejang, Kronjang,* and *Tungjang,* hold historical significance within the context under examination. In the complex social system of the period, it is worth noting that every clan was intricately subdivided into various sub-clans. The Karbi people's traditional and social governance structure is headed by a personality of great significance, referred to as the Lindokpo or Recho, which translates to 'King' in the Karbi language. Assisting the King in his duties are the Pinpos, who comprise the King's cabinet, and the Habes, who are the regional chiefs subordinate to the King. In the historical context, it is important to note that during certain periods, various authorities, commonly referred to as Habe, held distinct territories under their control. These territories were typically delineated based on factors such as political boundaries, traditions, cultural affiliations, or geographical features. It is important to note that in the administration of the village, it was the responsibility of the respected Rong Asar, who held the esteemed post of the Village Headman, to assure the well-being and proper functioning of the community.[3] The society in question possesses a remarkably abundant heritage of folklores. The enduring longevity of these folklores can be attributed to their preservation through a longstanding method of oral transmission. Because of the adoption of Roman script, the younger generation can document their folklore in writing. This change is also influenced by the fact that the majority of students nowadays attend English medium schools rather than Assamese medium schools.

RITES OF PASSAGE

Arnold Van Gannep's work in the field of cultural anthropology is highly regarded for his ideas outlined in the book 'Rites of Passage[4].' He has noted a noteworthy phenomenon in human existence, specifically in the form of individual ceremonies commonly referred to as 'life crises'. The term 'rites of passage' was used to refer to life crises. In every culture, individuals engage in activities that are associated with various ceremonies and rituals that hold significance in their lives. The ceremonial rite of passage can be delineated into three distinct stages, namely separation, transition, and incorporation. Rites of separation hold a significant position in burial ceremonies, while rites of inclusion are observed during marriage rituals. Transition rituals can hold significance in various life events such as pregnancy, betrothal, and initiation. However, in certain situations like adoption, the birth of a second child, remarriage, or the transition from the second to the third age group, these rituals may be minimised or omitted altogether. He comprehended the universal law of life as it pertains to humanity. In addition, he has recognised the correlation between the laws of nature and the seasonal changes in celestial bodies, particularly the moon. When examining Karbi society, one can also notice the occurrence of 'rites of passage.' I would like to delve into the main idea put forth by Van Gennep about the rituals of 'separation' in the context of the Karbi culture. Similarly, the Karbi community possesses a distinct and unique way of life, as well as a distinct worldview. The underlying structure within the human species following death encompasses a profound worldview regarding the departure of the soul from the physical body, resulting in a state of separation. The soul will ultimately arrive at its eternal destination known as *Chomrongme* (*Phu-Phi Arong*), commonly referred to as the ancestral village. However, what is intriguing is that the Karbi people possess a well-defined notion of the soul, which necessitates a process of sanctification in order for their souls to attain an eternal realm. According to Victor Turner, the soul exists in a 'liminal time'[5], which he described as being 'betwixt and between.' The Karbi people engage in a specific ceremonial practice known as *Chomkan* , *Karbi* or *Chomangkan*, which is conducted exclusively for individual participants following death rites. It is believed that if *Chomangkan* fails to fulfill its purpose for an individual, the sanctification of the soul will not be achieved, and the soul will not reach its destination, *Phu-Phi Arong*. The soul will neither exist in the specific location in *Ritlo Pharlo* nor the other worldly ancestral village.

SIGNIFICANCE OF RITUAL PRACTICES

The Karbis adhere steadfastly to their ancestral faith known as *Aronban* or *Aronbarim*, which encompasses a comprehensive system of beliefs and rituals rooted in the principles of animism. The rituals and practices of the Karbi people are intricately intertwined with their sacred convictions and the cycles of their agricultural endeavours. The majority of their celebratory events consist of communal festivals. The Karbi people partake in various festivals that hold significant cultural and spiritual importance. Among these is the *Rongker* ritual, which is observed to ensure the prosperity and welfare of the villagers. Likewise, the Karbis celebrate the *Chojun* ritual, during which they pay homage to their household deity and engage in ancestor spirit worship. Lastly, the *Chomangkan* ritual is held as a post-death ceremony, which is a secondary cremation ritual performed in festive grandeur, serving as a means to honour and remember the departed. These festivals serve as integral components of the Karbi traditions, fostering a sense of community and spiritual connection among the people. In addition to collective rituals such as *Tirim Kangduk*, which involves ancestral worship and includes offerings like food, rice beer, dry fish, betel nut, and betel leaves, there are also certain practices of a more individualistic nature.

In the realm of Karbi social folk customs, one encounters the profound practices of *Tirim/Chamburukso Kangduk*, *Sar Anthok* and *Chomkan*. These ceremonies, deeply intertwined with the essence of the departed soul, hold paramount significance within the cultural fabric of the Karbi people. *Sar Anthok* is an ancestral worship ritual that takes place during *Chojun*. During this ceremony, it is said that the spirit deities, the ancestors of the host, and the living families of *Chojun* will meet. The Karbis exhibit a profound adherence to the significance of these ceremonies. The religious performance serve as vessels of the cultural values, norms, and relationships that were prevalent within the Karbi society. The *Tirim Kangduk*, a traditional cultural practice, is observed through the participation of a solitary household belonging to a specific clan or sub-clans within the tribe. According to historical accounts, there exists a belief among certain cultures that the *Tirim*, regarded as ancestral spirits, possess powers comparable to those attributed to the divine entity known as God. The act of worshipping is undertaken with the intention of appeasing the *karjong*, or 'soul', of the departed individual, while also seeking blessings for the welfare and prosperity of the familial unit.

The *Chomangkan* is a traditional community festival enacted to honour and commemorate the departed soul/s. This age-old practice involves performing a series of sacred rituals through which it is believed that the soul reunites with those of the deceased family members in *Phu-Phi Arong*. The purpose of *Chomangkan* is to facilitate the reunion of a departed soul with the souls of the ancestors in the ancestral homeland. According to Karbi belief, the funeral festival practiced among the Karbi people is said to have been imparted by a mythical figure known as *Thireng-Vangreng*, who is attributed to Haja Bey. Haja Bey was known as Thireng-Vangreng. The individual possessing the ability to traverse between the mortal realm and the abode of their forebears, unencumbered by the finality of demise, undertakes this extraordinary journey.

KARBI'S CONCEPT OF SOUL

The concept of soul has been observed as a pervasive belief throughout the diverse tapestry of human cultures. In a similar vein, it is worth noting that the Karbis possess a profound belief in the immortality of the soul. According to the beliefs, the soul is not only immortal, but is reborn to the clan members in a phenomenon called *menchi-menvang*. This observation further attests to their understanding and recognition of the concept of mortality. The concept of death, as understood through historical lenses can be delineated into three distinct layers. These layers encompass the notions of the immortality of the soul, the existence of an afterlife and the phenomenon of rebirth. The concept of soul in the Karbi culture can be comprehended through the lens of liminality which holds significant historical and cultural significance. The prevailing belief among the Karbis is that the concept of life after death holds significant symbolic meaning and is regarded as a manifestation of their collective imagination and wisdom.

The significance of these phases, or 'rites of passage,' as proposed by Arnold Van Gennep identifies three phases which are also found in Karbi ceremonies: separation (*kithi kejang*), transition (*oso amahang kethek*), and reincarnation (*adam asar*). The Karbi people possess a notable and distinctive way of life, characterized by a worldview that sets them apart from other cultures. This distinctiveness is evident in their belief that individuals can communicate about their past lives and choose their parents for the next generation before they die. Throughout human history, it is clear that a prevailing belief system has existed regarding the fate of individuals after their mortal demise. This particular worldview, deeply ingrained within various cultures, revolves around the notion of the soul's departure from the physical vessel it once inhabited. This profound phenomenon, commonly referred to as 'separation,' holds great significance within the collective consciousness of humankind and is considered a universal experience among human beings. The notion of separation, as evidenced in the understanding of death is intricately tied to the belief in the soul's journey to a timeless realm known as phu-phi arong. This term, serving as a euphemism for the realm of the deceased, encapsulates the profound concept of the afterlife. According to the Karbi concept, it is believed that the soul possesses immortality and undergoes a cyclical process of returning to the earthly realm and being reborn within its own clan. In the context of the discussion, death can be regarded as a liminal space that represents a state of transition. Furthermore, it is important to note that according to historical accounts, the soul, upon departing from the mortal realm was believed to be unable to gain entry into the revered ancestral village known as *Phu-Phi Arong*. The state referred to as 'betwixt and between' has been designated by Victor Turner. The Karbi people, as part of their cultural practises, engage in a solemn ritual known as Chomkan, which serves as a post-funeral ceremony. In the absence of conducting the Chomkan ritual for the deceased, it is widely held in belief that the soul becomes ensnared within the interstitial realm, commonly referred to as *ritlo*. The location in question can be described as a peripheral area surrounding the primary settlement of the ancestral village. In this particular circumstance, one could argue that the essence of the individual is in a state of neither presence nor absence. During this particular era, the soul finds itself in a transitional state, existing on the threshold between the realm of the living and the ancestral village. This state of being can be described as an inter-structural situation, characterised by its inherent nature.

In this specific situation, the liminal soul finds itself situated at the periphery of established systems and frameworks at Ritlo Pharlo, a temporary place. The prevailing historical perspective suggests that this particular matter lacks a definitive location or categorization. The current circumstances present a challenging predicament. During the liminal period, it is noteworthy to observe that the Karbis held a worldview that attributed a structurally negative connotation to the concept of the liminal soul. The defining feature of this entity is its notable absence of any discernible characteristics, including the absence of a social structure.

Laurence Waddell (1900)[6] made significant observations on the belief systems of tribes in northeast India. He noted that the Mikirs, as a distinct ethnic community, had a distinctive belief in the quick departure of the spirit from the physical world. He observed that the Kacharis strongly believed that after the soul leaves the body, it would roam the earth for thirteen days. During this time, the soul was said to wander aimlessly, revisiting the very location where it had been liberated from its corporeal vessel. According to him, it is believed that a soul waits near the deceased individual's body for three days. This belief has led the Nagas to adopt a practise of diligently safeguarding the burial site for a period of two nights subsequent to the interment. Similarly, it was a prevailing belief among the Kukis and Lushais that the soul is forced to reside within the confines of the house it occupied during life for a certain period. The Mikir people, in contrast to many other tribes, do not hold the belief in the soul's ability to return to the earthly realm. Consequently, they perceive death as a state of being completely forgotten[7]. This statement by Waddell mentioned above is incorrect; the Karbis do not hold any such belief. The dead are not forgotten.

In light of the available evidence, it becomes apparent that according to Karbi beliefs, the soul of an individual promptly separates from their physical form and the earthly realm upon the occurrence of death. In the realm of Karbis, it will discern the existence of two distinct phases within the funeral ceremonies dedicated to the liminal soul. In the initial stage, commonly referred to as the first phase, an individual undergoes the cessation of vital functions, resulting in their demise. In accordance with the customs and traditions of the time, a sombre ceremony was held to commemorate the deceased individual's passing. This solemn occasion, known as a funeral, was conducted with the intention of facilitating the cremation process. The subsequent stage in the historical progression is known as the *Karhi*, which pertains to the post-funeral ceremony. In the initial stage, when a person dies, the body is prepared for cremation. However, *Karhi* is a highly dramatized performance. In the *Karhi* tradition, it is essential to recall and invite the deceased's maternal uncle and his relatives. Their presence is necessary for the *Karhi* festival, as the ritual or festival cannot be performed without them. In the *Karhi* tradition, a large network of people from the clan, including descendants, is required. While *Karhi* may be considered secondary in the present day, it was not always so. In the past, when a person died, only family members performed the *Karhi*, known as *Arpum Karhi*. Today, due to financial constraints, people perform *Karhi* according to their financial status. However, according to Karbi belief, it remains compulsory to perform Karhi. So they perform according to their financial status balance. But according to Karbi belief it is compulsory to perform Karhi. The aforementioned ritual can be identified as a rite of separation, aligning with the fundamental principles of Van Gannep's rite de passage. The 'uchepi', a revered figure within the Karbi community, assumes a significant role in the sacred rituals surrounding Karbi funerary ceremonies. The individual in question is a woman of advanced age who assumes the role of overseeing the proceedings of the funeral festival. In the wake of her ascension, a cohort of female assistants emerged, known collectively as the 'charhepimar'. In the annals of cultural practises, it is recorded that the people engage in the solemn act of singing the kacharhe, a poignant and lyrical composition dedicated to those who have departed from the realm of the living. This poetic song, with its profound emotional resonance, serves as a heartfelt tribute to the deceased, encapsulating their memory and honouring their legacy. The uchepi, elderly women engages in the performance and preservation of their traditions primarily through oral means. This includes the meticulous exploration of the soul's journey, a subject of great significance within their belief system. Adjacent to the Uchepi, one may observe the presence of the *rantini*, a venerable female figure entrusted with the solemn duty of preparing funeral meal for the departed souls. In ancient times, it was believed that the Uchepi played a crucial role in guiding the soul of the departed. *Charhepi* will sing the lament songs to guide the soul continuously for three or four days until it reaches *Phu-Phi Arong*. This song describes the soul's journey to the ancestral village. It recounts the geography of the 'other world' and explains the sacred realm of *Phu-Phi Arong*. According to prevalent beliefs, it has been postulated that the ethereal essence commonly referred to as the soul possesses the propensity to traverse the realms that lie betwixt and between the mortal plane and the realm of the deceased. Turner's utilisation of Van Gennep's notion of transition or liminality is evident in this instance.

KARBI'S CONCEPT OF LIMINALITY

Liminality is of great significance in the Karbi culture, relating to the profound spiritual journey of the soul. The concept of the journey or transitional stage holds significant importance within the belief systems of the Karbis. In the context of prevailing societal norms, the concept of the liminal soul is significant as an entity characterised by its lack of structure and definitive form. This means it cannot be clearly identified whether the soul is sanctified for *Phu-Phi Arong*. These people do not have any specific social class affiliation, and they do not possess any remarkable status or unique clothing. This particular entity holds no significant standing within the societal and cultural framework. According to oral narrative, there exists a belief surrounding the *Chomangkan* ritual and its significance for the soul. It is widely held that if the *Chomangkan* ceremony is not performed, the soul in question will be confined to a realm known as 'sanchom' or 'ritlo'. This particular realm is described as a liminal space, often referred to as the 'betwixt and between'. It is understood that for a deceased member for whom *Karhi* has already been performed, it is believed that they achieve eternal peace and will reside in *Phu-Phi Arong* (the main ancestral village). In contrast, a deceased member for whom Karhi has not been performed will remain in *Ritlo Pharlo* (a temporary place). Within this imaginary space, these souls are said to wander in close proximity to the outskirts of the primary ancestral village. In order to access the ancestral village known as *'Phu-Phi Arong'* it is imperative for the liminal soul to undergo the ritualistic observance of the individual *Chomangkan*, a funeral festival conducted by the family. The existence of accounts detailing the passage of the deceased soul and other ritualistic expeditions has been a subject of debate. These narratives have been documented across various cultural regions, including native North America, the Polynesian islands, and Southeast Asia. Likewise in native North American, Polynesian, and Southeast Asian belief systems, the concept of the ancestral village bear similarities with the Karbi traditions. The prevalence of this phenomenon, as evidenced by historical records, is notably concentrated in the regions of central and north Asia. Additionally, its influence is particularly pronounced within the Tibeto-Burman-speaking societies that span the vast expanse of the Himalayan Mountain range, extending from the nation of Nepal to the southwestern reaches of China.'[8] The notion of the soul and the existence of an afterlife is not exclusive to the Karbi people but rather can be observed within numerous other cultures as well.

The significance of *Chomangkan*'s practice in the Karbi tradition lies in its role as a pivotal socio-religious ceremony observed by the Karbi community. In the Karbi language, the term *Chomangkan* or 'Karhi' is used to refer to the same entity. The ritual known as *Chomangkan* holds significant cultural and spiritual importance, as it is traditionally performed to facilitate the soul's transition into its ultimate journey. The extensive ceremonial proceedings are presided over by the household of the deceased individual. The aforementioned event is a communal celebration that spans a duration of three to four consecutive days. Throughout history, Karbis have negotiated vast distances, hailing from various villages, to partake in the revered *Chomangkan* ceremony. This momentous event holds great significance, as it sees the convergence of diverse communities, each bringing with them their unique cultural heritage. Notably, among the participants, one can observe the presence of the *Jambili Athon*, a sacred totem revered by the Karbi people. According to Karbi belief systems, *Jambili Athon* can only be taken out during *Karhi* or to honor a dignitary person. Its inclusion in this grand gathering further accentuates the profound spiritual and communal nature of the *Chomangkan*. The intricate series of rituals spanning four days is dedicated to the liminal soul, with the ultimate aim of facilitating its reunion with the ancestors.

ROLE OF UCHEPI (DIRGE SINGER)

It is believed that the soul, the ethereal essence within each person, is influenced by a mournful tune called the dirge. This sorrowful lamentation, which carries with it a sense of mourning and introspection, is performed by a revered figure known as the *uchepi*. Through the haunting strains of the dirge singer's voice, the soul is believed to find solace and direction, as it navigates the intricate tapestry of existence. The composition attributed to Charhepi is characterised by its remarkable length and poetic qualities. The historical account of the poetic song of lamentation provides a comprehensive narrative of the soul's entire journey. Upon the recitation of the lyrical composition, the essence of the individual shall depart from its corporeal vessel. According to historical accounts, there exists a belief that upon departing from the earthly realm, the soul embarks on a journey to reunite with the village of the ancestors. Within the *Chomangkan*, a significant ensemble of ritual functionaries plays crucial roles in various ceremonial proceedings. Among these esteemed individuals are the *Rantini*, responsible for the culinary preparations dedicated to the departed souls; the *Kurusar*, serving as the priestly figure overseeing the spiritual aspects of the rituals; and the *Duhuidi*, a master drummer. Because duhuidi is the master of drummer (*cheng*), he is entrusted with the task of orchestrating the rhythmic cadences that accompanies the sacred observances.

SIGNIFICANCE OF DUHUIDI (MASTER DRUMMER)

The Duhuidi, along with his deputy assistant, the Duhuijang, hold significant positions within the Chomkan, exerting considerable influence and contributing to the functioning of the system. The commencement of the ritual is heralded by the rhythmic percussion of the drums, skilfully played by Duhuidi and Duhuijang, resonating throughout the sacred grounds of Chomkan. During the *Chomangkan*, a customary practice involves meticulously crafting a representation of the departed individual using paddy straw. This object symbolises the reanimated form of the deceased. In the ancient customs of certain cultures, there existed a solemn ceremony known as *Ru kihum*, which involved the collection of cowrie shells, also referred to as 'sobai'. These shells held great significance as they were gathered from the crematory grounds, where the remains of the departed were laid to rest. The act of collecting these shells was a symbolic gesture, representing the gathering of the deceased's bones. This ritualistic practice is deeply rooted in the cultural and spiritual belief of the Karbi.

THE IDEA OF DEATH

During the *Chomangkan* period, metaphorical social dramas are enacted through various acts. Following the *Chomangkan*, it became customary for the departed soul to find solace in *Phu-Phi Arong*, commonly referred to as *Rongsopi*, which denotes a place of perpetual joy and contentment. Upon the completion of the *Chomangkan*, it becomes apparent to individuals that the liminal soul has embarked upon its ultimate voyage to a realm known as *Phu-phi Arongsopi*. The aforementioned observation suggests that these transitional states of the soul, which hold cultural significance, will be identified and acknowledged. It is only at that moment that the soul shall find itself situated within a specific location.

Upon the arrival of the liminal soul at *Phu-phi Arongsopi* as it is also known, it is widely held that this ethereal entity is but a transient presence in this sacred place. The phenomenon can be attributed to the prevailing Karbi belief in the concept of rebirth. The notion of rebirth (*menchi-menvang*) holds a paramount and profound position within Karbi cultural beliefs. In accordance with the beliefs of the Karjong culture, it is postulated that upon the cessation of an individual's mortal existence, the Karjong, or soul, undergoes a process of rebirth. The phenomenon of rebirth, as observed within the context of Karbi societies, is found to be limited to individuals belonging to the same clan or sub-clan. Throughout history, it has been observed that the concept of rebirth has held a significant place in various belief systems and philosophical traditions. It is believed that the soul, an ethereal essence often associated with the individual, has the potential to undergo multiple rebirths. This notion suggests that the soul has agency in determining the frequency and occurrence of rebirths. For example, in Karbi belief, if a person's past life involved blindness, they might experience several lifetimes observing how blind people navigate, allowing for a seemingly limitless cycle of rebirths. Throughout history, it has been believed that individuals have the potential to undergo multiple rebirths in order to achieve their desired goals and aspirations. For example, it is believed that if a person is not satisfied with their wishes, they may be reborn several times to fulfill them. This concept suggests that one's journey towards fulfilment may extend beyond a single lifetime, allowing for the possibility of multiple opportunities for personal growth and the realisation of one's deepest desires. Throughout history, it has been widely acknowledged that the concept of the soul encompasses the possibility of rebirth. Referred to as a *menplak*, this phenomenon entails the soul's ability to undergo reincarnation, manifesting in various locations and within diverse familial contexts. When rebirth occurs, many believe that humans are able to uncover their previous identity through marks and signs. For instance, in Karbi belief, an *angthek* (mark) from a past life such as a cut on the head, might result in the hair not growing in the same area in the present life. The ancient practice known as *sang kelang*, commonly referred to as rice divination, was a ritual performed with the purpose of uncovering one's name. The traditional ritual known as *Sang Kelang* is a sacred performance carried out by a venerable individual from the Karbi community referred to as the *kurusar* or priest. Besides the Karbi, the Tiwa tribe also practices rice divination. In the realm of cultural beliefs, it is widely held that individuals possess the ability to fulfil their desires prior to experiencing rebirth. An intriguing aspect worth noting is that, in certain belief systems, individuals possess the ability to determine their future lineage through a verbal proclamation prior to their demise. This practice allows them to exercise agency in selecting their prospective parents for their subsequent rebirth. This assertion further reinforces the conviction that the soul possesses vitality.

KARBI'S CONCEPT OF REINCARNATION

According to the concept of rebirth, the Karbis adhere to a belief system that posits the cyclical nature of the soul's existence, referred to as *Menchi-Menvang*. Once more, the concept of the liminal soul emerges as an integral component within the intricate framework of the prevailing social structure. Throughout history, it has been observed that the soul has consistently regained a position of 'cultural significance'. Upon receiving the information, the individual is provided with the appellation of the departed individual. The act of bestowing a name upon a newly born child holds great cultural and historical significance within the Karbi community. In accordance with historical observations, it has been noted that a newly arrived infant may exhibit certain angthek, or indications, pertaining to their previous existence. In hypothetical instances, it is suggested that a person in a past life experienced an event that led to a unique mark on their forehead, observed by mark on skin or behaviour. If this person experiences reincarnation, it is believed that the described mark, known as an *angthek*, would appear as a visible imprint on their forehead in their next existence. The aforementioned evidence holds great significance in establishing a connection between the individual's past existence and their present life or essence. Based on the above-mentioned *angthek*, it can be discerned that the individual who has passed away has undergone the process of reincarnation, assuming a distinct identity in the present. The process of the liminal soul in transition and its role in the identification of Karbi culture is an argument of historical significance. The transition of the liminal soul is an important phase where its status is unknown while at *Ritlo Pharlo*. However, once the *Karhi* ritual is performed and the soul reaches Phu-Phi Arong, the phase changes, and the deceased *Karjong* (soul) is said to have reached its final destination.

CONCLUSION

It can be understood that in the context of Karhi, a post-funeral ritual concept of liminal soul and incorporation reflect of the Arnold van Gennep of 'Rite of Passage'[9]and VictorTurner[10] concept of 'betwixt and between'. The concept of 'angthek' or convincing proof of their prior existence is the primary reason that the Karbis include rebirth into their logical mind, connecting the past, present, and future. This relates from the concept of life cycle. So, the concept of cyclical process of life, death and rebirth is not only observed in Karbi but rather seen in Buddhism, Hinduism and so on. It is a universal belief system of the humankind. This means that the concept of rebirth is also practised in other traditions. Example the idea of 'separation' is the 'death'. In Karbi belief, after the soul separates from the physical body, the intangible soul remains alive and travels back to *Phu-Phi Arong*, which pertains to the afterlife. According to the Karbi people, death is seen as a moment of transition in which the soul returns to earth in a bodily form known as *menchi-menvang*. This is believed to be a rebirth within the same clan. The *Karhi* is a festival conducted to bring together the families of the departed, as well as to strengthen the bonds of kinship. Turner's concept of 'betwixt and between' is evident in both *Phu-Phi Rongsopi* indicating that they exist in a state that is neither in *Chom Rongsopi* nor on earth. The soul resides in a state of liminality within *Chom Rongsoso* or *Ritlo*. The soul is in a state of transition, existing at the boundary between the ancestral village (realm of death) and the realm of the living. The soul might be perceived as being in a state of being 'stuck' or 'trapped', thus referred to as a 'liminal soul'. Therefore, according to the Karbi worldview, if the *Chomangkan* ritual is not performed for the deceased, their soul will remain in a state of 'liminal space', trapped in *Ritlo Pharlo*. However, if the *Karhi* festival is performed, it is believed that the soul will reach *Phu-Phi Rongsopi*.

NOTES

1. Morningkeey Phangcho, 'About the Karbis' in DharamsingTeron (Ed.,), *Karbi Studies: Memories, Myths and Metaphors*, Vol. 1, Assam Book Hive, Guwahati, 2008, p. 4.
2. India Census 2011, 'District Census Handbook KårbiAnglong', *Assam*: Directorate of Census Operations, New Delhi, 2014.
3. RobindraTeron, 'Traditional Woodcraft Jambili Athon of the Karbis', *Indian Journal of Traditional Knowledge*, 7(1), 2008, pp. 103-107.

4. Arnold Van Gennep, *Rites of Passage*, The University of Chicago Press, Chicago, 1960.
5. Victor Turner, *Betwixt and Between*: The Liminal Period in Rites de Passage', The Forest of Symbols, Cornell University Pess, Ithaca and London, 1967, p. 93.
6. Laurence A Waddell, 'Proceeding of the Journal of the Asiatic Society of Bengal', Vol. LXIX Part-III, 1900. (Anthropology, &c.) and Edited by Anthropological Secretary, the Asiatic Society, Calcutta: the Asiatic Society, 1901, p. 34. Available at https://archive.org/stream/dli.ministry.19132/25025_djvu.txt (Accessed on 9-3-2024); Also see in Laurence A Waddell, *Tribes of The Brahmaputra Valley (the): A Contribution of their Physical Types And Affinities*, Concept Publishing Company, New Delhi, 1999.
7. Ibid.
8. Raju Pokhel, 'A Study of the Folklore of the Karbis: An Aesthetic Appraisal', PhD thesis submitted to Gauhati University, 2014, p. 25.
9. He observed a three-part pattern in ritual practices: separation, transition, and incorporation. Gennep provided insights into the importance of these rituals as mechanisms for societal renewal, drawing on symbolic representations like the cycle of life and death. (See https://www.britannica.com/biography/Arnold-van-Gennep (Accessed on 7/3/2024)
10. Victor Turner, 'Betwixt and Between: The Liminal Period in Rites of Passage' in Victor Turner (Ed), *The Forest of Symbols: Aspects of Ndembu*, Cornell University Press, New York, 1967. In 'Betwixt and Between,' Victor Turner examines rites of passage and the cultural customs associated with transitioning from one state to another, regardless of the specific stable or recurring condition being recognized within a particular culture. This transition encompasses the processes of separation, margin, and aggregation. (Cited in Jeri E. Wieringa, Victor Turner, 'Betwixt and Between: The Liminal Period', September, 2017) https://jeriwieringa.com/blog/2012/09/27/victor-turner-betwixt-and-between-the-liminal-period/ (Accessed on 12-12-2023).

CHAPTER 6

Exploring Gender Empowerment and Economic Self-Reliance among Karbi Women

An In-depth Study

BARNALI SARMAH

INTRODUCTION

India has the world's second largest tribal population[1], and the colourful cultures and traditions of the tribal people may be seen in the country's north-eastern region. Assam has a considerable tribal population, with the Karbis being one of the most prominent tribal residents in the two districts of Karbi Anglong Autonomous Council. Tribal women, especially Karbis, have played a vital role, particularly in terms of societal and familial economic progress. Gender empowerment can be apparent in local markets, where Karbi women predominate. Indigenous knowledge of the environment, participation in rituals, and expertise in traditional crafts have all been important factors in becoming economically self-sufficient, making Karbi women the backbone of their families and a potential contributor to the development of society. However, Karbi women face many challenges, particularly in the patrilineal structure of the Karbi community and in the neoliberal economy. As such, the present study attempts to investigate Karbi women as an example of empowerment, focusing specifically on the unacknowledged and undervalued economic dimension.

THE STATUS OF KARBI WOMEN AND CUSTOMARY LAWS

The Karbis, an indigenous community, have long adhered to a set of customary laws that serves as a framework for governing their society. These laws are designed to safeguard and perpetuate the community's vibrant culture and traditions, ensuring their transmission to future generations. Following the subjugation of the tribes residing in Assam by the British, the colonial authorities acknowledged the customary laws of these indigenous communities. This recognition was formalized through the enactment of the Scheduled District Act of 1874. The Assam General Clauses Act of 1915 was enacted with the purpose of safeguarding the tribal customs and practices prevalent in the hill areas of Assam. Its primary objective was to limit the application of Provincial Laws in these regions, thereby ensuring the preservation of the unique cultural traditions and practices of the indigenous tribes residing there. The Montague-Chelmsford Reforms of 1919 implemented comparable provisions. The Indian Statutory (Simon) Commission of 1928, in its recommendations, also emphasized the importance of safeguarding the customary rights of tribal communities. The Government of India Act of 1935, a significant legislative development, acknowledged and implemented a division of the hill areas into two distinct categories: *Excluded* and *Partially Excluded*. This division was accompanied by a crucial provision, which stated that no legislation passed by either the Central or Provincial Legislature would be applicable to these areas, unless the Governor, exercising his discretionary powers, deemed it necessary for the maintenance of peace and effective governance.Under the scheme of the Government of India Act, 1935, so far as the excluded areas , the Governor was to act in his discretion [vide section 93 (3)] and as regards the partially excluded areas, he had a special responsibility to make regulation for peace and good government [vide section 92 (2)][2]. The above-mentioned provisions subsequently evolved into what is now known as the 'Sixth Schedule' of the Indian constitution, which was later extended to include the region of Karbi Anglong[3]. The district is granted a certain degree of autonomy as stipulated by the Sixth Schedule.

Customary laws, in the context of legal systems, can be characterized as a collection of regulations that acquire legal validity due to their enduring and consistent observance by a society over an extended period. These customary practices are transmitted from one generation to the succeeding one, thereby solidifying their authority and influence within the societal framework. Customary law, in its essence, refers to the ingrained patterns of behavior exhibited by a given society. It encompasses a set of established norms, practices, and usages that govern various facets of social, cultural, and religious life. These customary laws dictate the acceptable and unacceptable behaviors within a community, shaping the very fabric of its existence. The hallmark of tribal customary laws lies in their inherent communal nature. The emergence of this particular aspect can be traced back to the practice of regionally-focused resource management, which was deeply intertwined with the sustenance of the local communities. The majority of these practices were instrumental in fostering self-sufficiency within their respective communities, with a particular focus on agricultural pursuits. Particularly, the practice of *jhum* cultivation emerged as a primary means of sustenance for these communities. The forest, serving as an additional element, played a significant role in the overall composition. Due to the profound significance of land and forests in their way of life, the ancient inhabitants meticulously structured their beliefs, customs, and practices to revolve around these natural resources. The legitimization of customary law is achieved through its acknowledgment by the community, whose adherence to the law stems from a combination of reverence or apprehension towards the divine, as well as the utilization of customary law by its leaders as a means of social regulation[4].

The significance of customary laws within tribal communities cannot be overstated, as they serve as a fundamental aspect of their collective identity. It is important to note that these customary laws also possess a gendered dimension, as they delineate and establish the specific roles and responsibilities of both men and women within the community. The allocation of roles within society serves as a reflection of the prevailing status of women during the given historical period. In accordance with the prevailing customary laws, it is noteworthy to mention that the Karbi society adheres to a patrilineal system, characterized by a steadfast adherence to patriarchal norms. Accordingly, they follow the patrilineal system tracing their descent in the male line. After the death of the father the eldest son becomes the household, the owner of father's all moveable and immoveable properties and owns the obligations to perform the rites. But if he marries a girl from the same clan, he loses all rights, and in such a case, the next son inherits the property and the household. If there is no son in the family, after the death of the father, a daughter can inherit the paternal property, but cannot become a household. In such a situation as per the customary law the nearest male relative from father's side owns[5]. Within this societal framework, it is important to acknowledge that women are not granted the right to inherit land. The Karbis follow established customary laws of patrilineal inheritance[6]. In accordance with the customary practices of the time, it was a prevailing tradition for the sons to inherit their father's land. However, it is worth noting that the eldest son was typically granted a more substantial portion of the inheritance. In accordance with the established protocol, the remaining portion is divided among the rest, with each individual receiving an equal share. If there is no son to inherit family property, the daughter or daughters can inherit ancestral land and other property, the right of inheritance also passes on to one's brothers's children and other patrikin, in the given order. However, the son has the first right of inheritance of property after the death of their father. Moveable properties, such as, ornaments, clothes, utensils, etc, are inherited by the daughter that are passed on to the male heirs of her husband[7].

It is noteworthy that the widow may be granted the right to inherit her deceased husband's property, albeit subject to specific conditions. A widow has right to enjoy her deceased husband's share of joint property and self-acquired property. The widow along with her sons, is entitled to the same share. But she is not entitled to inherit the entire property to exclusion of her sons and as such the woman has limited power over her husband's property. Also the widow cannot sell valuable property like land without the consent of her deceased husband's other family members or near kin. However, she can dispose of female properties like utensils, wools, etc., for fulfilling her petty economic needs. In case of a landed property that a woman possesses from her father passes on to her son[8]. In accordance with the prevailing customary law, it was stipulated that in the event of a widow's remarriage outside her deceased husband's clan, she would be disqualified from inheriting any property. In the realm of matrimonial customs, the institution of marriage finds its roots in the intricate framework of clan-based social structure[9]. It is imperative to comprehend that adherence to this societal norm necessitates individuals to seek a life partner from a clan different from their own. Any transgression of this established social edict is regarded as a grave offense, carrying the weighty consequence of excommunication. It is of historical significance to acknowledge that the Karbis, have traditionally organized themselves into five exogamous clans known as 'Kur.' These clans, namely Ingti, Terang, Teon, Inghi, and Timung, have played a crucial role in shaping the social structure and cultural practices of the Karbi people throughout history[10].

The International Conference on 'Oral Tradition of the Karbis: Remembering Kajir Ronghangpi: the 'Rhinoceros Lady' took place in Diphu from July 27th to July 29th, 2023. During this gathering, the matter of 'patriarchy' within the Karbi community was a subject of extensive deliberation and discourse. During the conference, a Karbi man made an observation regarding the local market, noting that it is a bustling hub where numerous women vendors actively engage in selling their locally produced goods and crafts. This observation serves as a reflection of the societal position. According to his assertion, within the Karbi community, it is a customary practice for Karbi women to preserve their surnames even after marriage, thereby upholding a certain degree of personal identity, which distinguishes this tradition from prevailing norms observed in other regions of India[11]. In rural and urban Maharashtra, owing to cultural traditions, many women change both their first and last names when they get married[12]. A Marathi family that lives nearby the author of the present paper had the chance to ask the lady regarding the tradition of changing names after marriage. She gave a positive response and informed that a tradition is there in the Marathi community of changing the names of the girl after marriage in Maharashtra. Generally, the name of the eldest daughter in law is not changed, the names of the younger daughter-in-laws gets changed by the husband's family after marriage. When the author asked if the family has only one son then does the name of the daughter in law get changed? She replied that then it's the choice of the husband's family. However, she stated that with the changing time, this tradition of changing names are not compulsory, but then it is still prevalent in the community.

It is noteworthy to observe the active participation of Karbi women in various economic activities. These activities encompassed a wide range of tasks, including cultivation, cutting, weeding, and the arduous task of clearing forest for *jhum* cultivation. Moreover, women were also engaged in the collection of fruits, tubers, and other valuable resources. Their significant contributions to these economic endeavors played a crucial role in the sustenance and development of their communities. It is imperative to acknowledge that the prevailing perception of the Karbi community as resolutely patriarchal is a mistaken assumption, especially in regard to rituals. The *Chomangkan* is one such important ritual, where women play a prominent role, especially the *Uchepi* and *Charhepi*. The *Uchepis* are the women who are assigned with the task of cooking for the deceased souls and it is the only *Uchepis* and no other person can take this task. Another group of women known as the *Charhepi* who laments for the deceased and talks about them and bless them in the form of a song[13].

In examining the gender dynamics within the Karbi community, it becomes apparent that a prevailing system of patriarchy persists, exerting its influence on the lives of women within this social context. It is evident that women have been actively engaged in a diverse range of activities that have direct implications for the economy. However, it is important to note that traditional norms and values have historically assigned the role of managing economic affairs to the male members of the family. In an interview at the Japaralangso weekly market, a Karbi woman stated that they have to remain busy throughout the agricultural cycle, but they become especially occupied from the time the crops are harvested until they are stored for consumption. R. Saikia and L. Das, in their article *'Tribal Women in Agriculture: A Study on Involvement of Karbi Women in Jhum Cultivation and their perceived Drudgery in Performance of Farm Operation'* wrote about the findings of their research in regard to the the involvement of Karbi women throughout the process of jhum cultivation. They found that out of the sample of 102 rural Karbi women nearly 80% of women showed high level of involvement in selection of seeds and cleaning of seeds. In cutting of jungle, women showed low level of involvement, 66.6% involved in hoeing of land and land levelling. In manure application women's involvement was found to be low. About 75.49% of the women are involved in cleaning boundaries, but when it comes to weeding, the participation of women is significantly higher at 92.16%. The findings shows that the contribution of women in jhum cultivation is significantly higher and are involved more or less throughout the period of jhum cultivation. They toil hard in performing labour intensive agricultural activities[14].

Uttam Bathari (2009) in his paper argued that the Karbi traditional land management system has changed due to both external and internal factors. The Karbis in the plains area shifted to ploughs after coming in contact with the Ahoms. This probably began in the early 19th century. Settled cultivation gradually filtered down to the valley district. Even in the hills where jhum cultivation is still practiced and wet cultivation is done in low marshy areas. This directed in the process of individual ownership, encouraged by the administration to get the people to abandon shifting cultivation. However, in the interior hilly areas where the people still are jhumiyas the land continues to be managed by the Village Council[15]. In the context of settled agricultural societies, it is noteworthy to observe that a prevailing practice emerged whereby women were strictly prohibited from engaging in the laborious task of operating the plough. This particular tradition entails that women are tasked with labour-intensive activities such as planting, hoeing, and weeding, which require arduous physical exertion and prolonged periods of bending in damp fields.

ECONOMIC SELF-RELIANCE OF RURAL KARBI WOMEN

In order to gain insight into the daily schedule of a Karbi woman, an interview was conducted amidst the bustling ambiance of the Japralangso weekly market, situated in the Karbi Anglong district of Assam. In accordance with historical accounts, a woman expressed her daily routine in the context of attending the local market. She revealed that in order to participate in the market activities, she would rise early in the morning and diligently complete various domestic tasks. These tasks included attending to household chores, preparing meals for her family members, and subsequently making her way to the market. Once there, she engaged in the sale of black tea, as well as the offering of steam rice cakes infused with black sesame seeds, commonly known as 'til diya tekeli pitha.' (*Him Sangtil Him Pum in Karbi*). Moreover, she would also vend pork meat, which was often cooked alongside medicinal herbs or occasionally combined with black sesame seeds. Following her time at the market, she would return home and resume her responsibilities, tending to her children and attending to other household duties. In accordance with the testimony of another woman, it is evident that during the period of harvesting, the female populace found themselves compelled to forgo attending the market, as their time and efforts were wholly dedicated to the arduous tasks associated with agricultural labor. Since time immemorial agriculture held a prominent position within the Karbi society, especially jhum cultivation. The Karbi women, as integral members of this agrarian community, would dutifully accompany their husbands to the *jhum* fields, which were strategically located in the hilly regions. Jhum cultivation is practised in Karbi Anglong since time immemorial. According to the Karbi Anglong Autonomous Council, this age old traditional system of farming is practised by 54,000 families in 2011[16]. In this arduous task, the women folk would actively contribute by assisting their husbands in the laborious process of cutting and clearing the dense forest. In the realm of agricultural pursuits, it is worth noting the active participation of women in various essential tasks. These tasks encompass a wide range of activities, including the dissemination of knowledge regarding crops, the meticulous process of weeding, the act of sowing seeds, the laborious task of uprooting unwanted plants, and the culmination of the agricultural cycle through the act of harvesting. Jhum cultivation (*Inglong Arit*) practiced by the Karbi community goes through the following phases of operation:[17]

a) *Ritkepan* – the felling of trees and undergrowth
b) *Me-Kekai* – the burning of the rubbishes
c) *Arikkarh*i – the clearance of half-burnt logs
d) *Rik* – Sowing of various types of seeds
e) *Sok-Karlu* – weeding of plants
f) *Sok Kerot* – harvesting

Land selection process starts in the month of February. The Village Council distributes jhum land to each family according to their need in Karbi Anglong district. Land preparation of Jhum cultivation includes cleaning of jhum plot, burning, land levelling and cleaning of jhum plot boundaries are the major activities usually starts from March. The dried vegetations and the fallen logs are burnt in the month of April and May. In May and June, as soon as the monsoon starts, the jhum fields become saturated, and sowing begins with the distribution of burning ashes across the jhum plot.[18] Jhum requires weeding. The Weeding operation takes place in the month of July[19]. Each and every cultivator in turn help neighbours in weeding. Harvesting, the crucial process of cutting and collecting crops in the jhum fields, begins in the month of November. The first crop to collect is maize in mid-July[20]. Majority of the women are highly involved in all the harvest and post-harvest activities like reaping of crops, making bundles, carrying of crops from field, threshing of grains, winnowing of grains, storage of grains, storage of grains for seed purpose, drying of grains, dehusking of grains and cleaning of grains[21]. It is to be mentioned that Karbis perform some ritulas and festivals before starting of jhum and at harvesting period. *Rongker* is the major spring time annual festival celebrated in the month of April before the starting of the jhum cultivation. This festival is organised by the elderly male folk so that people can be free from diseases and natural calamities for the entire year. However, the women are not allowed to enter the worship arena during the festival. *Haccha* is also a popular harvest dance which is also an all-male dance form[22].

The involvement of women in these vital agricultural endeavors is a testament to their indispensable role in the sustenance and prosperity of agricultural communities. During the early hours of the morning, the inhabitants engage in brewing rice beer, a customary practice of their time. They also diligently tend to their livestock and maintain the cleanliness of their sheds. Cattle and cows are reared for farming purpose only as the Karbis do not extensively draw milk from the cows[23]. In addition to their invaluable contribution to agricultural endeavors, Karbi women are known to engage in the gathering of various sustenance resources from the surrounding wilderness. These resources include but are not limited to wild roots, tubers, edible leaves, and firewood, all of which play a crucial role in supporting their households and communities. It is worth noting that the Karbi women possess a profound knowledge of the various wild roots, plants, leaves and fruits that are abundantly found within the dense forest[24]. In response to inquiries regarding the occupational pursuits of the male members, the Karbi women conveyed that agriculture stands as the primary means of livelihood. However, it is worth noting that the scarcity of land, burgeoning population and the advent of modern technology has collectively contributed to a shift in the occupation of many male individuals, who now engage in daily wage labor. The Karbis practice a diversified cropping system in jhum field. Paddy and maize are the main cereal crops cultivated. They also cultivate vegetables and fruits such as brinjal, tomato, pineaple, sweet potatoes, ginger, turmeric, chilli, etc[25] for the consumption of the household. These surplus produce, the vegetables that remains after consumption are traded by the women of the community in local markets. The exchange of agricultural and kitchen garden products in the local market serves as a consistent means of income for the individuals involved. In addition to cultivating agricultural crops, it is noteworthy that ancient societies also engaged in the practice of domesticating animals. These animals held great significance, serving not only as essential components of various ritualistic and social festivities but also as valuable sources of economic gain. Animal rearing, handicrafts, farming and selling of wild edibles plants are the main sources of income of the Karbi women. Laxmi Hansepi and Lena Laisram in their article *'Karbi Women and Environmental Conservation'* stated that *'The Karbi women perform multifarious tasks that include collecting and storing water, securing sources for fuel, collecting food and fodder for livestock as well as collect edible plants, etc. from the forest for their daily needs. In fact, it can be said that the whole community is dependent on the labour of the women due to their role in economy and also as caregivers to children, elderly and sick.* [26]. The evidence at hand provides a lucid depiction of the industriousness exhibited by Karbi women, who assume a diverse array of responsibilities ranging from the upkeep of domestic affairs to actively contributing to the financial advancement of their families.

Three key characteristics have been identified as the fundamental indicators of economic self-reliance among Karbi women. There are:

i. *The indigenous knowledge of the environmental surroundings:* The acquisition of comprehensive knowledge pertaining to the environment and its surroundings has proven to be a significant advantage for Karbi women in their pursuit of economic self-sufficiency. The Karbi women possess an extensive understanding of the medicinal and nutritional attributes associated with various plants and herbs. The acquisition of these botanical specimens from the adjacent jungles and hills, followed by their subsequent commercialization in the local marketplace, was a customary practice observed during the historical period under examination. Among the various plants that have been utilized throughout history, two notable examples are *Tihaso* (*boesenbergia rotunda*) and *Thesokeho* (*Solanum Indicum Linn*). *Tihaso*, a plant renowned for its aromatic properties, has been traditionally employed as a spice in the preparation of fish dishes. Additionally, it has been observed that *Tihaso* possesses remarkable healing properties, as it is known to expedite the recovery process of fresh cuts. Another noteworthy plant is *Thesokeho*, which has also been utilized as a spice. The significance of these plants lies in their contribution to culinary practices and their potential medicinal applications. During the field visit to the weekly market in Japralangso an assortment of uncommon medicinal herbs was observed. These herbs possessed the potential to enhance the flavor and nutritional value of various culinary dishes, such as curries and meat-based preparations. The encounter with *Tora Pator Gojali* or the tender shoot of *Tora* plants (*Alpinia allughas Retz.*) proved to be an extraordinary and distinctive occurrence. The indigenous inhabitants of Assam are well acquainted with the botanical specimen known as *Tora paat*. It is worth noting that this distinctive root appears to be exclusive to the aforementioned geographical area. The consumption of wild banana flower, garlic, brinjal, and ghost pepper (*bhutjolokia)* has been noted for its distinct and unparalleled flavor. Within the framework of the neo-liberal economic structure, it is evident that a significant number of Karbi individuals, both men and women, have actively engaged in diverse livelihood practices. However, it is noteworthy that a considerable portion of the population continues to adhere to their traditional agricultural method known as *'Inglong Arit'*, commonly referred to as *Jhum* cultivation. The area under *jhum* in the Karbi Anglong district, Assam, has increased from 54,000 farming families' hectares to 63,000 hectares in 2011. Around 54,000 farming families are involved in shifting cultivation in the district, cultivating 70,000 hectares of land annually, with around 70% of the population in the region depending on jhum cultivation[27]. In addition to this, it is worth noting that the gathering of wild edibles by the women of Karbi villages from the surrounding forest regions has long been a customary practice that continues to persist in the present day. While jhum cultivation may not yield significant monetary returns, it has emerged as a crucial means of income generation for numerous Karbi households in contemporary times. Within the given historical context, it is evident that Karbi women played a significant role as the primary breadwinners in numerous households. These women would embark on regular visits to local markets, either in groups or individually, with the purpose of selling gathered wild edibles. In addition, it is worth noting that the district has witnessed the emergence of numerous tourist lodges and restaurants, particularly in the vicinity of the renowned Kaziranga National Park. This development has provided a favorable opportunity for Karbi women to conveniently distribute their gathered resources in large quantities. Karbi women are highly dependent on the forests for their livelihood and sustenance. The forests provide them with readily available resources needed for their survival. Shrinking of forest due to deforestation, developmental projects and over explotation of forest resources poses a serious threat to the livelihood of rural tribal family forbidding the women folk to contribute financially along with the male member. During an era characterized by a dearth of educational qualifications and inadequate educational facilities, coupled with a scarcity of alternative means of livelihood, it is noteworthy that a significant number of individuals relied heavily on the trade of vegetables or wild edibles as their primary source of income[28]. During an insightful interview with a female Karbi vendor, it was revealed that their daily earnings in the weekly market amount to approximately Rs. 700-800/-. This figure represents the net income after deducting various expenses, such as payments to the Bazar committee, the collector for land usage, and a committee of Karbi women responsible for maintaining cleanliness within the market. The proceeds acquired from their endeavors were subsequently allocated towards the acquisition of essential household commodities. In her statement, she expressed her belief that by engaging in such activities, she actively participates in the management and maintenance of the household.

ii. *The expertise in traditional crafts:* In addition to engaging in agricultural pursuits and the gathering and commercialization of edible herbs, the Karbis have historically placed significant emphasis on the practice of weaving as a vital economic endeavor. The art of weaving has long been regarded as a cherished and esteemed skill among the women of the Karbi community, dating back to ancient times. Throughout history, it has been observed that the Karbi women have displayed remarkable skill in the art of weaving. This talent has been passed down through generations, resulting in a significant portion of the clothing used for domestic purposes being meticulously crafted by these women on their family looms. The utilization of a traditional weaving apparatus known as the *Kachivur atherang* also referred to as a Karbi loom, is a backstrap loom observed in the practice of weaving consisting of the following parts made of bamboo: *Therang* (loom bar), *Thening* (shed rod), *Thepun* (measuring rope), *Uvek* (bobbin), *Thelangpong* (heddle rod), *Barlim* (pattern sticks), *Ingthi* (reed/comp), *Hi-i* (Heddle), *Harpi* (batten), *Honthari langpong* (bobbin), *Thehu* (back strap), *Dang* (tightening stick), and *Lang vet* (sponging stick). With the help of this loom, the weavers make intricate designs[29]. Throughout history, it has been a common desire among parents to ensure that their daughters acquire the necessary skills in weaving and various household chores. During the formative years of a young girl, typically beginning at the tender age of five, it was customary for her to undergo a period of instruction in the art of weaving. This invaluable skill was imparted to her by either her mother or grandmother, who assumed the role of mentor and guide in this crucial aspect of her education.[30] The Karbi loom, it is widely believed, holds a position of utmost significance as a prominent emblem of the Karbi people's rich heritage and distinct cultural identity. Dharamsing Teron said that 'the Karbi loom is not just a piece of cultural symbol but provides the Karbi women subsistence, self-respect and pride and helps them to keep their homes and heritage alive'[31]. The annals of Karbi folklore recount a tale of great significance, one that venerates *Serdihun* as a seminal figure in the realm of weaving. *Selangdi* and *Rimsipi* are believed to have laid the foundation of the Karbi style of weaving. *Selangdi* was the woman who discovered the art of spinning yarn from the cotton flowers. Another women named *Rimsipi* discovered how the yarn could be woven into cloth. But *Dihun* was the woman who gave weaving the golden edge to become the patron of the weavers. Dihun used extracts of flowers, roots and seeds to dye the yarn in beautiful colours and created patterns and motifs. Therefore, She is immortalised as *Serdihun*, where *ser* means gold. Weavers today perform a ritual and pray for *Serdihun's* blessings to get rid of aches from long hours on the loom.[32] This legendary account, passed down through generations in the form of a melodious folksong, extols her as the pioneering woman who bestowed upon the Karbi people the invaluable knowledge and skill of this ancient craft. Henceforth, it was customary to partake in a ceremonial practice, wherein supplications were offered to *Serdihun*, beseeching for divine favor in alleviating the physical discomfort endured by the weaver due to the prolonged use of the back strap. In the realm of Karbi culture, it is worth noting the prominent role played by women in the domain of commerce. Specifically, the Karbi women engage in the practice of door-to-door selling, wherein they offer for sale a variety of traditional ethnic wears. These garments, known as *pini-vamkok*, *pekok,* and *blouse*, collectively form a three-piece ensemble that is considered the standard attire for Karbi females[33].

It is intriguing to observe that these items are not solely limited to door-to-door sales but are also commonly traded in the bustling weekly local markets. Such marketplaces serve as vital hubs of economic activity, facilitating the exchange of goods and fostering social interactions within the Karbi community. In the Japralangso weekly market, it is noteworthy that women have been observed engaging in the commerce of traditional attires.

iii. *The involvement in rituals:* The Karbi women holds a notable position within the ritualistic sphere of the tribe. Dr. Kamala Kanta Bori in his article 'The Rites of Passages of the Karbis and the role of Women: On Seeing Unlike a Feminist', stated that 'if one analyses the 'rites of passages' that form the corpus as well as the psyche of the tribe's traditional culture, the dominance of Karbi women over the male counterparts almost towards matriarchal social structure can be perceived'. He stated that the women folk in Karbi society dominate the entire lifecycle. Right from the rituals associated with the birth of a child (*Klongklo Athekar*), and marriage (*Adam Asar)* to the funerary (*Chomangkan ot Thikarhi)*, it is the Karbi women who take the lead. Accordingly, the ritual of *Klongklo Athekar* is performed to purify and protect the child from any kind of impurity and all kinds of evils, ghosts and spirits and satanic forces. In such ritual no male being can take part. The women folk gather together just after the delivery of the baby and recites the ritualistic chant in unison[34]. The women folk recites as under as a part of the ritual--

Karbi aso, karbak aso,
Hu aso kali, bang aso kali .
Rang ong kehang, jisi lok kehang,
Jisi pirthe kahache, mindar kahache.

(O, God! The baby just delivered is a human child, not animal. It has come to this world to establish relations with that of the human beings and to become human in all respects, etc.[35])

Similarly, during marriage ceremonies, known as *Adam Asar*, it is the Karbi women who assume a leading role. They oversee and orchestrate the various customs and traditions associated with this sacred union. The Karbi wedding ceremony is a system arranged in phase wise rituals. The system that enshrines these rituals is known as *'Piso Pangri'*. It means if a family of the groom wants to marry a Karbi girl, the Karbi women in the family can only approach and negotiate with the bride's family, that is, the house of the maternal uncle, three times taking necessary offerings along with them. The first phase is known as *'Nengpi-Nengso Kachingki* (The women's negotiation) where the mother of the groom is required to go to the house of the would-be-bride as a casual guest or visitor along with two or three married women and one bottle of Arak and she will express her desire to have the daughter as a bride for her son. The second phase is *'Kepatini'* (The word of confirmation) in which the negotiation is further resumed after getting the positive signals from the mother of the bride and at this stage a tentative date for the prospective marriage is decided. The third phase is *Ajo-Arni Kepha* (The fixation of the Date for the Wedding) where the mother of the groom would visit again to the bride's house with the requisite offerings and fix a date for the wedding[36].

Furthermore, when it comes to funerary practices, the Karbi women once again take the forefront. They are responsible for organizing and conducting the *Chomangkan*, the rituals performed to honor and bid farewell to the departed souls. The *Chomangkan* is one of the most important rituals of the Karbis and mirrors the philosophy of life and death. The first day starts with a ceremony called *Aru-kehum* (literally bringing back the deceased soul from the cremation ground to their ancestral house from the cremation ground). There is a procession by the family members to the cremation ground called the *tipit*, accompanied by the male drummers. A male member would dig the cowrie shells with a sword and with the indication of the drummers the cowrie which represents the bones of the dead body would be taken out. Then they offer food known as anjam (including rice beer, betel leaves, areca nut, and cooked food), prepared especially for the dead by the *Rantini*. An important aspect of this ritual is the singing of the oral epics *Kacharhe Alun* and *Mosera Kihir*, which are compositions that recount the migration history of the Karbis as the dead embarks on its journey to the 'village of the ancestors'. The most significant role in death rituals is that of the *Charhepi* (dirge singer) and se *karkli* abang (priests). The *Charhepi* sings about the life of the deceased, guides the soul to the routes to be taken, and recounts the Karbi's migration history. She is the official weeper who weeps on behalf of the family. She is the person responsible for guiding the soul to its proper abode.[37] These historical customs and traditions highlight the significant influence and leadership that Karbi women have exerted within their society, particularly in the realms of birth, marriage, and death. Their pivotal roles in these ceremonies reflect the deep-rooted cultural values and gender dynamics prevalent in Karbi history. According to a Karbi woman interviewed, women hold significant roles during these rites and their absence renders the rituals incomplete. Previously, the female participant who enacted the weeping segment in the *Chomangkan* ceremony received a modest remuneration in the form of '*Maan*' (*Nempo a-heem*), along with a bottle of rice beer, as part of the ritualistic proceedings. Nevertheless, as time and circumstances evolve, the *Uchepi* ritual has undergone changes. A Karbi women in an interview said that now-a-days it is difficult to find *Uchepi* and has to offer good amount of money to perform the ritual for the family.

ENTREPRENEURSHIP SKILL AND GENDER EMPOWERMENT: CHALLENGES AHEAD

The contributions of the Karbi women extend beyond the realm of domestic duties, as they also engage in entrepreneurial endeavors at the micro level, thereby making significant economic contributions to their families. Regrettably, it is evident that women in this particular context are predominantly involved in entrepreneurial endeavors solely as a means of generating income when no other viable options are available, or rather, as a means of sustaining their families in some capacity. The Japralangso weekly market of Karbi Anglong was primarily frequented by a significant number of women once in a week. These women also goes to sell their produce and items in the naearby markets as well once in the weekly haat (market). These women, predominantly falling within the age range of 35 to 60 years, were compelled to visit the market due to various necessities. In observing the aptitudes displayed by the Karbi women in the realm of agriculture, their expertise in medicinal herbs and their proficiency in various crafts, it becomes evident that fostering the growth of entrepreneurial abilities among these rural women is a pressing imperative. By doing so, we can empower them to cultivate greater confidence and self-sufficiency. The acquisition of entrepreneurial skills is crucial for rural women, as it enables them to effectively utilize available resources, thereby generating substantial income for their families and contributing to societal development. Furthermore, in response to the formidable obstacles presented by the neo-liberal market, the acquisition of entrepreneurial skills emerged as a crucial necessity. The neoliberal market refers to a single global free market that favours the liberalisation of trade and the global integration of markets. The rapid transformation of information, communication and transportation technology--a 'digital revolution' in the era of globalisation is a key factor in the spread of neo-liberal markets where it is expected that all people will be benefitted economically[38]. The rural Karbi women are engaged in household activities and agricultural activities throughout the year. After consumption whatever surplus agricultural produce is remained they bring to the weekly market to contribute economically in running the household along with the male member and that too for necessity. Once, when the author asked a Karbi rural woman vendor at the Japaralangso weekly market for her phone number, she replied that she couldn't provide it because she only knew how to make and receive calls and didn't know how to use the phone for anything else. Thus, the situation exemplifies that due to ignorance of the digital technology, illiteracy, and lack of entrpreneurship skills these hardworking women with the farming, weaving, cooking and craft making skills are not being able to reap the economic benefits of neo-liberal markets. The inquiry that emerges is as follows: what precisely constitutes the aptitude of entrepreneurship? The acquisition of entrepreneurship skills encompasses a diverse array of aptitudes, including but not limited to leadership, business management, time management, creative thinking, and problem-solving. The attainment of women's empowerment is contingent upon their attainment of financial independence, which in turn enables them to exercise agency in both the private and public domains. The acquisition of entrepreneurship skills by women would have facilitated their comprehension of the market dynamics, enabling them to make informed decisions and effectively harness the local resources at their disposal. Consequently, these women would have been empowered to transition into successful entrepreneurs, fully realizing their potential in the business realm. This development would have fostered the independence and confidence of women, enabling them to actively contribute to the advancement of society and the global cultural landscape.

Unfortunately, within the context of India, it can be observed that women's involvement in entrepreneurial activities in rural and tribal areas predominantly stems from a necessity-driven motivation, rather than an opportunity-driven one. The majority of individuals are primarily occupied with customary pursuits, such as agriculture, particularly the post-harvest procedures involved in the preservation and storage of agricultural goods and seeds. Additionally, they engage in poultry and livestock rearing, as well as the creation of handicrafts, embroidery, and garments. However, it is worth noting that these individuals lack the necessary expertise to transform these activities into profitable ventures. During periods of respite from their arduous agricultural labors and domestic responsibilities, individuals would contemplate venturing to the marketplace in order to sell the surplus agricultural produce such as fresh vegetables, ethnic food items like dried fish, traditional clothes for monetary gain. This income would then be utilized to procure essential household items. In addition to the prevailing system of patriarchy, Karbi women encounter a multitude of obstacles in their pursuit of becoming accomplished entrepreneurs. In examining the historical context, it becomes evident that a multitude of challenges were present during this period.

Illiteracy, a prevailing issue, has significantly impacted tribal women, rendering them unaware of government policies and programs. Consequently, they have been unable to fully avail themselves of the associated benefits. Indeed, it is noteworthy that a Karbi woman, situated within the Japralangso market, conveyed a significant observation. She revealed that every parent wants their children to be educated, but since the school in their village is not situated nearby, the children are compelled to attend a distant educational institution. She also admitted that the children shows less interest in attending schools. Consequently, this unfortunate circumstance has resulted in a considerable number of these young individuals abandoning their pursuit of knowledge. Kiran Teronpi in her article 'A case study on the school dropout reasons in Karbi Anglong district of Assam' stated that dropout rates of children from primary school has become one of the challenging issues for the Karbi Anglong district where right to education because of dropouts has been denied to a large number of children.[39] Mr. Binod Mochahari, Prof. T. Sangyu Yaden & Mr. Mindar Rongphar in their article *'Status of Educational Institutions in Karbi Anglong District, Assam, India'* argued that, with the formation of Karbi Anglong formally in 1951, initiated the process of establishing educations. In the year 1953, there were only 180 primary schools in the entire district which were increased to 1977 in 2016, that is, after a gap of almost 62 years. Out of these 1977 primary schools, 1870 are located in rural areas whereas 107 schools are in urban area. Presently, though the number of primary school is high in comparison to the geographical area, the distribution of primary school is very sparse and scattered in nature. Also it is observed that rural road connectivity is comparatively much lower due to undulating nature of topography which also hinder the school going children from attending their schools[40].

In an interview, a Karbi woman expressed her challenges in establishing a store during the rainy season due to the dearth of infrastructure. In addition, she expressed that the mere notion of establishing a dedicated establishment within the bustling market is inconceivable. Hence, in the event that the relevant Committee who supervises the market area were to establish a provisional repository, it would provide respite to the individuals involved, enabling them to sustain their commercial endeavors.

The Karbi women, in their pursuit of selling their products, have been observed to possess a limited understanding of marketing strategies. This deficiency of entrpreneurship skills has hindered their ability to effectively utilize the wealth of indigenous knowledge available to them within their immediate environment.

In the era characterized by globalization, neo-liberalism[41], and the advent of digitalization, it is evident that the market has undergone significant expansion and transformation. The strategic implementation of technology and utilization of digital platforms facilitated the expansion of businesses beyond local boundaries, propelling them to the national and international stage. Regrettably, it is evident that the tribal women, such as the Karbis, residing in rural villages, have not been exposed to the progress of technology and have not received adequate training. Consequently, they continue to be limited to the role of vendors at a micro-level within their communities. In the context of rural Karbi society, it is noteworthy to mention that when queried about the utilization of mobile phones, a Karbi woman candidly acknowledged her limited knowledge regarding the functionality of smartphones.

In an interview, a Karbi woman lamented the absence of vocational training within her village, highlighting the lack of specialized instruction provided to its residents. In the annals of rural life, it is recorded that a village, nestled amidst the verdant countryside, was bestowed with the noble endeavor of imparting the ancient art of handloom training. Alas, the fates conspired to place this village at a considerable distance from the abode of its inhabitants, thus presenting a formidable challenge to those seeking to partake in this venerable craft.

The phenomenon of tribal women engaging in entrepreneurship during their middle years has been explored through a comprehensive study. This investigation has shed light on the primary factors that drive these women towards such endeavors. It has been observed that a significant number of tribal women embark on entrepreneurial pursuits as a result of three key motivations. Firstly, the escalating demands within their families, including the need to meet growing household expenses, the pursuit of education for their children, and the financial responsibilities associated with the marriage of their daughters, have been identified as influential factors in their decision-making process. During this particular era, it is noteworthy that the tribal women exhibited a distinct inclination towards business pursuits. This phenomenon can be attributed to the fact that this period marked a significant phase in their lives, wherein they prioritized their personal interests and development. The maturation experienced during this stage equipped them with enhanced resilience in navigating the challenges posed by a society predominantly governed by males, particularly within the rural areas.[42]

In light of the circumstances mentioned above, several recommendations can be put forth in order to bolster the economic self-sufficiency of the Karbi women.

- In order to cultivate a broader understanding of diverse occupations within rural communities, it is imperative to provide vocational education and training at the village level.
- In an effort to encourage rural women to engage in entrepreneurial endeavors, it has been proposed to organize workshops on the subject of 'start-ups' within village communities. These workshops aim to provide the necessary motivation and guidance for rural women to embark upon their own business ventures. The organizers of historical events must demonstrate a willingness to embrace and foster innovative ideas and techniques.
- In the pursuit of fostering the development of women, a notable endeavor was the organization of periodic awareness programs within rural communities. This was achieved through the dissemination of informative leaflets and pamphlets, as well as the convening of formal gatherings. These initiatives aimed to apprise the local populace of the various programs and policies implemented for the advancement of women.
- During this period, it was recognized that the empowerment of young girls was crucial for their personal development and societal progress. To achieve this, a prevailing approach involves enrolling these girls in skill-based courses to make them financially empowered. The goal is to instil motivation, fostering self-reliance and financial independence as they embark on their journey to a brighter future.
- In light of the industrious nature and ecological acumen displayed by the Karbi women, it is imperative to provide them

with comprehensive instruction in the cultivation of entrepreneurial abilities. This training should encompass the utilization of modern technology and digital platforms, thereby equipping them to effectively contend with external markets.

CONCLUSION

In the context of the tribes residing in the North East region of India, it is noteworthy to highlight the profound significance of women within their tribal societies. These tribes have fostered a cultural environment wherein women play an indispensable role and exhibit remarkable economic self-sufficiency. The Karbi women exemplify the spirit of women's empowerment, confronting challenges with unwavering confidence and asserting their influence as the bedrock of their families. However, their contributions frequently go unnoticed, despite their significant impact. The Karbi women, possessing a wealth of traditional knowledge, skills, and expertise in agriculture, medicinal herbs, and weaving, hold great potential as successful entrepreneurs. With the provision of appropriate training in entrepreneurship skills, these women would undoubtedly make significant contributions to the advancement of their families and society at large. It must be acknowledged that the assessment of role and status cannot be uniformly quantified. In the context of the Karbi society, it is evident that rural women have historically assumed a significant role, surpassing that of men. It is truly a remarkable experience to observe the Karbi women as they endeavor to achieve self-sufficiency while adhering to the cultural norms of their society. They provide sustenance to the family on the individual level and broadly to the community through the judicious use and management of the natural resources. The irony is that despite the multifarious roles Karbi women play in society, they have no property rights, which places them at a disadvantage when it comes to economic security.[43] The customary laws that defines the role of male and female reflects the patriarchal structure where the women folk have to depend on the male member. Despite the obstacles posed by patriarchal structures, these women have demonstrated a profound understanding of their natural environment and have harnessed their expertise in the art of hand weaving. As a result, they have not only enhanced their own well-being but have also made significant contributions to the betterment of their community. The subject at hand presents ample opportunity for future scholarly inquiry, which would undoubtedly enhance our comprehension of the societal position held by Karbi women within the Karbi community residing in the Karbi Anglong district of Assam.

NOTES

1. 'History of Trifed', Retrieved from https://trifed.tribal.gov.in/history-of-trifed#:~:text=Home%20to%20a%20large%20number,tribal%20population%20in%20the%20world (11/06/2024).
2. 'Framing of the Sixth Schedule', retrieved from https://khadc.nic.in/acts_rules_regulations_bills/misc/Framing%20of%the206th%20SChedule.pdf (28/05/2024).
3. Walter Fernandes, 'Land as the Centre of the History of Karbi Anglong', in Vulli Dhanaraju and Dharamsing Teron (Ed.) *Karbi History: Past and Present,* Mittal Publications, New Delhi, 2020, pp.319-332.
4. Ibid.
5. Jatin Sharma, 'Minor Research Project on Women in Karbi Folk Literature', Retrieved from https://www.bkbcollege.in/upload/research_project/1655203633 (10/06/2024).
6. Rashmi Engtipi, 'The Concept of Landholding System: A Case Study of Karbi Tribe of Assam', in *National Journal of Advanced Research*, Vol.8, Issue 1, December 8, 2021, Retrieved from https://journals.indexcopernicus.com/api/file/viewByField/1805633 (08/05/2024).
7. Ibid.
8. Ibid.
9. 'Social Structure', Retrieved from https://karbi.wordpress.com/name-list-of-clans-kurs-in-karbis/ (30/05/2024)
10. Amphu Terangpi 'Folk Deities and Gender in Karbi Vernacular Religion', in *the Dwima Collective: A discursive space for all things indigenous,* December 8, 2021, Retrieved from https://dwima-collective.org/2021/12/08/ (30/06/2023).
11. 'Do Women Really Have to Change Their Surname After Marriage?' Retrieved from https://www.google.com/ampls/timesofindia.indiatimes.com/life-style/relationships/love-sex/

do-women-really-have-to-change-their-surname-after-marriage/photostory/86425228.cms (04/06/2024).

12. Kanitkar, Ajit & Gokhale, Suvarna Sunil, 'No identity for married women in Maharashtra', Retrieved from https://www.google.com/amp/s/idronline.org/ground-up-stories/ (04/06/2024).
13. Retrieved from http://dspace.cus.ac.in/jspui/bitstream/1/6973/1/Racheal%20CD.pdf (03/06/2024).
14. R.Saikia and L.Das, 'Tribal Women in Agriculture: A Study on involvement of Karbi Women in Jhum Cultivation and their Perceived Drudgery in Performance of Farm Operations', Retrieved from https://www.kiran.nic.in/pdf/IJHF/Vol11_1&2/3pdf (10/06/2024).
15. Rashmi Engtipi, 2021, op. cit.
16. Rashmi Sarkar and Ashok Kumar Bora, 'Role of Karbi People in Practicing Jhum Cultivation in Karbi Anglong District, Assam', Retrieved from https://www.xidxjxsu.asia/V17102-09.pdf (08/06/2024).
17. 'Jhum Cultivation in Karbi Anglong District', Chapter 3, Retrieved from https://www.shodhganga.inflibnet.ac.in/bitstream/10603/169794/8/08_chapter%203.pdf (06/06/2024)
18. Rashmi Sarkar and Ashok Kumar Bora, op. cit.
19. 'Jhum Cultivation in Karbi Anglong District', Chapter 3, Retrieved from https://www.shodhganga.inflibnet.ac.in/bitstream/10603/169794/8/08_chapter%203.pdf (06/06/2024.
20. Rashmi Sarkar and Ashok Kumar Bora, op. cit.
21. R.Saikia and L.Das, op. cit.
22. Rashmi Sarkar and Ashok Kumar Bora, op. cit.
23. Laxmi Hansepi and Rena Laisram, 'Karni Women and Environmental Conservation', in Grassroots Journal of Natural Resources, Vol.5, No.3, September, 2022, Retrieved from https://www.researchgate.net/publication/364725597_Karbi_Women_and_Environmental_Conservation (Accessed on 10/06/2024).
24. Indranoshree Das, 'Folk Medicine of the Karbis of Assam', Directorate of Assam Institute of Research for Tribals and Scheduled Castes, Guwahati, 2011.
25. Brota Sing Bey, Rizwan Ahmed, Ram Singh and Saddam Hossen Majumder in ' Crop diversification vis-á-vis shifting cultivation in Karbi Anglong district of Assam: an empirical analysis' in *Current Science,* 125 (5), September, 2023, pp. 1-8, Retrieved from https://www.researchgate.net/publication/373926347_Crop_diversification_vis-a-vis_shifting_cultivation_in_Karbi_Anglong (11/06/2024).

26. Laxmi Hansepi and Rena Laisram, 2022, op. cit.
27. Brota Sing Bey, Rizwan Ahmed, Ram Singh and Saddam Hossen Majumder , 2023, op. cit.
28. Trishita Shandilya, *'COVID 19 Pandemic and Livelihood Strategies-Practices of Karbi Women'*, Retrieved from https://www.google.com/amp/s/www.econe.in/amp (19/05/2023).
29. 'Three legendary women behind Karbi attires', Retrieved from https://www.nezine.com/info/QXBIUERSb1ArVnhoVld4b3RwNWlaQT09/three-legendary-women-behind-karbi-attires.htm (30/05/2024).
30. Indranoshree Das, 2011, op. cit.
31. Jatin Sharma, op. cit.
32. 'Three legendary women behind Karbi attires', Retrieved from https://www.nezine.com/info/QXBIUERSb1ArVnhoVld4b3RwNWlaQT09/three-legendary-women-behind-karbi-attires.htm (30/05/2024).
33. Ibid. The traditional attire of women consists of the following: Pini: It is basically black, worn around the waist and tied with a belt. Pekok: It is a square piece of cloth tied at the right shoulder. Vamkok: It is the belt used to tie the pin tight at the waist. Jiso: It was the long black cloth with designs and decorated fringes at the length ends. It was used by women in ancient time to tie around the bust but now it is replaced by short blouse for comfort and modern look.
34. K.K Bori, 'The Rites of Passages of the Karbis and the Role of Women: On seeing Unlike a Feminist', *The International Journal of Humanities & Social Studies,* Vol. 3, Issue 9, 2015, Retrieved from https://www.internationaljournalcorner.com/index.php/theijhss/article/view/126129 (31/05/2024).
35. Ibid.
36. Ibid.
37. https://www.mdpi.com/2077-1444/13/6/510 (03/06/2024).
38. Manfred B. Steger and Ravi K. Roy, *Neoliberalism: A Very Short Introduction*, Oxford University Press, 2010, pp. 52-53.
39. Kiran Teronpi, 'A case study on the school dropout reasons in Karbi Anglong district of Assam' in *International journal of Academic Research and Development*, Vol. 2, Issue 5, 2017, Retrieved form https://www.multidisciplinaryjournal.in/assets/archives/2017/vol2issue5/2-5-16-155.pdf (11/06/2024).
40. Binod Mochahari, T. Sangyu Yaden and Mindar Rongphar, 'Status of Educational Institutions in Karbi Anglong District, Assam, India',

IOSR Journal of Humanities And Social Science (IOSR-JHSS), Vol. 26, Issue 9, Series 2, September. 2021, pp. 59-64, Retrieved from https://www.iosrjournals.org/iosr-jhss/papers/Vol.26-Issues9/Ser-2/H2609025964.pdf (11/06/2024).

41. Neo-liberalism can be understood with the help of the 'D-L-P Formula' which means Deregulation (of the economy), Liberalisation (of trade and industry), Privatisation (of state-owned enterprises), cited in Steger, Manfred B. & Roy, Ravi K. (2010), 'Neoliberalism: A Very Short Introduction', Oxford University Press.
42. Budheshwar Prasad Singhraul, Sarika Agarwal and Mukesh Agarwal, 'An Analysis of Role of Tribal Female Entrepreneurship in Economical Development on Families' in *International Journal of Management Research and Development* ,Vol. 6, No. 1, January-April, 2016, pp. 1-9.
43. Laxmi Hansepi and Rena Laisram, 2022, *Op. cit.*

CHAPTER 7

Ecological Values of the Karbi Belief System

VULLI DHANARAJU and DAWATSHOGMO LAMA

INTRODUCTION

The relationship between nature and culture is interwoven in traditional worship practices, since they demonstrate symbolic connection[1]. The connection between 'nature' and 'culture,' as described by Dharamsing Teron (2008), is reflected in the beliefs and practices of the Karbi tribe who interact with and oversee natural ecosystems[2]. The management of natural resources is a debatable topic in the context of belief systems and its role in preservation of the local eco system. Natural resource management involves the administration and conservation of important resources found in nature. Multiple definitions exist for the concept of conservation, with some emphasizing the structural foundations of cultural interests, while others argue from an economic perspective. One such solution involves the utilization of conventional techniques that have enabled them to manage their interactions with the natural environment. The influence of traditional beliefs on the preservation of numerous components of local biodiversity, irrespective of their utilitarian worth, can be traced back to the time of creation[3]. Traditional conservation principles can effectively safeguard biodiversity and the environment overall, provided that local communities have a vested interest in it.

India is home to different tribes, each with distinct cultures that blend into the broader fabric of India's national identity. Since human history, people have always had a strong connection with their natural surroundings. The conventional religious traditions exemplify the mutually beneficial relationship between human beings and nature. India has revered nature since ancient times to establish a harmonious relationship between it and other living beings. Humans venerate and revere land, mountains, rivers, seas, trees, birds, and plants. It is simply a gesture of admiration towards the natural world that supports and nourishes us. Indigenous communities globally coexisted harmoniously with nature and diligently preserved its precious biodiversity. Indigenous societies, due to their direct connection with nature, possess a deep-rooted affinity with the plant and animal world. This affinity, in turn, fosters sustainable utilization and preservation of nature. Assam is a diverse region, home to multi-ethnic groups with diverse historical and cultural backgrounds. The Karbis, Bodos, Tiwas, Mising, Tai-Ahom, Nagas, Dimasa, Garos, Khasis, and Kukis are all prominent tribes of Northeast India. One of the common significant features of all these indigenous tribes is that they are the worshippers of nature and ecology has played a great role in shaping their traditional way of living, culture, beliefs and traditions. The Karbis are an ethnic tribal group scattered throughout Northeast India, with a concentration in the hills of central Assam.

In this context, this study is an attempt to explore the cultural traditions of the Karbis that are associated with nature and ecology while emphasizing their significance in the conservation or preservation of nature. The study aims to comprehend the cultural roots of ecology and traditional conservation practices among the Karbis of Assam. The study aims to examine the Karbi cosmologies, belief systems, myths, concepts of sacred locations, and their rites and rituals, all of which are closely connected to ecological preservation. For this work, data has been collected from elderly individuals of the Karbi community in Diphu, examined relevant secondary sources such as books, articles, and periodicals as well. This study utilized the interpretive method and a new ethnographic approach to establish the central argument for the paper. This is not an extensive analysis, but rather a concise exploration of the cultural roots of ecology and its importance.

A NOTE ON KARBI MIGRATION AND SETTLEMENT

Water is considered the foundation of numerous legends and myths in indigenous mythology[4]. Mythology includes various water deities and creatures, as well as tales of heroic figures associated with water. Rivers serve a vital role in the establishment and sustenance of human settlements. Karbis were thought to have resided along the banks of the rivers Kolong and Kopili and in the present-day Kaziranga areas, where the renowned Assam National Park is located. Indeed, the name 'Kaziranga' is thought to have originated from the Karbi language, combining the terms *Kajir*, which is a common name for a girl, and *rong*, which means village in Karbi. Thus, the name signifies the village where the Karbi girl lives. They are said to have originated from western China, namely near the Yang-Tse-Kiang and Hwang-ho rivers. From there, they traveled over the Chindwin, Irrawaddy and Brahmaputra rivers, eventually entering India[5]. The inhabitants of the mountainous area have a strong connection with their natural surroundings, witnessed by their folklore.

CORE CULTURAL VALUES

Tribal traditional values, also known as cultural values, serve as the fundamental basis for a community's viewpoints regarding culturally relevant flora, animals, or geographic areas. The manifestation of cultural values can be observed through the presence of religious sites, mythology, and local folklore[6]. Sacred locations consist of various natural features, including constructed buildings like burial sites, sacred groves, woods, mountains, and sources of water[7]. Sacred forests, also known as sacred groves, are locations that hold cultural or spiritual importance for the local communities. *Arnam Keso* (sacred grove[8]) are forest areas that remain undisturbed by the local population. Consequently, these areas possess abundant biodiversity and get protection from the local community as a result of cultural and religious convictions, as well as taboos associated with the residing deities. Trees generate elongated structures like spears that descend to the ground. The presence of sacredness, traditional religious beliefs, and taboos in certain areas significantly contribute to the sustainable utilization and conservation of plants and animals[9]. These beliefs are inseparable from the traditional knowledge system. The traditional knowledge system has the potential to offer society as a whole valuable information that is applicable to policy-making and administration. Moreover, lacking a fundamental comprehension of their value system, there is a high probability of misinterpreting their viewpoints and priorities regarding natural resources[10]. The breakdown of collaboration and negotiation involving tribes and natural resources sometimes stems from a mutual lack of understanding of underlying values or beliefs that shape perspectives on natural resources. Resource collaborations could be more enduring and yield superior results if they incorporated investigations into how worldviews shape natural resource values, which subsequently influence crucial moral assessments in decision-making and resource prioritizing.

Symbols are religious and cultural entities that possess profound significance beyond what can be directly perceived or understood. They serve as tangible representations of abstract concepts. Dukor (2006)[11] states that 'symbolic links are intrinsically connected to culture, as they demonstrate a fundamental aspect of human consciousness that is crucial for comprehending the language of a community, through which the world and reality are comprehensively grasped. In order for human consciousness to genuinely generate thoughts about realities, it is imperative for logic to establish a relationship and essential connection between this consciousness and reality'. Echekwube (2005)[12] asserts that symbolism involves interpreting an object to give it a meaning that it does not typically possess. In the African world, many elements such as trees, woods, animals, mountains, rivers, and canals serve as representations or symbols of different spiritual forces. Symbolism plays a crucial role in African eco-philosophy due to its use in symbolizing, representing, expressing, revealing, and indicating. These emblems provoke contemplation over the accuracy of the essence of the African world. And therefore, the social interactions between humans and non-human entities should be studied and examined within the particular ecosystem where the socio-cosmological framework originated.

The cultural traditions of the Karbis have significantly contributed to the preservation of the ecosystem. The Karbi people possess a comprehensive comprehension of nature, which is seen in the symbolism they employ and their utilization of natural resources. During the Rongker ritual held in the Donghap area, a specific ceremony called *thanarnam* was performed. This ceremony always involved the obligatory worship of three significant deities from the Karbi pantheon: *Hemphu*, *Mukrang*, and *Rasinja*. The following list exemplifies these deities.

1. *Hemphu Chingthong* (territorial deity)
2. *Rong Anglong* (the protective deity)
3. *Bulikang* (river deity)
4. *Langcherui* (river deity)
5. *Longri a-than* (territorial deity)
6. *Longle a-hi-i* (negative/evil spirit of the soil)
7. *Longri a-chekama* (protective spirit of the territory)
8. *Longri a-murti* (minor spirit)

Similar to other tribes, the Karbis consider the welfare of not only sentient beings but also the entirety of nature as a whole. The preference of species is influenced by both their practical usefulness and the symbolic significance and interpretations associated with their cosmic perspective. Their spiritual philosophy, much to other simple beliefs, revolves around the earth or the act of creation (Cosmogony). Taylor (1977)[13] stated that a fundamental characteristic of primordial religion is the perception of cosmic unity within African traditional faiths. In his 1966 work, M.M. Thomas explained that in the tribal worldview, there exists a belief in a continuous spiritual connection where all living beings, non-living objects, spirits, and gods are interconnected in a hierarchical unity of spiritual energy[14]. In this framework, an individual's sense of self is merely an extension of the universal self, actively engaged in all aspects of the whole. The traditional religious system of the Karbis involve direct interaction with the living, the dead, and the entirety of nature.

ECOLOGICAL VALUES OF THE KARBIS

The Karbi society is intricately intertwined with nature. This can be attributed to the presence of origin narratives, namely dealing with creation myths, generally referred to as *keplang*. Some examples are *Sok keplang* (the origin of rice), *Bong keplang* (the origin of Bottle Gourd), *Thap keplang* (the origin of fermented Rice-cake), *Phelo keplang* (the origin of cotton), *Hanso keplang* (the origin of Ginger), *Vo keplang* (the origin of poultry), *Lo keplang* (the origin of plantain leaf), and so on The nature of the Karbis' relationship with the natural environment is the primary reason for their deep affection towards it, which has persisted for generations. According to Karbi mythology, the universe of the Karbi ancestors represents a state of peaceful coexistence amongst animals, plants, demons, and deities, where the boundaries between the natural world and the human world occasionally overlap. It is universally acknowledged that the cosmos is collectively inhabited by all living and non-living entities. The Karbi forefathers sought to establish a state of peaceful coexistence between humans, animals, and plants, while also acknowledging the presence of protective deities and spirits. Prior to the inception of the cosmos, there was an immense and tumultuous expanse of water. According to DharamsingTeron (2008)[15], the Karbis believe that the 'Great Mother or Great Father', also known as *Pithe/Pothe* in Karbi language, is responsible for the creation of the universe, as portrayed in their version of the creation story. Consequently, the emergence of grasses and trees, hills and mountains, lakes and rivers, various animals, birds and avian species, ants and bees, maggots and flies occurred. The Karbi story elucidates the creation of Sang by the first Karbi progenitors, *Sum* and *Hemphu-Mukrang*. The five main clans of the Karbi tribe are *Kronjang*, *Ejang*, *Tungjang*, *Lijang*, and *Dingjang*. According to Robindra Teron and Ni-Et Teronpi (2020)[16], *Sibongpo* is the designated dog protector of the Karbis. According to the Karbi creation story, upon the gods' creation of Man (Karbis), malevolent spirits would consume them completely, leaving no evidence behind. Everything that God produced in the morning would vanish by the evening, and everything created at night would also vanish.

Another version of the myth is known as *Mosera*, which pertains to a mythical avian creature named *Voplakpi*. The bird produced numerous 'eggs' from which the Karbi ancestors and modern human populations originated. This exemplifies the profound spiritual bond that the Karbi ancestors had with their environment or nature[17]. The ecological vision of the Karbi forefathers is prominent in several interpretations of creation legends. The numerous origin myths vividly depict the environmental beliefs held by the Karbi forefathers. During the early spring, as per custom, the highest priest in the Karbi traditional kingdom, known as *Katharpo*, performs a ritual called *Botor Kikur* to invoke the monsoon. This ritual involves reciting the oral legend of *Ha'imu*, which serves as a way to appease the deified spirit of a peasant woman who chose death over submitting to a tyrannical chief. After her demise, the essence of *Ha'i* traversed the heavens, and her tears of torment came down as rainfall. The ritual involves the propitiation of several creatures, namely a grasshopper (*chanrik*), a cicada (*bengcheret*), a golden beetle (*arni aharling*), a *vo-krokchur* (a specific bird species), and a frog (*chongho*). According to Karbi ancestors, the hills, mountains, rivers, lakes, and other natural features are considered living entities and are believed to be under the ownership of invisible spirits. A Karbi engages in spiritual communion with invisible forces and venerates them as guardian deities through various yearly ceremonies. Specific locations within Karbi society are recognized as *arnam keso*, signifying the influence of a 'angry deity'. Consequently, these places are regarded as sacred and are accompanied by numerous stringent prohibitions. Taboos serve as cautionary measures, requiring the complete abstention from offensive language and behavior in order to preserve the sanctity of a location and avoid displeasing the residing deity. It is widely thought that committing such a breach can result in divine retribution, which may manifest as sudden illness and even death.

According to this study, the taboos that safeguard sacred woods form indigenous conservation systems. In Karbi society, *arnam-keso* is a prevalent phenomenon. The sacred groves might be regarded as exemplars of the symbiotic relationship between culture and ecology. Household deities, village deities, and territorial deities share distinct similarities. Each of them holds equal significance inside the community's belief system. The deities have angry counterparts known as *hi`i*, and they are worshipped together with *arnam* as *hi-i-arnam*. Consequently, arnam-keso is handled in a similar manner. The Karbis hold the belief that sacred groves possess extraordinary abilities, therefore safeguarding particular plant and animal species. *Garuga pinnata*, a plant commonly known in the local population, is widely regarded for its remarkable therapeutic properties[18]. The presence of a female dirge singer, also known as a *charhepi*, is crucial throughout the funeral ceremony. She performs the *Arni-Arve Kesai alun*, a song specifically designed to dispel rain clouds, in order to prevent any disruption to death ceremonies that are about to take place.

The Karbis possess a wealth of varied cultures that stem from their profound spiritual connection with their land and natural resources. They perceive themselves not as separate from nature, but as an integral part of it. They possess a distinct connection to their land and region, and employ their own methods of production that are informed by their specialized understanding of the surrounding environment. Soul (*Karjong*) has been attributed to several phenomena, particularly living and non-living forces in Karbi society. The Karbis consider all life forms and supernatural creatures as *Arnam Keso* because to the existence of *Karjong*, which is believed to be a part of the creator residing in all his works. The Karbi hold the belief that it is considered an offense to end the life of any living being without a specific ritualistic intention, as it is believed to possess the Karjong. Even when domestic animals such as poultry, goat, or pig are slaughtered for food, a brief ritual is performed to seek forgiveness from the gods and ensure that no wrongdoing is attributed to people. In order to kill such an animal, a *Alon* or a banana leaf is placed on the courtyard. Prior to cutting, the neck is adorned with sang, also known as rice, and then sliced with a knife.

The Karbi people, who follow the animist belief system, traditionally worship the deities known as *Hemphu-Mukrang*, as well as numerous territorial deities and ancestral spirits called *tirim*. The phrase 'Hi-i-Arnam' can be roughly translated to signify both 'devil' and 'deity', and they hold equal importance in folk rites. The term 'Hi-i-Arnam' was created by the Karbi ancestors and does not refer to a 'devil' or 'Satan', but rather represents the coexistence of 'negative' and 'positive' energies and the equilibrium between them, which forms the conceptual foundation of Karbi folk religions. Their animistic belief exhibits a profound connection between the deities, souls, spirits, and various flora, avifauna, aquatic creatures, and animals. The Karbi society practices various major religious rites, such as *Peng*, *Chojun*, *Longri Arnam Karkli*, *Wophong Rongker*, *Tirim Kipi*, and *Sang kimi-kipi*, as a way to show reverence to their nature deity. These rituals are mostly interconnected with nature. The sacred location known as *Longri Arnam* is situated near the house or just beyond the hamlet, where the rituals of *Wophong Rongker*, *Chojun*, and *Arnam Karkli* take place. Accessing the 'Than' site, harvesting fruits, or damaging the preserved trees is strictly forbidden. Prior to conducting the rituals, they collect all the essential items either one day in advance or on the day of the rites from the neighboring forest, where they are stored in their *Arnam Keso*. They gather various sacred flora, fauna, and even aquatic organisms for the purpose of making offerings. The preservation of this *Arnam Keso* can be attributed to the unwavering cultural and faith-based convictions of the local community, as well as their deep spiritual, religious, and cultural connections to the *Arnam Keso*. The primary advantage of this rich culture-oriented practice is that it promotes community engagement in the preservation of natural resources and fosters a lasting appreciation for nature and the interconnectedness between humans and the natural world.

SIGNIFICANCE OF TOTEMIC BELIEF SYSTEM

It is a type of religious and social structure seen among tribes that connects individuals with particular animals or items. The phrase has its origins in the language and practices of indigenous communities[19]. Yet, their distinct manifestation of *totemism* deviated from the anthropologists' understanding of the concept. A totemic tribe consists of distinct totem groups, each intricately linked to a particular totem, which can either be an animal or an inanimate object. Each member of a 'tribe' possesses a unique totem that is distinctive to their particular group. Therefore, although every tribe member has their own distinct totem, it will differ from the *totems* of other groups within the same tribes in the same location. In specific geographical areas, plants are highly respected as totems, yet in other instances, totems may encompass only a little symbolic element of an animal. Various theories concerning totems have offered valuable perspectives on distinct facets. These theoretical frameworks have been established based on 'unilateral models' employed in Western Europe. However, they may not completely support the evidence that aligns with the totemic belief system of the Karbis. Western researchers have employed the concept of totems to analyze the intricate relationship between 'civilized' and 'primitive' communities. These concepts illustrate the faith in totems and the ceremonial practice of animal sacrifices. Frazer (1910)[20]defines totemism as a religious and social framework wherein individuals or clans identify themselves as being linked to a particular object. It defines totemism as a belief system that cultivates a profound sense of interconnectedness between the follower and all other sentient entities in existence. Frazer's work provides a delineation of totemism as a religious and social framework in which people or clans view themselves as having a profound connection to a particular object. According to Frazer's idea, it can be deduced that a totem is not perceived as an invisible guardian, but rather as a tangible being that dwell alongside humans and shares their mortal existence. Therefore, it is crucial for the believers to actively refrain from inflicting damage onto other beings that possess a like essence to their totem. The term 'totemism' was initially coined by James Long in 1791 in his book *Voyages and Travels of an Indian Interpreter and Trader*[21]. James Long defines *totems* as ethereal entities that materialize in the form of animals and are revered by native populations as their individual protectors. Contrarily, Lévi-Strauss (1963)[22] posits the notion that animals and plants might function as totems, symbolizing either a civilization or an individual. Sigmund Freud examines the complex structure of clan differentiation and marriage, which is determined by the distinct totems of each clan and the restriction against marrying within one's own totem. Freud's research indicates that the Totem functions as a protective measure against sexual desires, given that tribal communities frequently lack distinct paternal lineage. *Totemism* is a spiritual belief system in which a community or individual is believed to have a mystical connection with a totem. It is also held that humans have a kinship with a totem. Nevertheless, it has unquestionably impacted the psychological conduct, socialization customs, and the formation of human character across diverse ethnicities. A distinct correlation is there between a totem and the individuals within a group, frequently encompassing a belief in a common ancestry with the totem. Masks and images have the potential to enhance this relationship. Individuals belonging to a particular totemic group exhibit profound veneration for the animal or thing that functions as their totem. They enforce a stringent taboo on destroying it inside their own group, but this prohibition does not apply to other members of the tribe. Thus, each member of the group who possesses the animal gene of their totem not only identifies as a human, but also embodies their totem as a tangible and mortal entity.

Totemic belief is a distinctive and special quality of Karbi community. Generally, tribes have *totemic* traits. They attribute mystical and mischievous characteristics to many physical objects, such as plants, animals, birds, and sometimes even aquatic life. The Karbi people see some artifacts as their totemic symbols, taboos, or curses, known as *Kertang* in the Karbi dialect. The belief in *Kertang* or 'taboo' is passed down through generations and is upheld in every household of each Karbi clan. This belief prohibits the killing or consumption of totemic artifacts. Failure to comply with these constraints could result in unfortunate consequences, both for the current and future generations. The Karbis hold a significant reverence for various plants and animal species, considering them sacred. One example is the plant *Garuga pinnata*, sometimes known as *Teji* or *Timur*, which is considered to have extraordinary abilities. According to the words of the Karbi folk song (*Keplang*), it is widely believed that 'Arnam' was the initial creator of human beings on this world. According to the traditional values of the Karbis, every aspect of creation holds sacred significance as it is deeply intertwined with their beliefs and rituals. Natural items possess religious importance due to their association with people's religious system, thereby earning them a position of reverence.

Various clans' worship distinct species as sacred, often with beliefs and myths that ascribe a special connection to specific flora and animals. For example, the Terang clan holds great admiration for the hornbill, considering its killing to be a serious transgression. In addition, the Karbi people hold several totemic beliefs, one of which is the prohibition of killing tigers, elephants, and other members of the feline family for individuals who worship the spirits of these animals. This kind of worship is referred to as *Sonpi-Sonbon.*

As previously said, Karbis believe in *Arnam Keso* as part of their belief system, and those who live in an area known for violence refrain from killing cats. Similarly, families that engage in the rites of *Dor* refrain from harming any species of snakes. The Teron clan holds the Rui-Teron, who aassumes the guise of a snake in high reverence[23].

The Tokbi clan refrains from both killing and consuming eagles. Despite its quality as an excellent source of firewood, the Lo Teron tree holds holy significance for the Teron clan[24] . As a result, it is considered prohibited for them to use the tree or even touch it, as stated by Sarma and Borpujari (2014)[25]. The *Ingsum leaves,* known for their sour taste and consumed as a vegetable by the Karbis, hold religious significance to the Ingti clan and are therefore forbidden to be consumed. In addition to these particular flora and fauna, the Karbi people also venerate the bovine, pachyderm, and feline. Once again, the act of slaughtering a pregnant animal for the purpose of obtaining food is prohibited. According to Timung and Singh (2016)[26], the Rongpi clan believes that it has historically offered direction to its members in jhum cultivations. The Timung clan believes that animals played a key part in safeguarding their lives during times of conflict. The enemies proceeded to set the house on fire, but luckily, they stumbled upon a pangolin digging a hole to escape capture. They chased the pangolin and ended up in the forest. Consequently, starting from that day, they refrained from killing the pangolin and regarded it as a vital element of their clan[27].

CONCLUSION

Like other tribal communities, the Karbis preserve their customs by practicing the worship of their deities, beginning from birth and persisting until the mourning of death. They engage in precise religious rituals accompanied by meticulous offerings. Karbis strongly believe that any failing to show respect towards spirits and ancestral worship will lead to the complete destruction of their clan. They maintain the plants that they consider sacred for social, cultural, and religious reasons. The cultural life of Karbis has been greatly shaped by the ecology of their environment, as previously stated. They possess a strong devotion to nature, similar to other tribes, and maintain a distinct bond, as previously mentioned, with specific plant and animal species. In addition, they adhere to their customary practice of preserving *Arnam Keso* in order to safeguard and preserve rare, endangered, vulnerable, and endemic species that inhabit these sacred areas. Therefore, it is essential to protect the unique practice of conserving sacred trees as a vital step for ecological importance, requiring conservation and preservation efforts.

The sacred groves and cultural traditions are currently in a deteriorated situation due to various factors. The maintenance and adherence to traditional beliefs have been diminishing. The vegetation in sacred groves is identical. As the belief system has gradually weakened, the vegetation in these groves has likewise deteriorated. The primary factors contributing to this phenomenon are the declining state of the sacred groves, limited awareness, the growing desire of the local populace for improved living standards in light of modernity and shifts in local religious practices. In addition to these considerations, there have been recent alterations in the administration of *Arnam Keso*. In the past, there was a lack of awareness regarding the vast number of species, which therefore hindered the recognition of their degradation or economic potential. That said, the customs and traditions of the Karbis indicate that the traditional resource management is well harmonized within the existing socio-political and socio-economic framework of the society. This study revealed that the local belief systems associated with sacred *Arnam Keso* have a crucial impact on the comprehension and formulation of sustainable conservation measures within a given community. Also, it highlights the interconnectedness of culture and environment, highlighting their mutual influence on each other. The sacred groves (arnam keso) of the Karbis have significant roles in the preservation of ecological diversity. Therefore, it is crucial to safeguard and develop the traditional values and systems that support biodiversity conservation, in addition to conventional conservation efforts.

NOTES

1. K. Kato, 'Community, connection and conservation: Intangible cultural values in Natural Heritage: The case of Shirakami-sanchi World Heritage Area' in *International Journal of Heritage Studies*, 12(5), 2006, pp. 458-473.
2. Dharamsing Teron, 'The Mosera Tradition and the egg origin of the Karbis in DharamsingTeron (Ed.), *Karbi Studies: Memories, Myth and Metaphors*, Vol. 1, Assam Book Hive, Guwahati, 2008.
3. F.Berkes, *Sacred Ecology: Traditional Ecological Knowledge and Resource Management*, Routledge, New York & London, 1999.
4. June-Ann Greeley, 'Water in Native American Spirituality: Liquid Life—Blood of the Earth and Life of the Community Earth and Life of the Community' in *Green Humanities*, vol. 2 (2017), pp. 156-179.
5. Durmily Hansepi, 'Traditional Belief and Ecological Preservation among The Karbis' in Vulli Dhanaraju and Dharamsing Teron (Ed.), *Karbi History: Past and Present*, Mittal Publications, New Delhi, 2020, p. 394.
6. W.Jackson and A. Ormsby, 'Urban Sacred Natural Sites: A Call for Research', in *Urban Ecosystems*, Vol. 20(3), 2017, pp. 675-681.
7. Bas Verschuuren, Robert Wild, Jeffrey McNeely and Gonzalo Oviedo, 'Introduction:Sacred Natural Sites the Foundations of Conservation' in Bas Verschuure (et.al.), *Sacred Natural Sites: Conserving Nature and Culture*, Routledge, 2010, pp. 1-13.
8. Sacred groves are parts of forests or natural flora ranging in size from a few trees to many acres that are typically dedicated to local folk deities. Local communities maintain these sites because of their religious beliefs and long-standing traditions. However, mainstem scholars have defined this term to refer to the local belief system for the preservation of the local environment. The Karbis used the term 'Arnam Keso' to describe similar conservation initiatives.
9. M.L. Khan, A.D. Khumbongmayum and R.S. Tripathi, 'The Sacred Groves and their Significance in Conserving Biodiversity: An Overview', in *International Journal of Ecology and Environmental Sciences*, Vol.34(3),2008, pp. 277-291.

10. C.R. Menzies and C. Butler, 'Introduction: Understanding Ecological Knowledge' in Charles R. Menzies (Ed.), *Traditional Ecological Knowledge and Natural Resource Management*, University of Nebraska Press, Lincoln, 2006, pp. i-vii.
11. M. Dukor, 'Theistic Panpsychic Animism of African Medicine' in *Essence-Interdisciplinary International Journal*, No. 3, 2006, pp. VI-XXX.
12. A.O. Echekwube, 'The Basic Principles of African Philosophy' in *Essence-Interdisciplinary International Journal*, No. 2, 2005, p. 2.
13. John.VTaylor, *The Primal Vision: Christian Presence Amid African Religion*, SCM Press, London, 1977.
14. M.M. Thomas, 'Modernization of Traditional Societies and Struggle for New Cultural Ethos', in *Ecumenical Review*, Vol. XVIII, No.4, October 1966, p.429. (Cited in Kailash Kumar Chatry, 'Ecological Significance of the Traditional Beliefs and Practices of Dimasa Kachari Tribe', *Indian Journal of Theology*, 43.1& 2, 2001, pp. 63-69.
15. Dharamsing Teron, 'The Mosera Tradition and the egg origin of the Karbis' in Dharamsing Teron (Ed.,), *Karbi Studies: Memories, Myth and Metaphors*, Vol. I. Assam Book Hive, Guwahati, 2008
16. Robindra Teron and Ni-Et Teronpi, 'Conservation Ethos In Karbi Folklore in Vulli Dhanaraju and Dharamsing Teron (Ed.), *Karbi History: Past and Present*, Mittal Publications, New Delhi, 2020, p. 394.
17. DharamsingTeron, *op.cit.*, 2008.
18. U. Sarma, B. Indrani, 'Eco-Cosmologies and Biodiversity Conservation: Continuity and Change among the Karbis of Assam' in *International Indigenous Policy Journal*, 2 (4), 2011, pp. 1-10.
19. Josef Haekel, 'Totemism-Religion' in *Brittanica*, Available at https://www.britannica.com/topic/totemism-religion (Accessed on 10/5/2024).
20. J.G Frazer, *Totemism and Exogamy-A Treatise on Certain Early Forms of Superstition and Society*, Severus Verlag, 1910 (2011).
21. James Long, *Voyages and Travels of an Indian Interpreter and Trader*, Kessinger Publication, 1791 (2005).
22. Claude Lévi-Strauss, *Totemism*, Penguin Books, London, 1963.
23. Durmily Hansepi, op. cit., 2020, p. 397.
24. Ibid.
25. U.K. Sarma and I. Borpujari, 'Eco-Cosmologies and Biodiversity Conservation: Continuity and Change among the Karbis of Assam' in *the International Indigenous Policy Journal*, Vol.2, 2014, pp. 1-7.

26. L.Timung, L and N.Singh, 'Totemic Beliefs and Biodiversity Conservation Among the Karbis of Assam, India' in *Research on Humanities and Social Sciences*, Vol. 6, No. 11, 2016, pp. 26-30.
27. Durmily Hansepi, op. cit., 2020, p. 394.

CHAPTER 8

Traditional Ecological Knowledge and Skills (TEKS) of the Karbis

The Case of Magursila Village of Kamrup Metro District, Assam

BARASHA RANI DAS and NITYANANDA DEKA

INTRODUCTION

The concept of Traditional Ecological Knowledge and Skills (TEKS) pertains to a specific body of knowledge, practices, and beliefs that have been passed down through generations within indigenous communities residing in a particular region.[1] These TEKS have developed and evolved over time as a result of the intimate and intricate relationship between these communities and their surrounding natural environment.[2] The issue at hand encompasses a profound comprehension of ecosystems, biodiversity, the management of resources, and the implementation of sustainable practices. The TEKS hold considerable importance within the contemporary framework of ecological restoration and conservation. They provide invaluable perspectives and remedies for confronting newly arisen environmental difficulties, while also advocating for the advancement of sustainable development.[3] One of the fundamental principles of TEKS lies in its recognition of the intricate interdependencies between the natural world and human civilizations. Indigenous and local communities have maintained enduring connections with various species, habitats, and ecosystems in their immediate surroundings.[4] The TEKS have a vital role in facilitating the implementation of sustainable resource management practices. Indigenous and local communities have carried out distinctive practices and methods pertaining to land utilization, agriculture, resource extraction, seed preservation, water resource management, textile production, and architectural design of their dwellings. These practices are intricately aligned with the specific characteristics of their surrounding ecosystems, thereby fostering enduring sustainability.[5] The implementation of these practices frequently stems from a profound comprehension of ecological contexts, encompassing patterns and processes within ecosystems, the evolutionary dynamics of these systems, the reproductive cycles of species, migratory behaviors, and the inherent regenerative potential of ecosystems.[6]

Currently, researchers and policy makers have acknowledged the potential benefits of incorporating TEKS (Traditional Ecological Knowledge and Skills) into resource management strategies. This integration holds promise for bolstering the resilience of ecosystems, safeguarding the uninterrupted availability of critical resources, and mitigating the perils associated with excessive exploitation and depletion of ecological resources.[7] Moreover, it is worth noting that TEKS have considerable cultural and social importance. The profound intertwining of cultural heritage, identity, and spirituality within the indigenous and local communities of a given region is evident. Traditional knowledge systems embody a deep reverence for the natural world and recognition of the intricate interdependencies within ecological contexts.[8]

Similar to ecosystems found in different locations, the diverse ethnic communities dwelling in the state of Assam, India preserve specific traditional ecological skills and knowledge that have been passed down through past generations. The development of the state's expansive cultural landscapes can be attributed to the intricate interplay between its diverse ethnic groups and the abundant and varied physical environments. This interaction has been shaped by the utilization of traditional knowledge, skills, and belief systems.[9] The diverse indigenous tribal and non-tribal ethnic groups within the state have harmoniously interacted with their surrounding environment, drawing upon its natural resources while adhering to their distinct cultural practices and traditions. This symbiotic relationship has given rise to intricate land utilization patterns, resulting in the creation of composite cultural landscapes across various geographical locations within the state over the passage of time.[10] Similar to other rural ecosystems, the inhabitants of Assam have been effectively harnessing the natural resources available to meet their daily requirements and essentialities, while minimizing the detrimental impact on their surrounding natural environment.[11] The state provides numerous examples that demonstrate the significant impact of natural environments on the socio-cultural dynamics of its diverse ethnic groups, as well as the reciprocal influence of these groups on the natural settings.

The Karbis, an indigenous community residing in Assam, have successfully cultivated a variety of traditional ecological knowledge and skills (TEKS). These TEKS have played a crucial role in enabling the Karbis to maintain their way of life and sustain their livelihoods, even in the face of modern socio-economic influences. The Karbi people exhibit a strong affinity for residing within elevated terrains such as hills and plateaus, consequently acquiring a multitude of ecological traits specific to these particular ecosystems. The lifestyle and culture of the Karbi community exhibit distinct characteristics when compared to other tribal and non-tribal ethnic communities residing in the floodplain regions of the state of Assam. The indigenous communities residing in mountainous regions rely on the forest resources to meet their basic needs. Conversely, the inhabitants of flat terrains prioritize the floodplain resources, particularly the riverine ecological resources, as their means of supporting their livelihoods. The indigenous communities residing in the state exhibit a profound affection for the pristine ecological landscapes, particularly the forests and wetlands, fostering a harmonious connection with these natural habitats. Their values are intricately intertwined with the reverence and sanctity bestowed upon every manifestation of life and the inanimate components within the ecological milieu[12].

Karbis, the predominant indigenous community, inhabit the East Karbi Anglong and West Karbi Anglong districts of Assam. In addition to the aforementioned districts, the Karbi community can also be found residing in various other districts of Assam, such as Dima Hasao, Kamrup Metro, Morigaon, Nagaon, Golaghat, Karimganj, and Sonitpur districts. It is widely believed that they have established a profound connection with the hill environment, as well as the diverse plant and animal life that inhabit it. Over time, they have developed various traditional ecological knowledge and skills (TEKS) to responsibly acquire the necessary resources from the hill ecosystem in order to sustain themselves. The predominant agricultural practice observed in their region continues to be the traditional jhum (shifting) cultivation method. The intricate dynamics and progression of embracing and adjusting to the distinct hill ecological landscapes have resulted in the emergence of invaluable Traditional Ecological Knowledge and Skills.[13]

Currently, the traditional ecological knowledge and skills (TEKS) held by the ethnic communities in Assam are experiencing a decline, with some already lost due to the impact of emerging modern socio-economic processes. Moreover, it has been noted that due to the impact of altering physical and social landscapes within the region, the ecological systems have experienced swift deterioration, leading to a gradual disconnection and decline in the symbiotic relationship between humans and their environment. The preservation and safeguarding of traditional ecological knowledge and skills (TEKS) holds great importance in the realm of managing and alleviating environmental degradation. Amidst the pressing environmental issues of climate change, habitat destruction, pollution, and biodiversity loss, it is crucial to acknowledge the valuable contribution of traditional ecological knowledge and skills (TEKS) in fostering sustainable and resilient conservation practices. The preservation of traditional ecological knowledge and skills is not solely a matter of cultural conservation, but also holds equal significance in advancing sustainable and efficient conservation endeavors. Through the acknowledgement and incorporation of TEKS (Traditional Ecological Knowledge and Skills), researchers and policy makers who are invested in environmental conservation can promote a comprehensive and all-encompassing strategy towards achieving a sustainable ecosystem. In this particular context, the Karbis have developed numerous distinctive traditional ecological knowledge and skills that have enabled them to sustain their natural environment in a manner that is harmonious with ecological principles. If the TEKS were to be embraced and implemented within the realm of environmental management practices in comparable ecosystems, it is plausible that the pursuit of sustainable socio-economic and environmental objectives could be realized.

The current investigation aims to record the traditional ecological knowledge and skills of the Karbis residing in a representative Karbi village called Magursila village, located in the Kamrup Metro district of Assam. Additionally, it seeks to emphasize the significance of traditional ecological knowledge and skills in the contemporary context of environmental deterioration and conservation efforts. The Karbis residing in Magursila village, located in the Sonapur Revenue circle of Kamrup Metro district, Assam, demonstrate a profound and interconnected bond with the hill ecosystems. Even within the contemporary framework of modern human societies, the village remains relatively unaffected by the extensive modern socio-economic processes. Their existence and means of sustenance remain intricately intertwined with the natural world. Therefore, the current investigation possesses considerable academic importance in documenting the existing culture, livelihood patterns, traditional ecological knowledge, skills, and belief systems, traditional dietary practices, traditional attire, housing structures, and other aspects of folk culture observed among the residents of Magursila village.

DATABASE AND METHODOLOGY

The Magursila village of Kamrup Metro District of Assam has been selected as a case study village in order to make a thorough investigation on the traditional ecological knowledge and skills (TEKS) of the Karbis. The study is mainly based on the primary data and information collected from each household of the village. Different physical and cultural components of the village were studied on the basis of field investigation and primary surveys through well-structured questionnaire cum schedule. The village was intensively surveyed through different types of primary surveys, viz. benchmark household survey, ecological survey, plot survey during 2019-2022 to have a clear-cut picture on the existing ecological and social conditions of the village. With the help of GPS, the latitudinal and longitudinal positions of the village were obtained based on which the demarcation of the village has been made to prepare some required maps of the village.

THE VILLAGE

Magursila village, located under the Sonapur Revenue Circle in Assam, is one of the largest Karbi villages in the sub-district. Confining within 26 o03'12.20" N to 26o04'39.29" N latitude and 91o59'35.42" E to 92o02'8.64"E longitude, the village is situated on the southern side of the sub-district. The village covers an area of 4.5 sq. km with a population of 653 persons as per 2011 Census. It is located at a distance of about 14 km from Sonapur Circle and about 30 km from Guwahati city. The village is about 12 km away from the Kolong River which flows along the north-eastern side of the Circle. The village consists of 4 *chuburis* (hamlets) with a total household of 126 (as per field survey, 2019).The village is characterized by a hilly landscape, encompassing three major hills and numerous smaller ones scattered throughout its surrounding. It is filled with mesmerizing natural beauty, characterized by dense forest cover, rich ecological diversity, streams, and man-made canals (dongs), which have sprinkled a beautiful texture across the village landscape. The hills serve as the feeder to the villagers. A cordial and sustainable relation with the natural environment is being maintained by the local people.

While many villages of the Brahmaputra valley have been experiencing negative implications of environmental degradation, Magursila village under study stands unique example regarding the maintenance and conservation of ecological settings by the villagers. In the present-day context of rapid loss of TEKS in many ethnic villages, the people of Magursila village have been still practicing the TEKS in conserving and managing the village ecology for their sustainable livelihoods. Hence the selection of the present village for investigation.

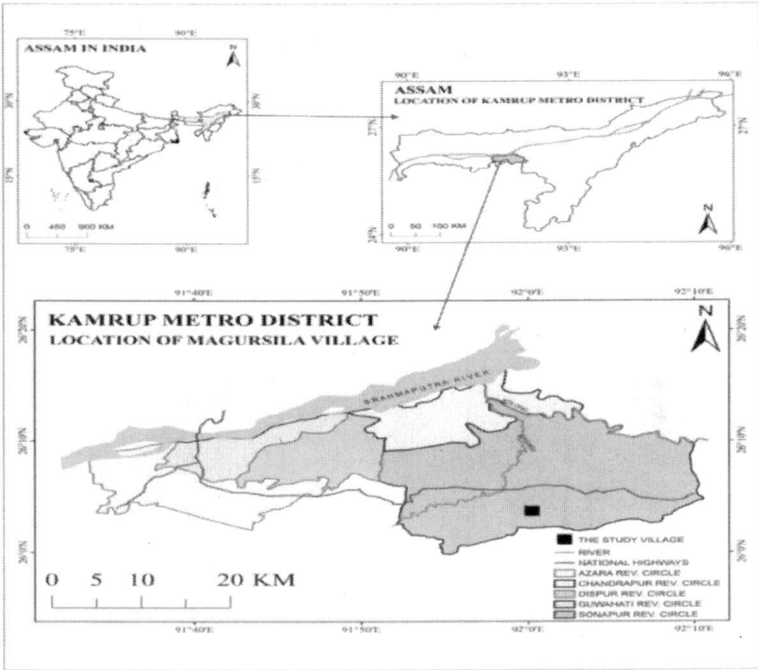

FIG. 1: LOCATION OF MAGURSILA VILLAGE

Mapping: Some maps depicting the physical elements, such as hills, plains, vegetation cover, streams, along with the cultural ones were drawn with the help of participatory rural appraisal (PRA) method and ground survey. The village is shown in Kamrup Metro District taking its GPS points, and the location map has been prepared taking help of ArcGIS software.

Household Survey: The study is mainly based on the primary data/information obtained by surveying all the 126 households of the village through a well-structured questionnaire. Data on TEKS related to agroforestry practices, land use and cropping practices, housing and homestead design, management of hill ecosystem, weaving and crafting, water resource management practices etc. were collected.

Other Methods: Information on the use, management, and conservation of ecological resources was collected from the villagers through personal interactions and interviews with people of different age groups. The Participatory Rural Appraisal (PRA) and Rapid Rural Appraisal (RRA) methods were applied for documenting their TEKS. Focus Group Discussions (FGDs) among the people of different age-sex structure and occupations were conducted to acquire relevant information and perception towards the natural landscapes and their changes over time. Information and data about various floral and faunal species were also collected and tabulated to show their impacts on rural life and livelihoods. Besides, information about their traditional food habits, dressing pattern, traditional agricultural inputs and implements, house building materials, culturally important tree species were gathered. Information regarding their culture and traditional practices were collected through the survey schedule. In addition, relevant photographs were taken, and various physio-cultural aspects were documented to authenticate the findings.

TRADITIONAL KNOWLEDGE AND SKILLS IN LAND USE

The land use patterns in the rural areas of the Brahmaputra valley vary spatially. The spatial variations of land use in the rural areas of the Brahmaputra valley are mainly caused by its natural and cultural factors. The locational characteristics, physical configurations, soil types, micro-climate, water bodies, flood dynamics are some of the prominent physical factors that govern the pattern of land use and production systems. Additionally, land use patterns vary among the ethnic communities of the valley, as their traditions, customs, food habits, and traditional ecological knowledge and skills (TEKS) play important roles in shaping their rural land use practices. It is worth mentioning that the typology of land use patterns of Magursila village reflects the close interaction of inhabitants with its ecological elements. Based on local ecological knowledge and skills, the villagers have traditionally made some unique land use patterns which can be typified as i) residential lands (*Gharveti*), ii) home gardens *(bari-basti)*, iii) the winter rice fields (*Salikhetimati*) iv) kitchen garden

(*Sakonibari*), v) seedbeds (*Kothiatoli*), vi) grazing lands (*Bakorimati*), vii) ponds, viii) *jhum* fields, ix) orange gardens, x) bamboo patches xi) broom fields, xii) betel nut gardens, xiii) rubber gardens, xiv) pineapple garden etc. It is found that the winter rice fields (*Salikhetimati*), which are made in low lying lands of the village cover the largest area of the village (33.285%). The bamboo patches, orange gardens, *jhum* fields, betel nut gardens, rubber gardens, pineapple gardens, and broom fields etc. have brought a peculiarity in the land use pattern of the village unlike many floodplain villages of the Brahmaputra valley. In the recent years, the lands used for cultivating/planting bamboo, broom, rubber, betel-nut, orange, pineapple etc. have been providing remarkable earnings to the villagers. The nearby hills, rich in diverse tree species, provide the villagers with ample resources, so unlike many other floodplain dwellers, they do not feel the need to plant trees in their home gardens. As a result, only a few plant species are found in their home gardens, which the villagers use frequently to meet their daily needs. Some of these plant species include coconut trees, betel nut, black pepper (*golmoris*), lychee, mango, jamun and drumstick. Additionally, various types of flowers, such as roses and hibiscus, which are typically found in the plains, have recently been planted by some villagers in their homesteads to enhance aesthetic beauty. This change reflects the assimilation of hill dwellers with people from nearby plain areas. Consequently, based on traditional knowledge and ongoing interaction with their ecological surroundings, the villagers have used natural elements to meet their needs, creating a unique cultural landscape within the village.[14]

TRADITIONAL ECOLOGICAL KNOWLEDGE AND HOMESTEAD DESIGN

The homestead designs of Karbi villages are different from other ethnic communities of the Brahmaputra valley. The homestead designs which include the house types, fencing style, courtyard, home gadens, kitchen garden and flower gardens etc. reflect traditional ecological knowledge and skills of the Karbis about their natural envirionment. Various elements of their traditional houses vividly exhibit the utili-

FIG. 2: DIFFERENT LAND USE PATTERNS IN THE VILLAGE,

Note: A-pineapple garden; B-bamboo cultivation; C-rubber plantation; D-broom cultivation; E-betel nut garden; F-jhum field

zation of locally sourced materials such as wood from nearby trees, bamboo, and thatch. Various fruits and wood trees that are planted in the surrounding areas of their residence mainly include betel nut, coconut, *robabtanga (citrus grandis), golnemu (citrus limon), modhuriam (psidium guajava), gomari (gmelina arborea), silikha (terminalia chebula), kothal (artocarpus integer), bokul (mimusops elengi), segun (tectona grandis), banana (musa paradisiacal),* mango *(magnifera indica)* etc. The residences in the study village are traditionally protected by bamboo fencing. The cactus and dried betel nut leaves are mainly used by the villagers for fencing. Various fruits and wood trees that are planted in the surrounding areas of their residence mainly include betel nut, coconut, *robabtanga (citrus grandis), golnemu (citrus limon), modhuriam (psidium guajava), gomari (gmelina arborea), silikha (terminalia chebula), kothal (artocarpus integer), bokul (mimusops elengi), segun (tectona grandis), banana (musa paradisiacal),* mango *(magnifera indica)* etc. Various trees, both planted and naturally grown, around the residence have added an aesthetic beauty to the village landscape.

TEKS AND VILLAGE WATERSCAPE

It is very interesting to note that the people of Magursila village have designed a peculiar dong (man-made canal) system by diverting the stream water of the hills to their agricultural and residential lands. This *dong* system has been used as a traditional way of irrigating their agricultural fields and is a beautiful example of human response to the natural set up. Besides, the *dong* water is also diverted to the man-made ponds, especially during winter, for the survival of fishes and other aquatic floral and faunal species[15]. As the village is a hilly one and the groundwater level is very deep, no tube well could be set up for consumption of drinking water. Earlier, the *dong* water was used for all purposes like washing, drinking, bathing, soaking seeds and some construction materials, irrigating agricultural fields and so on. Although the villagers currently use ring wells for drinking water and other household needs, use of *dong* water for drinking and other purposes is still common in the village.

A

B

C

D

E

F

FIG. 3: DIFFERENT HOMESTEAD DESIGNS OF THE VILLAGE

Note: A-courtyard; B-bamboo fencing around the residence; C-paddy straw heap; D-trees around the residence; E-cowshed; F-broomshed

DYEING OF TRADITIONAL COSTUMES WITH NATURAL DYES

The various communities in Assam have a long history of using natural dyes to colour fabrics. Many native inhabitants of Assam have identified numerous plants that are used for dying[16]. The majority of the indigenous people of the state still use natural plant dyes in place of the synthetic dyes that are commonly used today. To make dyes, they use the entire plant, including the leaves, fruits, barks, and leaves. The fabrics have been coloured using natural dyes. The various ethnic communities of the state continue to use traditional dyes to colour their clothing and textiles.[17]

Similarly, according to the village elders, the blue color of their traditional dresses is derived from a plant locally known as the Chubu plant[18], which bears tiny blue flowers.[19] First of all, the leaves and flowers of that plant are pasted with the help of traditional grinding tools such as '*urol*' and '*dheki*' and the fluid part is then separated and then it is mixed with local *Khar* (alkaline). In the final mix, the cotton threads are soaked for 2-3 weeks. Once properly soaked, the threads are dried in the sunlight. Finally, the homemade blue-colored cotton threads are ready for weaving new clothes 20. However, the number of people using this plant species for dyeing has declined somewhat due to the availability of artificial dyes in the market.

FIG. 5: *CHUBU* PLANT

INDIGENOUS KNOWLEDGE AND SKILLS OF TRADITIONAL FOOD

The people of rural areas all over the world have always been depending on ecological elements for their life and livelihoods and this dependency on nature has been providing economic assistance to the rural dwellers.[21] Similarly, the people living in the hilly areas of the Brahmaputra valley are also intimately connected with the forest resources for their daily needs and necessities and they have been maintaining a balanced relationship with nature, thus forming beautiful cultural landscapes.[22] Correspondingly, the people of the concerned village have also been using the ecological elements for various purposes, such as diet, dress, agricultural tools, house-building materials, organic fertilizers, traditional medicines and so on.

The use of ecological elements in the food items of Karbis in the concerned village has been occupying a significant place since the beginning of the evolution of the village in that area. The diverse floral and faunal resources found in the hills have been the sources of their diet and also means of earning to the villagers. The plain areas of the village help the local people to produce different types of *Sali* rice, such as *Mekrasali, Aijungsali, Ranjit, Baahadur, Haaldhimaguri* etc. Besides, the vegetables collected from the hills are inseparable part of traditional food habit of the villagers of which *pahariyaaloo, kosu (Dioscore alata), dhekia (Diplazium esculentum), mestatenga (Hibiscus sabdariffa), kolphul, bahorgaja (Bambusa vulgaris), bahakatita (Phologocanthus thyrsiflorus), kumura (Benincasa hispida), rongalau (Cucurbita moschata),*etc. are prominent. The hills also provide them different types of fruits such as banana, mango, guava etc.They also include roots and leaves of certain trees in their traditional diet.[23]

Apart from these, the traditional knowledge and skills in preparing dried fishes, dried pork and dried *sophing, dried bahakatita, bahorgaja (bamboo shoot), dried mestatenga (Hibiscus sabdariffa)* etc. are very significant in their culture. Besides, boiled pork and chicken also hold an important place in their food habit. Even today, the use of oil, salt, turmeric, onion and other spices are very less in their cooking. They mostly consume boiled items with little salt or without any kind of oil and spices. However, some people have now started using small amounts of salt and oil in preparing certain food items. The villagers still use traditional methods of cooking in bamboo hollows (*sunga*) to cook food items in an open fire.

TRADITIONAL KNOWLEDGE AND SKILLS OF CROP MANAGEMENT

The ethnic communities of Assam have evoloved some unique TEKS in managing their crops in the farm lands and in the granary after harvest[24].The traditional knowledge and skills of agriculture is well reflected in folklore such as folk songs, rituals, proverbs, riddles, and several other traditions through which the art of humanity is passed down to successive generations[25]. Besides these, farmers of various indigenous communities in Assam possess a deep understanding of the floral species in their environment and have identified a wide range of plants that can be used for pest control. The Karbis in the study village, like other ethnic communities in the state, use various traditional ecological knowledge in pest control, crop management and crop preservation[26].

The use of ecological elements in agricultural systems is very much significant in the concerned Karbi village. The people of the village have been using various natural elements as insecticides, among which the use of *robabtenga (Citrus maxima)* is prominent. To get rid of the attack of insects, they throw small pieces of *robab-tenga* (*Citrus maxima)* on the paddy fields. Additionally, they plant a floral species known as *jomnempocholuk* in the rice fields to combat a rice disease locally referred to as *Pessam*, which causes the rice leaves to turn red or white. They also throw pieces of *Robabtenga* in the rice fields to cure this disease. During the panicle formation stage of rice, an insect called *Gandhipuk* can severely damage the crops. To address this issue, the local people place dead crabs on bamboo sticks throughout the paddy fields. This strategy diverts the insects away from the crops and towards the crabs, helping to protect the rice from pest damage. The villagers make a mixture of '*Patsadha*', '*Bihdhekia*' and '*Jonotasabun*' and spray it on agricultural fields to kill all kinds of insects that ingest the rice crops.

TRADITIONAL KNOWLEDGE OF MEDICINAL HERBS

The various ethnic communities that inhabit the state of Assam have inherited vast amounts of traditional medicinal knowledge. The ethnic groups and tribals who live in remote forest villages and forest fringe villages continue to rely heavily on indigenous medicinal plants.[27] It is found that many floral species availabe in Magursila village have immense medicinal values. These plants are the prime means of remedy to different ailments faced by the villagers. Since the evolution of the village, nature has been serving as a traditional ailment healer to the concerned locality. Even in this era of development and modernization, the villagers, lacking modern health facilities, remain wholly dependent on various floral and faunal species to treat their illnesses. This dependency on nature shows an intimate eco-friendly bonding between nature and people in the village.

Some of the selected floral species being used as natural disease healer in Magursila village are enlisted in the following table.

TABLE 1: MEDICINAL FLORAL SPECIES AVAILABLE IN THE VILLAGE

Category	*Local name (Karbi, Assamese)/Scientific name*	*Purpose of use*
Creepers	Kongwan-aringkan	(i)The fluid of this creeper is used in dysentery. (ii) People while working in the hills consume this creeper's fluid as water.
	Rijanglen	Used in waist pain.
	Pethongsek (Haajuralota)	Bone fracture
	Ritarmeringkang	Used in a disease locally called '*aar-ko-pali*' in which headache starts with the sunrise.
	Aalaringkang	Consumed in body pain.
	Samphrat-aringkang	The root of this creeper is used in body injury to stop bleeding.
	Ripumplum-aringkang	Used in lesion.

Ximepeasulang	The small potatoes found in the root of this plant are used to increase milk of the newborn's mother.
Rikang-akipo	Leaves of this creeper are consumed to cure body pain and waist pain.
Ripeshawat – aringkang	Jaundice
Tike-adeh-aringkang	Used to cure lesion in cows.
Bith/Paan*(Piper betle)*	Itching
Hiphe-aringkang*(Paederia foetida)*	Consumed to cure stomach pain and acidity.
Lojangthu	Its leaf is used to cure piles and Jaundice.
Rikang-angllang (Joibangla)	Paste of this creeeper's leaves is used in injury. It is also consumed in stomach pain.
Xurupanari (Roghumola)	The paste of this creeper's leaves is used to cure the vitiligo disease (loss of skin colour in blotches)
Jangphung-ouksukuri	Used to cure the poisonous effect of snake bite.
Phillangtu	The root of this creeper is used to cure urine burning
Nengpehrekthi	Fluid of the potatoes of this creeper is used in hair to remove louse.
Arlonglureu (Xilpoat)	Consumed to increase blood in human body.
Althe/Pipoli (Piper longum)	Leaf is consumed in cough and stomach pain.
Birik/Golmoris*(Piper nigrum)*	Consumed in cold and cough.
Arlongaathe	Used to cure wound, external injury , paralysis
Riting	Wound

(Contd.)

Category	*Local name (Karbi, Assamese)/Scientific name*	*Purpose of use*
	Nirket	Stomach pain
	Bonkaarol	Used to stop nosal bleeding.
	Chomangperampa	Consumed in jaundice.
	Amoaakee/ Aporajita*(Clitoria ternatea)*	Leaves are consumed to cure diabetes
	Richangkru	Potato found in the root of this creeper is consumed in dysentery.
	Gorgaang/ Modhuriam (*Psidium guajava)*	Leaves and bark of this fruit are used to cure dysentery.
	Theimuthia (Aathiakol)	The potatoes found in the root of this fruit are used in fatigue.
	Lopo-Kengtong (Raamkol)	Dysentery
	Kochari-aazangphong	Ear disease
	Hanthor-aakidouk/ Komola*(Citrus sinensis)*	The peel of *Citrus sinensis* or orange is used to cure wound. Dried peel is used as spice.
Fruits	Hanchopha-aa/ Golnemu*(Citrus aurantifolia)*	Used to cure high blood pressure, dysentery and headache.
	KaziNemu*(Citrus limon)*	Vomiting, dysentery
	Hesotume	Liquid extracted from the root of this tree is consumed to cure breathing problems.
	Thelu/PahariaAmlokhi *(Phyllanthusemblica)*	Stomach pain, cough
	Xilikha*(Terminalia chebula)*	Cough, Indigestion
	Chumeng/ Amora*(Spondius pinnata)*	Leaf of this tree is used to cure dysentery
	Pumpiri/Thekera (*Garcinia pedunculata)*	Dried *Garciniapedunculata* is consumed in dysentery.

Tortey/Kordoi*(Averrhoa carambola)*	Consumed in Jaundice.
Taapilip/Bel*(Aegle marmelos)*	Cures constipation.
Therpaal/Poniyol *(Flacourita jangomas)*	Consumed to cure breathing problem.
Barla	Used in fungal infection.
Dalim*(Punica granatum)*	Consumption of young leaves of this fruit is good to cure low blood pressure and vomiting.
Baap-nemthu*(Ageratum conizoides)*	External body injury
Bengsaar/Noroxingho *(Murraya koenigii)*	Stomach problem
Baatsokori *(Chromolaena odorata)*	External body injury
Nempocholuk *(Pogostemon benghalensis)*	Leaves are consumed to cure bone breakage.
Titiri-aakik*(Justicia gendarussa)*	Leg fracture, leg pain
Nukicho*(Cyperus brevifolius)*	External injury
Ingphaat	Stomach pain

Source: Field Survey, 2019-2022.

TRADITIONAL ECOLOGICAL KNOWLEDGE AND CRAFTS

The hills and hillocks of Assam support a wide variety of floral species. The primary raw materials for making a variety of crafts in the area are basically the wood trees and bamboo plants[28]. The presence of ecological elements is well reflected in various forms of crafts prepared by various communities of the region. Similarly, the local people of Magursila village prepare many beautiful craft items from bamboo available in their surrounding. They create various craft

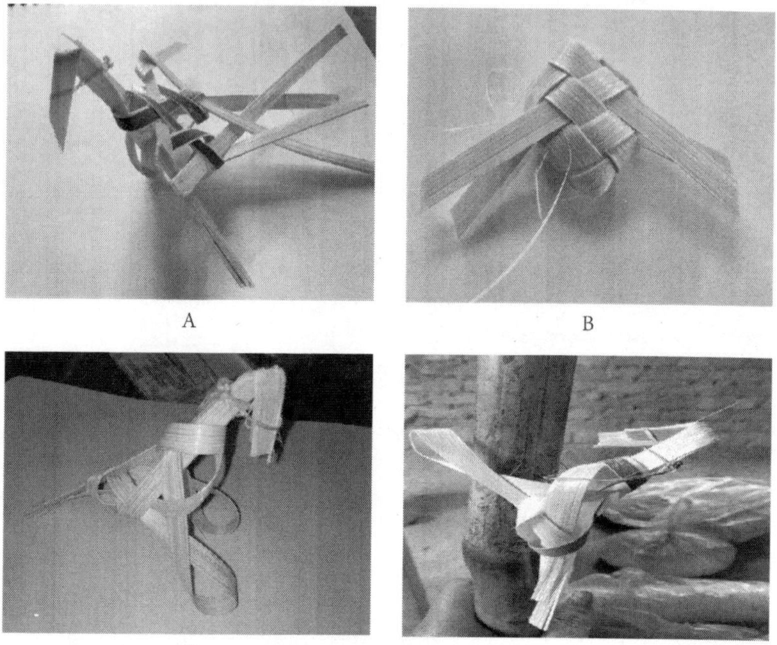

A B C D

FIG. 6: SOME OF THE SELECTED CRAFT ITEMS PREPARED BY THE VILLAGERS

Note: A-an insect; B-kupotibird; C, D-kaathrukabird

items resembling insects, birds, animals, and other elements of their local ecology.[2]

TRADITIONAL ECOLOGICAL KNOWLEDGE AND BELIEF SYSTEM

The traditional ecological knowledge and belief systems prevalent among different ethnic communities have immense ecological significance in protecting the natural resources of the world.[30] Similarly, in the Brahmaputra valley, different indigenous communities have been practising their own ecological knowledge and belief systems. The most popular belief systems in the study village include the avoidance of cutting selected trees in particular time and day. They avoid leaving their homes at certain specific times. Besides, they don't visit some selected parts of the hills which they consider as the habitat of spirits. These belief systems have been helping the villagers in conserving the ecological elements and thus in maintaining a balanced relation with nature.

The people of the village have also some ecological knowledge and belief systems which help them in maintaining an eco-friendly relation with its natural setup. Even in this era of industrialization, when nature is being exploited at a rapid rate in various parts of the valley, these ecological beliefs have been helping the villagers to conserve the concerned natural environment. Some of the ecological knowledge and belief systems pursued by the villagers can be documented as follows:

- The people of the village refrain from cutting the old trees such as jackfruit trees, mango trees, peepal, banyan trees etc. as they are thought to be planted and maintained by their forefathers and therefore, cutting them would be a kind of disrespect to them.
- The religious *ahoi tree* (Vitex peduncularis) which is worshipped by the villagers to cure various diseases should not be cut as per their customary laws. And if someone does so, he/she has to pay a fine to the Village Council.
- The villagers do not begin planting rice on Tuesday, Wednesday, Thursday, and Saturday because these days are reserved for their rituals and cultural ceremonies. They believe that planting rice on these days results in lower crop productivity, so they avoid doing so. On these days, they also refrain from selling rice to others.
- They also believe that the croaking of frogs signifies the imminent arrival of rains.
- The villagers put *'paning'* (a traditional dress of Karbi women which is tied up in the waist) and broken earthen pot on the trees to protect the fruits from any kind of negativity. When trees don't produce fruits for long period, they create human figures made from rice thatch and place them on the trees.
- The villagers consider the screaming of cows, dogs, hen, vulture, crow, etc as a sign of bad days.

TOPOPHOBIA

It is interesting to note that in all the ethnic villages of the Brahmaputra Valley, there are certain places within the villages that the inhabitants fear to visit alone or use as operational landholdings. Similarly, the people of Magursila village avoid visiting specific areas at certain times of the day, as these places are believed to be inhabited by negative spirits. Consequently, they avoid cutting trees in these areas, which helps preserve the ecological richness of these regions compared to places with significant human intervention. Therefore, the role of 'Topophobia' – the fear of visiting particular places, is ecologically very much significant as a result of which the biodiversity of these areas remain in an undisturbed and balanced state.

Moreover, the people of the concerned village avoid cutting trees of the sacred places. As a result, the Karbi community in the village has been conserving the ecology of these areas, and thus the villagers have maintained an eco-friendly relationship with nature.

TRADITIONAL NATURE-CONSERVATION STRATEGIES

The indigenous measures being practiced by the rural dwellers in many parts of the world have immense ecological significance in conserving the concerned natural resources[31]. People living in different parts of the Brahmaputra valley have also been following various traditional nature-conservative strategies. Similarly, the people of the study village have also been practising different indigenous methods to conserve the floral and faunal species among which the following methods are worth mentioning.

Traditional Bird Conservation Methods: Since the evolution of settlements in Magursila village, the local people have been maintaining an ecological relationship with nature. They are very concerned regarding the conservation of various bird species available in the village. The villagers have set a remarkable example of natural conservation in their village. Some of the villagers bring chicks of birds like *xalika (Acridotheres tristis), moina, bhatou (Pisttaciformes)*etc. into their home from the hills which they find injured, and thereafter nurture them very carefully. They have also created wooden bird nests and placed them in large trees within their home gardens. This reflects the villagers' strong, nature-friendly relationship with their environment. The villagers have restrictions on cutting the large trees of hills which are the habitats of birds like *bhatou (Psittaciformes), barhoituka (Dinopium benghalense),moina, xalika (Acridotheres tristis),* etc. Besides, they have been rearing chicken, which they use in various religious ceremonies. The conservation and nurturing of bees among the villagers also reflect their care and love for nature. These examples clearly reflect the traditional nature conservation practices of the villagers and their remarkable contribution towards conserving the ecology of the concerned village.

Traditional Ecological Knowledge of Tree Conservation: The villagers have been conserving the various tree species by planting them within their home gardens. Those plant species are surrounded by bamboo fencing and proper care is being taken by the households. The plant and grass species such as rubber, betel nut, orange, bamboo, broom, etc. are being cultivated and maintained by the villagers in the hills to get some amount of financial assistance from them. The villagers avoid cutting down large trees in the hills, as these trees serve as habitats for various faunal species. They believe that cutting them would result in the loss of these species from their local ecology. Besides, the villagers give cow dung and ash to plant roots to make them grow faster and turn productive.

Traditional Fish Conservation Practice: The villagers refrain from fishing in their ponds during June and July, which are considered the breeding seasons for fish. The people of the village provide cow dung, rice flour, *kholihoi, sapor, grass,* banana leaf, etc as fish foods. They cut the banana trees into some small pieces and put them into water. They believe that this will purify the pond water.

It has been observed that the village people lack in scientific preventive measures for any kind of fish disease. Most still use traditional fish conservation methods Only a few households are using lime. It is important to mention that no harmful diseases have occurred in recent years. Therefore, the role of the people in this Karbi village is highly significant towards conserving the natural resources and maintaining a sustainable relationship with nature.

TEKS AND CHANGING SOCIO-ECONOMIC LANDSCAPE

Based on traditional ecological knowledge and skills (TEKS), the villagers have been maintaining a balanced and cordial relationship with the natural elements. However, in the recent years, few changes have been observed in the socio-economic life of the local people. These transformations, driven by modernization, industrialization, rural-urban relations, public policy intervention, etc. have brought changes in occupational structure, livelihood pattern, social relations, traditional belief and knowledge systems etc.as a result of which the traditional socio-cultural landscape of the village has got altered.

Modernization in the traditional socio-economic life of the people has brought ecological changes in the concerned locality. The use of pesticides has contaminated water and soil, as a result of which some of the insect, bird, fish, and tree species are getting lost from the village ecology. Loss of floral and faunal species breaks up the food-chain and thus has led to the loss of other dependent species from the environment. Due to degradation of wetlands, number of some aquatic bird species such as bogoli (*Bubulcus ibis*), hargila (*Leptopilos javanicus*), masruka, pani kauri (*Phalacrocorax niger*), etc. are declining. Additionally, the cultivation of economically beneficial plants like bamboo, rubber, betel nut, broom, and orange has led to the clearing of large trees such as gomari (*Gmelina arborea*), ahot (*Ficus religiosa*) in the hills. As a result, the ecological conditions of the village have deteriorated to some extent. Moreover, as a result of social transformation, the hill dependency of the villagers is getting declined and the importance of market-based products has induced. The use of medicinal plants has also decreased among the villagers. Dependency on the market based items can also be considered as the cause behind the inattentive behaviour of the local people towards the natural elements, as a result of which their importance towards conserving some of the natural elements have been slowly declining which in future may lead to loss of many floral and faunal species as well as loss of traditional ecological conservative measures in the concerned village.Therefore, all these existing social transformations within the village have been depleting the traditional rural landscape thereby deteriorating the concerned village ecology.

CONCLUSION

The traditional ecological knowledge and skills (TEKS) are deeply rooted in the folk life and culture of the Karbi people living in Magursila village. Their day-to-day life and traditional activities are overwhelmingly dependent on the natural resources available in their environment. They try to maintain an intimate and balanced relationship with nature as they are aware of the fact that nature continues to sustain their life and culture spontaneously. The reflection of nature in their folk culture is, therefore, very much prominent. However, the ethnic life in this village has also started getting transformed under the influence of modern material culture. The spread of sub-urban transport and communication development has already reduced the time distance between the city and the village area. Interestingly, the changes already occurred in the traditional farming practice, green cover and housing in the village have now started affecting the ecological system of the village. Thus, the emerging changes in the cultural landscapes will obviously overshadow the otherwise vibrant natural setting of the village. Therefore, maintaining a sustainable relation with nature, it is essential to ensure preservation of traditional ecological knowledge and skills for a sustainable socio-cultural life and a sustainable environment in the present-day context of environmental degradation. The TEKS practiced in different aspects of rural life and livelihoods which they have evolved through generations based on their ecological knowledge, have been playing a great role towards achieving socio-ecological sustainability. Therefore, thorough documentation of the traditional ecological knowledge and skills (TEKS) practiced by the villagers is essential. If this knowledge is shared with other similar areas, it will not only aid in managing ecological settings but also contribute to the sustainability of rural livelihoods.

NOTES

1. F. Berkes, *Sacred Ecology: Traditional Ecological Knowledge And Resource Management*(3rd Ed.), Taylor and Francis, London, 2012.
2. Ibid..
3. F. Berkes, J. Colding and C. Folke, in 'Rediscovery of Traditional Ecological Knowledge As Adaptive Management', *Ecological Applications,* 10(5), 2000, pp. 1251-1262.
4. F. Berkes, *Sacred Ecology: Traditional Ecological Knowledge and Management Systems,* Taylor & Francis, Philadelphia and London, 1999.
5. F. Berkes, J. Colding and C. Folke, 2000, op. cit.
6. R. Johannes, 'The Case for Data-Less Marine Resource Management: Examples from Tropical Nearshore Finfisheries', in *Trends in Ecology & Evolution* 13, 1998, pp. 243–246.
7. C.R. Menzies (Ed), *Traditional Ecological Knowledge and Natural Resource Management,* University of Nebreska Press, London, 2006.
8. M. Gadgil and R. Guha, *Ecology and Equity: The Use and Abuse of Nature in Contemporary India,* Routledge, London and New York, 1995.
9. N. Deka and A.K Bhagabati,'Farming Practice in a Flood Plain Village of Assam (India): Continuity and Change' in *Indonesian Journal of Geography,* Vol. 42, No. 1, 2010, pp. 13-34.
10. N. Deka and A.K Bhagabati and A. Kazuo, 'Floral resources in a village environment of the Brahmaputra valley, Assam: inventory, use and conservation' in *Journal of Agroforestry and Environment,* Vol. 5 (Special Isssue), 2011, pp. 75-82.
11. Ibid.
12. P. Ghosh, 'Nature, Culture and Tribal Behavior: A study of the Social Transformation in Jharkhand State' in *Pallicharcha,*2014, pp. 1-16.
13. R.Teron and S.K Borthakur, 'Traditional Knowledge relating to use of flora and fauna as indicators in predicting annual seasons among Karbi tribe of Assam', in *Indian Journal of Traditional Knowledge,* Vol. 8 (4), 2009, pp. 518-524.
14. B.R. Das, 'Nature-culture interactions in an ethnic village of Kamrup (M) district, Assam: present status and future prospects', Unpublished M.PhilDissertation, Gauhati University, Guwahati, 2020.
15. B.R. Das, 2020, op. cit.
16. D. Baishya, *Traditional Science & Material Culture of Early Assam,* EBH Publishers, Guwahati, 2009, p. 261.

17. B.K. Barua, *Asomia Bhasa Aru Sanskriti*, Guwahati, 1957, p. 134.
18. The villagers used to call it as 'Chubu,' although in the hills of Karbi Anglong, this plant is known as Sibu Marsdenia tinctoria R. Br. (*Apocynaceae*).
19. B.R. Das, N. Deka and A.K Bhagabati, 2022, op. cit.
20. B.R. Das, 2020, op. cit.
21. T. Kizos, J. Primdahl, L. Kristensen and A. Busck, 'Introduction: Landscape Change and Rural Development' in *Landscape Research*, Vol. 35, No. 6, 2010, pp. 571-576.
22. N. Deka, A.K. Bhagabati and K. Ando, 'Rural Land Use in Brahmaputra Floodplain Environment, Assam: A case of Muktapur Village' in *Contemporary India*, Vol. 1, 2011, pp. 177-193.
23. B.R. Das, 2020, op. cit.
24. N. Deka and A.K. Bhagabati, 'Farming Practice in a Floodplain Village of Assam (India): Continuity and Change'in *Indonesian Journal of Geography*, Vol.42, No. 1, 2010, pp. 13-34.
25. N. Deka, *Legal Aspects of Traditional Knowledge in North-East India*, Publication Board Assam, Guwahati, 2020.
26. B.R. Das, 2020, op. cit.
27. N. Deka, 2020, op. cit.
28. D. Baishya, 2009, op. cit.
29. B.R. Das, 2020, op. cit.
30. J.T. Inglis, *Traditional Ecological Knowledge: Concepts and Cases*, Canada, 1993.
31. C. Sobrevila, *The Role of Indigenous Peoples in Biodiversity Conservation the Natural but Often Forgotten Partners*, Washington D.C., USA, 2008.

SECTION II

MYTH AND HISTORY OF KAJIR RONGHANGPI

CHAPTER 9

Kajir Ronghangpi
The Legends in Rongkhang

ELWIN TERON

INTRODUCTION

The academic interest in the life and time of the legendary Karbi lady, Kajir Ronghangpi, has increased due to the elaborate celebration planned by the Karbi Anglong Autonomous Council (KAAC) to honor her. It is believed that the Kaziranga National Park was named after her. However, apart from the few articles written by Ajit Timung and Dhaneswar Engti from among the Karbi authors, there are very few reliable resources available to learn about the renowned individual. It is crucial to thoroughly investigate the extensive collective knowledge of the public in order to gather any available information that can be used to construct a reliable historical, mythical, or legendary account of the topic. This includes details on her family lineage, her accomplishments, exploits, or myths. Based on the belief that any events, achievements, or tragedies that contribute to the lasting remembrance of the Karbi people would have a significant impact in the Rongkhang region, which is considered the cultural center of the Karbi people, the author has recently tried to gather some information from oral sources in Rongkhang. Oralists with established reputations were found through a gradual process, and interviews were organized and carried out in Hamren. The finding has surprisingly opened up new avenues for storytelling, where additional investigation may uncover fresh insights into the life and era of Kajir Ronghangpi. This concise paper may provide a fresh perspective on understanding and valuing the topic matter. The inscription beneath the statue of Kajir Ronghangpi, which is situated in Kajir Ronghangpi Park in Kohora (near the KNP), raises several inquiries:

1. The inscription specifies that Kajir Ronghangpi was the offspring of Hok Ronghang. Who was Hok Ronghang and what was the name of his mother?
2. The inscription also states that Kajir Ronghangpi was 'transported to and raised in the dwelling place of the deities.' It has more of a mythological quality than a legendary one. What is the truth? Is this story or folklore universally recognized in all locations inhabited by the Karbis?
3. The inscription also states that 'Kajir Ronghangpi reconstructed the land established by her father within and nearby the current Kaziranga National Park region.' This suggests that Hok Ronghang was probably a Chieftain who ruled over a kingdom or a leader who governed a certain territory. Who were the individuals responsible for establishing the Karbi kingdom or dominion in and around the Kaziranga National Park area, and what were the specific methods and timing of its establishment?

It is therefore necessary to make an effort to answer the questions in order to verify the claim of the Kajir Ranghangpi story as told by the Karbis. If not about the divinity that is assigned to her, then at least regarding her life and the time period in which she lived. In this context, the purpose of this study has been to investigate the Kajir Ronghangpi story within the Karbi territory of Rongkhang, which is widely regarded as the cultural epicenter of the Karbi people.

THE SEARCH FOR THE LEGEND

According to traditions, Rongkhang is the principal Karbi cultural and political dominion, considered higher than that of the Chinthong and the Amri where the highest political functionary, attributed by the Karbis as a whole as the King, governs. Historically, the Karbis were divided into four groups according to their geographical location: Chinthong, Ronghang, Amri, and Dumrali[1]. The first three territorial divisions are regarded as 'customary provinces' since they have traditional governments who continue to practice Karbi customs while living in hilly environments. All of these territorial units preserve their distinctness and differences from one another. The Rongkhang dominion has four territorial divisions, each governed by a *Lindokpo*; and so, it has been referred to in the Jaintia language as *Sow Lyngdoh*, meaning four Lyngdohs, later on corrupted by the Karbis as *Solangdo* to refer to the Karbis of Rongkhang dominion. In comparison the Chinthong dominion has three *Lindokpo* territories and reverentially referred to as *Le Lyngdoh*, Le being 'three' in Jaintia language. Similarly, Amri has two *Lindokpo* territories and is referred to as *Ar Lyngdoh*, Ar being 'two' in the Jaintia language. These three dominions, that is, Rongkhang, Chinthong and Amri have been the roots of Karbi culture and polity and each Karbi man anywhere would identify himself with either of the three territorial dominions. Gurdon had referred to them as *Ryngkhang*, *Jynthong* and *Mynri*.[2] It is therefore assumed that any Karbi myths or legends would ordinarily have traces in all or either of the dominions.

In the initial stage, inquiries were made to ascertain the availability of resources and resource persons. Obviously, there is no written records to find the answers to the questions posed here; and so, the search is heavily dependent on the oral tradition of the Karbi people. Various known oralists were contacted from all the dominions but the Chinthong and Amri oralists appeared to have no clue. The focus therefore shifted entirely on the oralists from Rongkhang where three persons volunteered to share their memories about the legend of Kajir Ronghangpi. When this writer finally arranged the interview with them on the 26th April, 2023 at Hamren, only two turned up as the third person was indisposed.

The Oral Interview-1: The first person to be interviewed was Harsing Ronghang, the 41st Karbi King according to his family tradition and now retired from the post[3]. He is the son of late Basa Ronghang, and is now about 75 years of age. He presently lives in Ronghidi, Hamren, West Karbi Anglong. The source of his information, he claims, is the oral tradition of his family passed on through the generations. According to him the legend of Kajir

Ronghangpi is found in the annals of the migration story of the Karbis. In his account of migration, the Karbis having been pushed from Tibet reached the northern bank of the Brahmaputra in the vicinity of the present Sonitpur district and settled there. Some had then crossed the Brahmaputra called Lut at the Kaziranga point and settled on the southern banks there. The Karbis had built their first settlement there and Kajir Ronghangpi's parents lived there. Her father's name was Sereng Ronghang and the mother's name was Kare Engtipi. Sereng had a brother whose name was Dok Ronghang. The couple had two lovely daughters and a son. The eldest one was Kareng Ronghangpi followed by Kajir Ronghangpi.

It so came to pass that the exquisite beauty of the sisters was noticed by the Ahom dominant power of the area known by the name of Medhibura who wanted to marry Kareng Ronghangpi, but she rejected the proposal. Having been slighted, Medhibura got furious and in his rage killed Kareng. The distraught family cremated her at Kuthuri. Later on, Medhibura was known to have regretted his action and wanted to perpetuate her memory by erecting the Kareng *ghar* and a *mandir* at Sivsagar. The attention was now on the beauty of Kajir Ronghangpi whom the Ahom suitors were determined to possess. Sereng and his wife were faced with the dire prospect of losing their daughter forever. They therefore hatched a plan before the Ahoms came to take her away. A solution of lac was prepared which was poured over her and immediately she became red from head to toe. When the Ahoms saw her, they exclaimed what had befallen her; her exquisite beauty had now been destroyed. She had become *Kajir-ronga*. In utter desperation, the Ahoms took her life also.

There are some who say that Kajir Ronghangpi was not killed, that she attained divinity and was transported to heaven. But this resource person did not agree with this theory. He said that the oral tradition on which he relied always maintained that the Ahoms killed her and it was in the manner of speaking that she had been transported to heaven to live among the Gods and Goddesses. The Karbis believe that all men, great or small, become gods and goddesses after death. He said that the truth about her elimination was the fact that there is no information about her husband or the children that she could have progenerated. According to him, Kajir Ronghangpi did exist and the chilly plant she planted near the Brahmaputra bank had grown into a big tree which is believed to exist till today. Kaziranga is a protected reserve now and an exploration to find the chilly tree may not be allowed, but it is still there, the former Karbi King insisted.

Relying on the royal version of the oral tradition, the former King also described the divine power of Kare Engtipi, the mother of Kajir Ronghangpi. Kajir Ronghangpi had a brother when they were living on the bank of the Brahmaputra who got drowned. A search of the body was launched but the river did not relent. So, the mother mourned and sang the dirge inconsolably and persisted till the water parted to reveal the sandy bed where they found the dead son which they retrieved and cremated according to tradition. This scene is reminiscent of the Biblical parting of the water of the Red Sea through the divine power of Moses as described in the book of Exodus.

According to tradition, the tragedy in the Ronghang household forced the community to move over to Burapahar where they settled and later on migrated to the present Rongkhang. 'Let us not forget that since the beginning of time, and all along our migration from Tibet our oppressors always followed us and forced us to move on to new settlement. We have had countless of abandoned settlements all along the way till we reached the *Lut* (*Luit* in Assamese version). We crossed the Lut to settle on its southern bank and moved on to Burapahar. Our people then dispersed in different directions, some remained in Sonitpur area, some groups moved on to the present Karbi Anglong. All this movement ultimately making our tribe a divided people', he lamented. Today Kaziranga is populated by other communities, 'but the entire stretch belonged to the Karbi people. It is our place', the former King asserted.

This assertion is not without basis. Even British ethnographers, Edward Stack and Charles Lyall, in the book *The Mikirs* had recorded the northern boundary of the Karbi settlement[4]. This book stated:

> To the north from Koliabor to Kaziranga, they are on the Brahmaputra, only a narrow strip of country, traversed by the southern Grand Trunk Road intervening between them and the river. This strip has few inhabitants and

little cultivation and is covered with high grass and cotton tree (*semul*) jungle, the haunt of wild buffaloes and rhinoceros.

This testifies that even after the present National Highway was constructed as Grand Trunk Road, the inhabitants abutting the river Brahmaputra were the Karbis. Stack and Lyall also mentioned that mouzas around the Kaziranga – Duar Baguri, Duar Bamuni and Duar Salona – were Mikir Mouzas. Each Mouza had a Mikir mouzadar or bikhoya.[5]

The Oral Interview-2: The second resource person whose statement has been recorded is Sri Rupsing Ronghang (Basapo)[6]. He lives at the Pinpo-Ritlo, which is the land held by the royal households, as the Guardian of the land. He (the Basapo) holds the unique office of introducing Gods to the royal families[7]. Whenever any royal person desires to find a God or deity whom he may adulate, propitiate or deify, it is his responsibility to take him to the spot where he may find the family deity. He and his predecessors have been fulfilling this duty for generations. For the purpose of general understanding, one may compare it to the office of the Levites in the Old Testament, the line of priestly family who served royal household.

This resource person laments that he could not foresee information such as Kajir Ronghangpi would one day be of any use. If he had been a bit more attentive as a boy, he would have been able to offer more information today. But he was just a curious but casual listener when the village elders would sit around the fireplace of their ante-house called *hong-pharla* in the evening to drink and to while away their time. Or during social occasions, the elderly group would discuss folk tales, migration stories and even indulge in singing and wise-cracking over their drinks. It was in one of those times that he heard about Kajir Ronghangpi. He could not remember what made Kajir Ronghangpi a legend, but she was the daughter of Chere Ronghang, a Karbi King who left Socheng to establish his kingdom at Kathalguri. Kajir was beautiful and she would always wear red garments, that was why she was called Kajir Ronga.

Now, according to the genealogy compiled by the Ronghang Nok`hum Chingrum Amei (Estd 2012) in their publication called

Ronghang Keplang lapen Ser Anghoi Kelong Aphurkimo (January 2023) at page 13, Chere Ronghang was the 5th Ronghang King and was believed to have ruled between 1206 to 1243 A.D. It was believed that serious differences had cropped up within the royal household and the King, Chere Ronghang, who was not inclined to argue and fight and even liked to choose his words, decided to move away to Kathalguri (Rongcheden), taking with him the Kingdom's Golden Seat. The Golden Seat had mystic power on which only the fit and the destined person could sit. It was so hot for the others that even mustard seeds thrown on it would pop. But at Kathalguri, the Ahom King got to know about the Golden Seat and asked the Karbi King to surrender failing which they were threatened to be killed. Chere Ronghang had no choice but to surrender the Golden Seat to the Ahom King, so that today even at Rongkhang, the King had only a symbolic wooden seat in place of the Golden Seat.

CONCLUSION

In analyzing the two sources, serious time anomaly is detected. While the former King Harsing Ronghang (2008-2018) maintained that the legend of Kajir Ronghangpi is part of the annals of the Karbi migration story. But he has also maintained that the perpetrators against Kareng Ronghangpi and Kajir Ronghangpi at Kaziranga were the Ahom nobles and the Ahom Kingdom was established by Chaolung Sukapha only in the year 1228 AD. So, the incidents surrounding the legend could have taken place only after 1228. On the other hand, the genealogy of the Ronghang Dynasty (*Ronghang Keplang lapen Ser Anghoi Kelong Aphurkimo*) (January 2023), began with Har (Pokang) Ronghang in the year 1127, a century before the Ahom arrived; and before that also the Rongphar Dynasty already existed from whom the Ronghang Dynasty took over. This points to the fact that the Karbi migration must have taken much earlier than the advent of the Ahom dynasty. There is also a difference in the identity of the parentage of Kajir Ronghangpi. The inscription says the father was Hok Ronghang which has no mention in the genealogy of the Ronghang Dynasty while Sereng Ronghang and Chere Ronghang were the other claims.

However, it must be said that the accounts given by both the resource persons agree that a legendary figure named as Kajir Ronghangpi exists in the oral narrative of the Karbis, in the Rongkhang region and that she was known as 'Ronga' due to either because of habitually wearing red garment or because of the application of a lac solution. Both also agree that the name Kaziranga originated with the legend of Kajir Ronghangpi.

NOTES

1. C.J. Lyall, *Report on the Census of Assam for 1881*, Office of the Superintendent of Government Printing, Calcutta, 1883, p. 81.
2. P.R.T. Gurdon, *The Khasis,* 1914, Macmillan, London, p. 62.
3. Interview with Harsing Ronghang (75), Retired Karbi King, S/O Late Basa Ronghang, Ronghidi, Hamren, West Karbi Anglong, conducted on April 26, 2023.
4. Edward Stack, *The Mikirs*, David Nutt, London, 1908, p. 2 (This book had been edited, arranged and supplemented by Charles Lyall, 1908).
5. Ibid., p. 21.
6. Interview with Rupsing Ronghang (Basapo), (Age 81), S/o Late Lindok Ronghang, Langtukthepi (PinpoRitlo), Hamren, West Karbi Anglong, conducted on April 26, 2023.
7. In the Karbi religious tradition, each household has an exclusive presiding deity, called *Peng Arnam* who is propitiated and worshipped by the family. The name of the presiding deity is kept secret by the family priest and not supposed to be divulged to others. As the office of the *Lindokpo* (King) is not strictly hereditary to a family but selected from the hereditary clan, a new incumbent may not be aware of the name of the presiding deity of the royal household; and in such situation the Basapo introduces the new King to the presiding deity of the royal household.

CHAPTER 10

The Legend of Kajir Ronghangpi through the Lens of Collective Karbi Memory

SERDIHUN TERONPI, BEENA RONGPIPI, RENGKA TIMUNGPI and MAGGIE KATHARPI

INTRODUCTION

Myths and folktales serve as valuable resources for uncovering the 'distorted history' of one's own cultural identity, such as the Karbis, while also perpetuating opposing perspectives through the portrayal of the 'other'. The dynamic nature of language and migration contributes to the evolution of culture and history within a society, leading to the potential representation as well as distortion of 'collective memories' over time. Numerous narratives exalt the figure of Kajir Ronghangpi, presenting diverse nuances and variations in the conduct of the 'Rhinoceros Lady.' Kajir Ronghangpi is a person who is consistently remembered by the Karbis. According to local belief, it is believed that the appellation 'Kaziranga' originates from the term 'Kajir Ronghangpi.' She has garnered recognition and acclaim among regional legends and traditional narratives due to her personality and bold actions. The naming of the sanctuary Kaziranga after a female figure is, therefore, really remarkable and awe-inspiring.

According to Dhanaraju and Teron[1], 'The discovery of present history of the Karbis is not an accidental affair. It has evolved through several forces in the past. Therefore, an understanding of present history of the Karbis will certainly lead to the study of their past. But reconstruction of the past accurately is a very difficult task where there are no written records, especially by themselves'.[1] Considering this statement, we need to understand that the revelation of the current historical understanding of the Karbis is not a coincidental occurrence. The phenomenon under consideration has undergone a series of transformative influences in previous periods. Consequently, a comprehensive comprehension of the contemporary historical context of the Karbis is likely to facilitate the investigation of their historical background. Reconstructing the past with precision is a formidable challenge, particularly in cases where written documents are absent and rely only on their own merits. While there is a lack of written documentation regarding the existence of the Rhino Lady, it is imperative to acknowledge the significant role that oral tradition has in shaping human experiences. In the words of Kathar (1997), 'The traditional history of the Karbi as orally passed on from father to son, from generation to generation…'[2] shows the transmission of Karbi history by oral tradition from fathers to sons and between generations stand practical, accurate, and significant till today.

According to scholarly discourse and in the words of David Henige, oral tradition serves as a means of reconstructing the past[2]. The following narratives to be shared herein have been gathered from four distinct individuals residing in disparate regions in close proximity to Kaziranga. The examination of the four narratives will contribute to the expansion of our understanding of the 'Rhino Lady', thereby facilitating the identification of any potential connections or patterns that exist. Thereby, helping us locate her place in history via the delineation of the narratives. The different constructed series of historical narratives will also aid in our comprehension of Kajir Ronghangpi's disposition and the reasons behind Karbi veneration of her.

HISTORICIZING ORAL NARRATIVES ON KAJIR RONGHANGPI

Oral Narrative-1: One of the historical narratives told by Mr. Devinson Terang, the village headman of Bachekrang Amreng

Terang Village and also the current chairman of the Biodiversity Management Committee, Minority Board President, and Vice President of the Dolamara Town Committee, narrates that Karbi women always forged ahead in life, to which he cited the examples of Rongpharpi Rongbe and Kabon Neli Timungpi Khongmen in support of this assertion. Like these leaders, Kajir Ronghangpi too was a leader and a warrior in her own way. The reason why she is more proclaimed is because she was more courageous than the rest. In addition to being brave, she was also smart, intelligent, and had excellent communication skills. When it came to resolving issues in the village, she exuded authority. People started looking up to her as a result. She was reported to have been incredibly attractive, achieving fame and glory because of her beauty, intelligence, and excellent communication skills. Kaziranga is, according to him, a compound of Kajir Ronghangpi. The Assamese simply uttered Kajir Ronghang without the 'pi'. The source also revealed about Kajir's connection to rhinos – that many claim she was responsible for bringing them to Earth, endowing her with supernatural abilities. In this, he isn't entirely confident in the stories being circulated, adding that fanciful and imaginative shades have been added to the life of Kajir Ronghangpi. Several contend that rhinos were imported, which, in his opinion, lacks a logical conclusion to the assertion. He also shared that a couple may have existed by the names of Kaji and Ronga. Many claim these two names are connected with Kaziranga. The informant/source asserts, however, that Kajir Ronghangpi is where the term Kaziranga originated from. Prior to the restricted forest sanctuary's official formation in 1908–1910, Karbis resided in those regions. The numerous jackfruit, mango, and bamboo trees are proof that Karbis once resided there. Mass eviction of the Karbis occurred as a result of their forced departure under the guise of preservation of a wildlife sanctuary in 1908-1910.

Oral Narrative-2: Another historical narrative was obtained from Mr. Darsing Hanse S/O Lt. Dhonsing Hanse, the current Sarkari Gaonbura (government village headman). Since the time of his great grandfather, this headship has been passed down from generation to generation. The source revealed that they had come from Daphlang, which was a section of the protected forest at the time. They called it *Phu Longkoi ahidi daplang*, which translates to 'Grandfather Longkoi's paddy field.' Five tufts of rice plants generated one basket's worth of rice – all due to the fertile land resulting in the paddy's excessive production. According to Longkoi Hanse, Arimora was the name of the village. Now, the word *Daphplang* originated from the word *ingdeiplang*, which indicate shallow, level, and plain. They had been there since the Arimora days, a place that was inside the reserve when villages were standing tall then. It was in 1890-1892 that they left the place. This is tangible evidence that the Karbis were the first to live in the area that is today known as Kaziranga. Additionally, he emphasized that many jackfruit trees still exist. They were forced to depart because of the rising water level, followed by the disclosure that a wildlife sanctuary would soon be established therein. Owing to displacement and the floods, numerous documents were lost along the way. The first person to see a rhinoceros among them was the informant's great-grandmother Kadom Terangpi, who was married to Longkoi Hanse. They called the rhino *pi langno* (ugly creature) since it wasn't a particularly attractive animal. They didn't start referring to it as *kindu* until much later. The informant received all the details on Kajir Ronghangpi's story from a man by the name of Langtuk Killing. Jarle Rongpi, on the other hand, related the story to Langtuk Killing. He claims that various narratives are connected to it. His account reveals that Ha`i, Sai Ronghang's eldest daughter, was the sister of Kajir. Kache Tokbipi was Sai's spouse. Everyone is aware of Ha'i's story and tribulation.

The account of *Ha'imu*, is important enough to include here as many will reiterate the impossibility of the connection of *Ha'imu* with Kajir Ronghangpi. But that's what the informant had to share with the presenters. So, she was forcibly separated from her spouse because she did not conform to societal conventions. Pinpo Dilli of Ronghang Rongbong was regaled with the narratives of Ha`imu. So, he decided to wed her forcibly despite the fact that she'd already married having a child. Herein, Pinpo Dilli controlled Ha'imu's individual rights. He suppressed and behaved like a power unto himself, demonstrating an authoritarian behaviour. Despite being obliged and coerced by an influential man, she did not give up. She did not fall for it. She did not eat anything and died in this manner. Kajir was heartbroken that her sister had to separate and die. Thinking the same would happen to her, she left home, her father and mother. She moved towards the plains, crying. As she was drinking from a nearby stream, she got caught in a whirlwind that arrived at that same moment. She was brought to Hemphu arnam in heaven wherein she started handling all of the chores there, including serving, sweeping, and washing. One day, she revealed that she was missing home and her parents. They promised to take her home, but the years passed. She sobbed and pined. This time, after seeing her condition, Songsar Recho sent her back to earth. She arrived on earth along with the rhino sitting atop on it. On reaching earth, she was met by white soldiers. She could utter nothing more than her name when she was persistently questioned by the soldiers. So, one of the soldiers inscribed her name on a notebook. In this manner, the name Kaziranga was created. Nobody witnessed or heard about her passing away, nor did they see her enter heaven or any other place.

Oral Narrative-3: The subsequent historical narrative was obtained from Mr. Chatrasing Bey, son of Kania Bey and Kade Teronpi, Kahora Phumen Engti village (Jilangso). His spouse's name is Phudang Engtipi. This account narrativizes that Kajir Ronghangpi was a typical simple village girl. She was deemed *thekser* (able), but why? This was due to the fact that she had excellent Assamese communication skills and was always willing to provide a hand in her village or in neighbouring villages upon requirement.

To validate his narration, the informant shares about his own personal experiences. He started with the fact that parents frequently kept their sons or daughters with wealthy families so they could receive both financial support and education. He further added that there used to be an Assamese village close to Diring (informant's village). Because of his father's friendship with one of the Assamese families there, Kania Bey (the father), used to travel to that village often. Subsequently, he shifted Chatra Bey (our informant), his son, into one of the Kothuri Assamese homes. During his stay there, he learned and developed effective Assamese communication skill. The reason as to why he shared about this is to tell us that the same happened with Kajir Ronghangpi. The major information that our informant provided to us was provided to him by Bakring Engti and his father Kania Bey. It seems, everyone from the hills, including Kajir, descended to Hulmora (Huimora), Mihimukh – a place close to Kaziranga. The place Mihimukh is named after Mihi Tokbi, the spouse of Kajir Ronghangpi, who was cremated there. This location is also known as Mihibil. A tiny bridge inside the sanctuary goes by the name of Mihimukh dolong (Mihimukh's bridge). Now, it is no longer accessible. This is the precise location where Mihi Tokbi's *Langtuk Chomangkan* was performed. *Chomangkan* is an extensive ritual performed in commemoration of the dead. Some claim that Mukoi Tokbi and Mihi Tokbi can be related; the former resided close to Hatikhuli. It is said, later this Tokbi family as well as another Ronghang family moved to Tarabasa (Phuloni Constituency) and Virvar (a place within the periphery of Mahamaya, about 8 kms from Dengaon).

He proceeded to elaborate that Kajir's father and his Assamese acquaintance had a harmonious rapport. They would consistently engage in reciprocal visits, effectively nurturing their connection. On a particular day, Kajir accompanied her father. That event was a pivotal moment in her life. By that time, Kajir had already attained proficiency in several manual jobs. The wife of the Assamese friend, upon coming into contact with Kajir, sought permission from Kajir's father that she be allowed to stay with them throughout the sowing season so that she would assist them in the paddy field. The father conveyed to them that she had not acquired the proficiency in the practice of paddy farming. This Assamese family provided reassurance that she would receive instruction and attain proficiency in the skill. Upon obtaining unequivocal reassurance from both his friend and the wife, the father acquiesced to granting them custody of his daughter. Kajir showed commendable performance in her task. She successfully assimilated and acquired proficiency in the Assamese language, comparable to that of a native Assamese speaker. The passage of time progressed from months to years. She ultimately embarked on a journey (after several years) to Hulmora alongside her family, where they established a colony some two centuries ago. Certain individuals engaged in the rearing of cattle, whilst others were involved in the cultivation of pigs, goats, and poultry. Individuals who were acquainted with the hamlet arrived with the intention of engaging in commercial activities. However, the indigenous population encountered difficulties in establishing effective communication due to their lack of proficiency in the Assamese language. In this particular scenario, the designation 'Kajir' would be employed. She engaged in dialogue with the traders, providing them with information on the pricing, so facilitating her community's ability to establish commercial relationships with other factions. Due to Kajir's exceptional fluency in Assamese, she was much sought for in many circumstances within the community of Hulmora. Her name gained prominence and achieved widespread recognition throughout the region. Furthermore, the merchants would respond with the phrase *Kajirgaon* when queried about the origin of the commodities they acquired. The village in which our informant Bey dwells was intended to have been designated as *Mastor Gaon* in recognition of his prominent status, which stems from his influential role, exceptional capabilities, and distinguished occupation, that is teaching. Similarly, the inhabitants began referring to Kajir's settlement as 'Kajir Gaon'. *Kor pora anile?* (from where have you brought them?) *Kajiror Gaon* (from Kajir's village). *Kot goise?* (where are you going?) *Kajiror Gaon* (to Kajir's village). As such, Kajir Gaon became Kajironga – Kajironga from Kajir Ronghangpi. According to the informant, there is no correlation between Kajir Ronghangpi and rhinoceros or *kindu* (Karbi word for rhino). Similarly, the settlement associated with Kajir became well recognized as 'Kajir Gaon' among the local inhabitants. 'Kajir Gaon' and 'Kajir Ronghangpi' experienced a linguistic alteration and afterwards came to be recognized as 'Kaziranga,' with the exclusion of the suffix 'pi.' Herein, he expressed a strong and unwavering belief that there exists no conceivable correlation between Kajir Ronghangpi and rhinoceroses or kindu. The existence of rhinos may be traced back to prehistoric times, as shown by the *Pirthe Keplang Alun* (Origin of Earth Song). According to the song, a traditional song that chronicles the creation of the earth, rhinoceroses have existed since the very beginning of time.

There were a number of Karbi settlements in those regions, which have since been transformed into a wildlife sanctuary. Similar to the other informants, he also emphasizes that the presence of bamboo plants and other edible fruit plants serves as proof of human occupancy. Also, the *Ok Kipru*, an annual fishing festival, was conducted inside the confines of the reserve during that time. Rhinoceroses inhabited in a wide range of habitats. He would frequently traverse such regions while conducting official or personal tasks. The place boasts significant dimensions, creating a sense of the vastness of the sky appearing much smaller up close (as the narrator describes it – *Sining ta akangdaipi* meaning the sky was very low) On his way to Arimora to carry out an official duty (specifically, distributing payment to the personnel stationed there), he observed numerous settlements located within the reserve.

He also had a vivid recollection of encountering a group of rhinoceroses. He successfully procured transportation aboard a truck. He recounted of facing a life-threatening situation had he been required to continue riding the bicycle. It may be inferred that Kajir maintained consistent proximity to rhinoceroses throughout her life, both during her youth and after her marriage, since she resided in regions inhabited by these creatures. It is possible that she participated in the skill of domesticating rhinoceroses, similar to the methods used for taming other animal species. It is probable that she assumed the responsibility for the care of the rhinoceroses from the time of their birth, so facilitating the development of a strong emotional connection between her and the animals. Therefore, the connection between Kajir Ronghangpi and rhinoceroses. There were several sightings of rhinoceroses, which were reported to navigate the landscape regularly, including ascending slopes. During that time period, it was common for rhinoceroses to migrate to regions extending as far as Dokmoka and Langlokso towards Korkanthi Constituency. Nevertheless, due to the growing poaching cases, there was a notable decrease in the number of these species. Today, no rhinos are found therein.

Oral Narrative-4: The next narrative was provided by Sar-et Killing, a farmer from Panbari, Kaziranga. According to his account, the term 'Kaziranga' is derived from the combination of the words *Kajir* and *Ronghangpi.* During the historical period of the Ahom dynasty, there existed a notable Karbi warrior by the name of Bikha Tokbi. The individual resided in the locality of Kohora, namely in and around the area known as Mihimukh. He entered into matrimony with Kajir Ronghangpi, the daughter of Kang Ronghang.

Bikha Tokbi, acquired the additional appellation of *Kang* due to his affiliation with Kang Ronghang, his father-in-law. Consequently, he became recognized as 'Bikha Kang Tokbi'. The Ahoms bestowed upon this hero a golden crown, known as *ser aphutup*, as a token of their appreciation. He later acquired the appellation of Bikha Kangburva. His title 'Tokbi' was then revoked, resulting in his new designation as 'Bikha Kangburva.' It is worth noting that the term 'burva' is a variant of 'Boruah' that has undergone linguistic corruption. The removal of Karbi surnames had become a practice in those days which resulted in a diminished Karbi identity.

According to this narrative, during the initial years of the 1820s, Bikha had a friendly relationship with the Burmese amidst their invasion in Assam. He relinquished his sister-in-law, Tahin, to the Burmese.[3] The recipients of this action expressed great satisfaction, from Luit-Kolong to the north, the southern boundaries of Nagaland, the eastern Dhansiri region, till the western Kopili area, bestowed upon him as a gift. The term *Bikha alongri* (Bikha's territory) was used to refer to that certain location or territory associated with him. Despite the Burmese government's formal agreement with the English through the Treaty of Yandaboo in 1826, he persisted in levying taxes on the English. In the year 1831, specifically in the Terang village of Rangsali, located in Numaligarh, an incident occurred while tax collection activity was conducted by him. As he proceeded with the tax collection process, the local inhabitants offered him food and beverages, which he consumed. Being incapacitated, he met with his death at the hands of the inhabitants of Terang's hamlet. The one responsible for the death of Bikha in the traditional ballad *Mir Tahin Alun* is identified as Chalut Singnot[4]. The deceased was buried in that place. However, because of his exceptional physical prowess, he managed to emerge from the subterranean confinement in a state of vitality.

Though subjected to many instances of lethal harm, he consistently revived thereafter. The people then considered it to be most advantageous to terminate and afterwards dismember his physical form into two separate halves. So, the mortal remains of the dead Bikha were interred in two distinct sites, whereby his physical corpse was laid to rest in Rangsali, while his head was buried in Behora. Following the demise of Bikha, representatives from the British government arrived at Mihimukh, presently situated inside the Kaziranga sanctuary, with the intention of seeing Kajir, the wife of the deceased Bikha. She was assured that the land would remain under her jurisdiction, as was the case throughout her husband's tenure. Consequently, the entire region acquired the appellation of Kaziranga (from Kajir Ronghangpi). According to the narrator, her subsequent departure remains undisclosed, leaving both her destination and mode of transportation unknown.

Based on the narrator's account, it may be inferred that the Karbis continue to retain proprietary rights over the land situated inside and in the vicinity of the Kaziranga area. Majority of the Karbi are now settled elsewhere. Furthermore, it may be asserted that there is no likelihood of their return to assert ownership over that particular portion of the land. The land held by the Numaligarh Refinery Limited (NRL) was under the patronage of the Karbis – mention may be made of Samuri Bordoloi and Rondon Mondol. The etymology of the name 'Samuri Bordoloi' may be traced back to the term *Bordili*, which specifically denotes to the Terang clan – Terang Dili. Samuri and Rondon Mondol are recognized as the pioneers amongst the Karbi to be assigned with official land work.

In 'The Myth Behind The name Kaziranga' (2010) by Ajit Timung[5], a respected Karbi social activist and politician, it is narrated that Hok Ronghang fled from *Bithi Arlok* (west Karbi Anglong) to *Tovar Kethom* (present day Kaziranga). Having settled there, he married Bong-eh Teronpi, who birthed Khoi Ronghang, Kajir Ronghangpi and Kading Ronghangpi. Kajir runs away from home after a fight. The seven daughters of the god found her hungry, thirsty and in a disoriented condition. They took the lonely Kajir to their abode wherein she grows up into a beautiful girl. She now possesses super-natural powers. In the meantime, her parents are sent elsewhere and they are left to fend for themselves. Her brother is an able leader but there are some who dislike him so he's killed twice but each time, Kajir brings him back to life. The third time she couldn't help him as the body was cut into two. One part was boiled so that

Kajir wouldn't be able to save him. It is also written that Sarsomon Ronghang accompanied Kajir to earth. In order to cultivate rice on earth, he brought *kindu* (rhino) to plough with it. When he tried to take it back to heaven, the rhinos ran into the jungle. Ever since then the rhinos are believed to have remained here on earth.

The following is an excerpt from *Pirthe Keplang Alun*[6] wherein mention has been made of animals' creation in the beginning. In this song, rhino is also specifically mentioned. The lines are as follows:

Pirthe Keplang Alun
(Origin of Earth Song)

'*Pirthe longle avelang....*
(when there was no trace of earth and land)
E...Ansi bang Mon pen Jon kipha
(The creator called upon Mon and Jon, the wind gods)
Ansi Mon pen Jon kivang
(Then Mon and Jon came)
Ansi nangbut pachitang
(They blew the wind)
Ansi nangja pachitang
(It was made known to all)
E... ansi bang Durminang'ingtang...
(Then the earth hardened)
Se... nangjuthip kuru abang
(The creator then said)
Sorji ma kindu pen ingnar
(Shall we create rhino and elephant)
Nangsorji lo kindu pen ingnar
(So rhino and elephant were created)
Pirthe bang do rengdok rengphang
(They lived peacefully on earth)'

According to this version, rhinos were created by the creator. If this is so, then the association of Kajir Ronghangpi as the Rhino Lady would remain with the fact that she tamed and cared for rhinos, reared them and domesticated them very well. She passed on the word to preserve the rhinos. Another important aspect one has to consider is how well she took care of this particular wild animal. She reared them, took very good care of them, spoke on the importance of preserving them – and she tamed them. This very aspect could make her an *uchepi*. The role of an *ucha/uchepi* in Karbi culture is a unique and revered one, as they are believed to have a special connection with animals and nature. Through their rituals and ceremonies, uchas are able to communicate with and control animals (all forms of animals), ensuring harmony between humans and the animal kingdom. Their abilities and knowledge are passed down through generations, making them essential figures in Karbi society. The *ucha/uchepis* also play a crucial role in healing and spiritual guidance for the community, using their connection with nature to provide wisdom and insight. They are respected for their ability to maintain the delicate balance between humans and the natural world, ensuring prosperity and well-being for all. The rhinos being wild, disturbed people like any other wild animals. Now if Kajir could tame and ride on it, it's an indication that she could've been an 'uchapi' and this could be one of the reasons why she is deified till today.

EXPOSITORY AND CONCLUSION

Kajir Ronghangpi and the narratives surrounding her are clearly an etiological myth. In certain narratives, the origin of the rhino on earth is explained, making it etiological in this respect. Who or what brought it here, who made it, why was it brought to earth, and by whom? In this sense, it is necessary to take into account Sarsomon Ronghang, Kajir Ronghangpi, the divine world from which it was taken, and the divine component of Kajir's superpower abilities. It is also a historical myth because Kajir Ronghangpi's life speaks about specific locations. It discusses historical locations which include Mihimukh, Mihibil, Mihimukh dolong, Daphlang, Arimora, and the surrounding regions. It tells the story of a group of people moving from the hills to settle on the Halmora plains (within Kaziranga). Though the people have scattered owing to the establishment of the sanctuary yet the names of the places remain in their memory. The names of the places remain unchanged till today.

The accounts in this article are also examples of psychological myth because they describe in detail giving a clear explanation how and why individuals felt the way they did both then and today, especially the Karbis. It's all integrated into the belief system. Even now, all may be seen experiencing subjugation, dread, and eventual displacement. The government clearly prioritized and placed greater value on the lives of animals over people, who were the original settlers, as seen by the fact that the Karbis were forced to abandon their land, farms and homes in order to make room for the establishment of the Wildlife Sanctuary. This is a clear case of oppression and dehumanization. The dread of being driven away, the fear of being told, the fear of being singled out, and the fear of not being free are still present in the Karbi thought and existence today – to the extent that they would rather be under domination. Relocation of the people continues. The phenomenon does not seem to come to an end. Is this the reason why individuals continue to exhibit susceptibility, diminished agency, apprehension, and reside within a state of fear-induced psychological distress? Is it possible for individuals to maintain resilience and perseverance in the face of significant loss or deprivation? The pivotal relevance of the notion of 'displacement and relocation' in creating the historical trajectory of the Karbi people is without dispute. In contrast, the historical figure known as Kajir Ronghangpi has a contrasting propensity. The subject under consideration displayed a notable absence of fear and a tendency towards expressing her opinions openly. Moreover, she exhibited remarkable proficiency in interpersonal and professional communication, with adeptness in entrepreneurial acumen. Furthermore, she had a unique aptitude in the domestication of various fauna, with a special emphasis on the management of rhinoceros species. In addition, she possessed expertise in providing care and fostering the development of persons. How did she manage to complete these tasks? Her proficiency in these can be attributed to her early exposure and teaching in each of them. When a child or adolescent is exposed to diverse environments and receives instruction in skill acquisition during her/his developmental years, she/he undergoes a transformative process that equips her/him to become influential agents and valuable contributors to personal growth. According to Sigmund Freud[7], the formation and maturation of personality occur from early infancy and are significantly influenced by a series of five psychosexual phases. So, if a learner successfully acquires the ability to integrate into society and has a strong sense of safety consciousness, it may be said that this individual has achieved a well-developed ego. The ego, in contrast to the instinctive id and the rule-based superego, represents the reasoning component of an individual's identity. Freud posits that an individual possessing a robust ego, capable of effectively reconciling the conflicting desires of the id and the superego, has a psychologically sound disposition. Every stage presents the child with a conflict between his own biologically driven needs and social expectations. According to him, the successful negotiation of these internal conflicts will lead to the progressive mastery of each developmental stage, and thus lead ultimately to the development of a fully mature personality.[6] The observed phenomenon aligns precisely with the psychological developmental progression seen in the case of Kajir Ronghangpi. She had excellent care and guidance from her parents, as well as from the extended family, which played a significant role in her acquisition of essential skills throughout her formative years. These experiences greatly influenced her personal development and contributed to the person she ultimately transformed into.

This paper is a deliberate endeavour to reconstruct the historical segment that has been inadvertently omitted. The purpose of Kajir Ronghangpi's life narratives is to provide a historical perspective on past events and happenings, seeking to revitalize historical narratives, aiming to deeply engrave and cement Karbi history into our collective consciousness. The historical and mythological narratives mentioning a woman by the name of Kajir Ronghangpi, establishes that such a person actually did exist. She was beautiful, fluent not only in Karbi but in Assamese as well, was competent and savvy in managing commercial affairs. Her fame spread so wide that the location was named in honour of her. The fact that Mihimukh is named after Kajir's spouse is unmistakable proof that Karbis used to live in that forest back then. If Kajir is the person we know today, one must be grateful to her parents for helping her become who she is in our memory. Not to be forgotten is the family, who helped her learn knowledge in the areas of farming and language acquisition. It was a woman who raised, domesticated, and kept rhinos thriving.

She was a woman who expertly handled business matters and helped the villagers in it. It was a woman whose fame was widespread. This observation highlights the role and position of women within the Karbi society. Women occupy a significant position throughout society. To this day, no woman has had a village named after her. However, Kajir Ronghangpi has effectively refuted her critics, since the very mention of Kaziranga serves as a commemoration of her accomplishments. The fact that a specific location has been designated with her name serves as evidence that women are capable of achieving noteworthy recognition. This speaks positively of the Karbi, which has always accorded women special importance – this in itself is praise worthy. Kajir Ronghangpi is a legend – a historical legend and a mythical legend. The repetitive elaborations chronicle Karbi History through the life of Kajir Ronghangpi. The myth has become a reality. This assertion remains valid in contemporary times, as articulated by Teron and Katharpi[8], 'Karbi folklore, with all its diverse myths and legends, is an important area of academic research to address important historical issues which nobody can deny'.[7]

NOTES

1. Vulli Dhanaraju and Dharamsing Teron (Ed.,), *Karbi History: Past and Present*, Mittal Publications, New Delhi, 2020, p. 2.
2. Cited in John Edward Philips (Ed.,), *Writing African History*, University of Rochester Press, Rochester, 2005, p 169.
3. Mon Timung, *Pengsomir*, Anthology of Poetry published by Karbi Lammet Amei, Monjir Press, Diphu, 1995.
4. Dharamsing Teron and Maggie Katharpi; Singing the Past – Historical Episodes in Karbi Traditional Verses; Vulli Dhanaraju and Dharamsing Teron (Ed.,), *Karbi History: Past and Present*, Mittal Publications, New Delhi,2020, p. 113.
5. Ajit Timung, *The Myth behind the name Kaziranga* , Booklet published by Bhuban Chandra Terang, Integrated Tribal Development Project, Rongmongve Block, Karbi AnglongAtonomous Council, Diphu, 2006.
6. We recorded this song while it was being sung by Babu Terang, a farmer and folk singer by profession from Sarthe Terang village (Dadhora), Karbi Anglong, on July 20, 2023.
7. 'Child Development Theories: Sigmund Freud', Available at:

https://www.firstdiscoverers.co.uk/child-development-theories-sigmund-freud/#:~:text=In%20Freud%27s%20view%2C%20personality%20is,Freudian%20psychosexual%20theory%20of%20development – (Accessed on 17/10/2023).

8. Dharamsing Teron and Maggie Katharpi, 'Singing the Past – Historical Episodes in Karbi Traditional Verses' in Vulli Dhanaraju and Dharamsing Teron (Ed.), *Karbi History: Past and Present*, Mittal Publication, New Delhi, 2020, p. 116.

CHAPTER 11

Exploring the Multiple Narratives of Kajir Ronghangpi

JUNMONI HANSEPI and SUMI DAA-DHORA

INTRODUCTION

Perspective is a key concept in academic discipline and plays a vital role in the comprehension of epistemologies of phenomena. At the same time, there are two premises in history writing.

The first premise, that history is written based on empirical sources, is known as 'scientific history.' The other premise is that 'histories' are narratives recounted from the perspective of groups marginalized in history writing. Keeping these two premises in mind, the argument of this paper relies on oral narratives that continue to be recounted by the locals of the surrounding areas in and around Kaziranga, which is the main area of the current paper. In this context, this chapter is to re-locate the legendary figure of the Karbis, Kajir Ronghangpi, also known as the 'Rhinoceros Lady', through the perspective of multiple narratives. This paper constructs the argument on the oral history discourse. This discourse often serves to amplify the voices of marginalized or overlooked individuals or communities, providing a platform for them to share their stories and express their perspectives.[1] Thus, the core discussion of this paper is to comprehend the narratives of Kajir Ronghangpi and how these narratives contribute to the reconstruction of the Karbis' past, potentially leading to a more accurate 'representation' of the Karbi people in current historical discourse.

CONTESTING NARRATIVES

Narrative is defined as a verbal or written account of any related occurrences. Legend can be studied as a narrative reading since it is a collection of interconnected stories with the goal of expressing a message or meaning. For example, *The Mahabharata* and *The Ramayana*, the two ancient epics from India, have numerous narratives that are employed to communicate meaning to readers or listeners. Jean Francois Lyotard (1984)[2] refers to narrative as a method of knowledge since it is used to produce, articulate, and disseminate knowledge. Narratives, thus, define the potential for knowledge and action in each given community. Narrative serves both epistemological and explanatory purposes.

To what extent does this narrative mode accurately depict the perspectives of the local communities? In his work, D.D Kosambi (1962)[3] pointed out that Indian historiography has overlooked the historical significance of certain smaller communities. One of the primary reasons for this is the absence of a 'historical sense' in Indian historiography. One reason for this oversight in conventional Indian historiography is the lack of attention given to smaller tribes and their cultural and ritual practices, which are often overlooked in the broader scope of Indian history. Consequently, the academic discourse has overlooked the histories of small communities. This is relevant to the Karbis as well. The question at grasp pertains to the portrayal of the Karbi people in the narratives of colonial and post-colonial ethnographers. It is evident that these depictions have led to a distorted understanding of their true identity. During the British period, several researchers and missionaries conducted studies on the history of the Karbi people. These individuals included B.C. Allen[4], Edward Stack and Charles Lyall[5], G.D. Walker[6] etc. They engaged in conversations with the Karbi people to gather valuable insights into their past. These records could be seen as important sources for studying the Karbis during the colonial period. Several Indian scholars, such as P.C. Choudhary[7], K.L. Baruah[8], and S.K Chatterjee[9] have written about Karbis in a negative light. For example, S.K. Chatterjee uses the term *Kiratajana* to refer to the 'Indo-Mongoloid tribes' (including the Karbis) living in mountainous regions, characterizing them as the 'children of rakshasa'[10]. Recently, a number of scholars from the Karbi community have been motivated to independently pursue research due to the critical and disparaging nature of scholarly discussions about them. Narratives are the essential building blocks that form the foundation of our understanding of knowledge. However, the true nature of narratives has been subject to critical examination in the recent writings of Karbi scholars. These narratives have been constructed based on oral accounts passed down through generations. In recent times, Karbi scholars have been delving into the long history of their community, drawing from the oral traditions of *Mosera Kihir* and *Kecharhe Alun*. These traditions, which involve recounting the past through memorization and funeral dirges, provide valuable insights into the migration memories of the Karbi people. In his work *Karbi Studies*, Dharamsing Teron (2008)[11] discusses the importance of oral narratives among the Karbi community. According to his statement, in the past, Karbi ancestors could recite endless poems about the universe, religion, and their unique surroundings and descendants. The Karbi forefathers' simple, repetitive melodies and precise metrical structure told stories about the creation of the universe, the origins of their ancestors, elaborate wedding and funeral traditions, sorrowful migrations, and more. Karbi oral tradition covers various aspects of the tribe's lifestyle. Rural areas have preserved these verses despite a lack of documentation. History in Karbi is limited to myths, legends, and hearsay.

In the context of the scenario, oral narratives, often referred to as histories, played a significant role in the process of moulding the attitudes and viewpoints of the common people. The oral narrative is an important component of the cultural inheritance of all communities, tribes, and other groups, and it carries a substantial amount of value. The transfer of traditional knowledge and cultural legacy is one of the ways in which they contribute to the enhancement of perceptions by individuals and their ethnic and social identities. Oral histories are extremely important in the process of putting together the history of a society. This is because every cultural group has a common understanding and interpretation of its history, which in turn influences the beliefs, behaviours, and customs of its members. The significance of a group's past is established through these narratives, and they also determine the information that must be transmitted to future generations regarding the ways in which history has influenced the present. The materials are not only supplemental to written records; rather, they have an inherent historical worth that cannot be denied. As a result, the said history of the Karbi people remains entangled in the realm of myths, legends, and hearsay. Therefore, one may say that personal narratives of migration and settlement by Karbis in the current day of Karbi Anglong are an important source of history. For this reason, it is possible to make this argument. They are cherished recollections that can be passed down from one generation to the next, and they provide the voice of actual experience to the backbone of deeper histories of the Karbis. Verrier Elwin, for example, created an enormous body of oral stories during his extended excursions across the hills and woods of India over a three-decade period. He published nearly two thousand of these stories in his five collections: *Folktales of Mahakoshal*, *Myths of Middle India*, *Tribal Myths of Orissa*, *Myths of the North-East Frontiers of India*, and *The Baiga*. In the book *When the World was Young*,[12] Verrier Elwin carefully selected stories from the collections listed above and placed them in a logical sequence based on the issues they addressed, beginning with 'The beginning of things' and finishing with 'The end of things.' This book is organized into six sections, each focusing on a particular motif. The title implies that readers will be exposed to the vivid imagination of the storytellers, who convey us to a time when the world was in its infancy and the foundations were only starting to form. The anthology of stories encapsulates the cognitive processes of the storytellers who freely let their imaginative faculties to explore various themes, so provoking intellectual engagement and contemplation among the audience. These stories were transmitted from one generation to the next through oral tradition. Elwin has documented several tales that center on the origin motif. Every story is creatively linked to the creation of various elements that contribute to the vastness of our universe: the earth, the sun and moon, thunder and lightning, the rainbow, snowflakes, rivers, and earthquakes. The stories delve into the intricacies and depths of human emotions and interpersonal connections. Verrier

Elwin diligently gathered a significant collection of tribal tales from various regions in India, faithfully transcribing them without any personal bias or interpretation. He faithfully conveyed the tales exactly as they were recounted by the storytellers of his era, providing readers with a glimpse into the imaginative intellects of many tribal cultures.

KEEPING KARBI HISTORY ALIVE THROUGH THE LEGENDS

Myths and legends can be challenging to categorize and frequently exhibit overlapping characteristics. In a historical context, myth and legend refer to the widely accepted story or narrative that is associated with a specific community. Every culture commonly engages in the act of narrativizing stories. The majority of people derive pleasure from engaging in narrative experiences. Narrators have fulfilled the need for a compelling narrative since the beginning of humankind. However, the scholars frequently employed myth and legend interchangeably or in a continuous fashion to provide justification for the narrative. A myth conveys a deep truth to both those who share it and those who hear it, going beyond a mere record of events. Myths often provide explanations for the origins of both the world and specific places, involving supernatural beings. A legend usually includes an element of truth or is based on real historical events, but is enhanced with imaginative elements. Legends often center on brave individuals or remarkable places and often reflect the spiritual beliefs of the community they originate from. However, due to the cultural specificity of oral genres and the inherent ambiguity surrounding concepts of the past and truth, distinguishing legends from other oral narratives can be a challenging task. Given their focus on the past, legends often obscure the line between fact and fiction. They are intertwined with history, as they convey what is believed to be true. Furthermore, their origins can be traced back in a manner similar to ancestry, and occasionally, they integrate aspects of folklore, which adds a mysterious quality to them. Therefore, a legend is a story of human events that are believed by the storyteller and the audience to have occurred in the past. The actions of the legend are not beyond the realm of possibility, but they do involve miraculous events that are believed to have actually occurred within the tradition. Jacob Grimm's definition of a legend highlights its key traits – its specific setting, relatable nature, and historical accuracy[13]. A legend serves a purpose beyond mere entertainment – it imparts knowledge about one's surroundings and equips individuals with the means to safeguard themselves. Even though scholars have categorized legends into different types, such as local, etiological, and historical, it's important to consider the societal impact of these legends. In 1963, a committee of experts created four preliminary categories of legends, taking into account the existing collections[14]. These categories include etiological legends, historical legends, mythical legends, and religious legends. However, these models have been constructed using Western concepts and therefore, may not be applicable to the field of indigenous studies.

Exploring the fascinating history of the Karbis involves delving into one of their earliest renowned legends, which provides insight into their origins. The extensive past of the Karbi people comes alive through the exploration of the legends that form the very essence of their way of life. There are many 'mythical legends' that can be found in the history of the Karbis, including the story of Kajir Ronghangpi. There are several types of mythical legends in the world of the Karbis, one of which is the well-known Kajir Ronghangpi, who can be called a legendary character of mythical proportions.

A fascinating legend in the historical past of the Karbis is Hemphu. Oral tradition holds that Hemphu and his sister Rasinja emerged on the riverbank of Kuleng, where they encountered the two brothers Long Mukrang and Bang Mukrang. They sought accommodation in the house of the two brothers and were graciously received by Rang Mukrang, their father. Since Hemphu did not reveal his identity, he was referred to as Langmingpo or Langmipo (someone who glanced sideways). He was also known by the title *Vo-hangpo*. This individual was later identified as Hemphu, who played a significant role in introducing the Karbis to new forms of worship.

Sot Richo can be regarded as a historical legend. This classification is made by the narrative and essence of the story, as well as its relevance to the present-day society. The Sot Richo legend serves as a significant reference for determining the initial location of the Karbis. According to the myth of *Sot Richo Karkli*, there was once a man called Kathang Rongphar, also known as Sot Richo.[15] As the Karbis resided in the area known as *Longle Achete*[16], they maintained connections with neighbouring communities. Sot Richo was a remarkable individual among the Karbis rallying his people to unite and defend their very existence. He was recognized as the inaugural ruler of the Karbis. Thanks to his guidance, the Karbis successfully defended themselves from external threats as they migrated from *Longle Achete* to various regions across the globe. Thus, he implored the Karbi people to always remember his presence, as he had led them to relocate to ensure their safety. There is also a ritual in Karbi society, often performed once in each generation, to remember the contributions and sacrifices of *Sot Richo Karkli*.

Sambepo is a significant figure in Karbi society, credited with establishing the practice of ancestor worship among the Karbis. The legend of Sambepo maintains that ancestral spirits persistently remain involved in the affairs of their living descendants, exerting either beneficial or detrimental influence based on how well they were appeased. The story of Sambepo is honoured through the *Chojun* ritual in traditional Karbi society.

In the history of the Karbis, the art of weaving has been passed down from generation to generation. Even today, many women continue this tradition, using their skills to create beautiful textiles for their households. Therefore, Serdihun was revered as a legendary figure who introduced the tradition of weaving, and their significant contribution to the formation of the Karbi identity.

Apart from the above mythical and historical legends, there are some popular legendary figures which have been witnessed by contemporary historical sources.

Aon Teron maintains significant historical significance as a legendary figure among the Karbi community. The folk song *Parok bang van akengkethe* recounts the saga of Aon Teron, a pivotal figure in the resistance against the Dimasas in Maibong around the mid-16th century.[17] During that period, Govinda Chandra held the position of ruler in Dimasa.

'Parok bang van akeng kethe
Ramu lakhapo neke.
Parok aphan lakhadet anke
Karbi adengnang pale.
Afrang do dun Aon Nokbe
Pa-phelok akeng kethe;
Ra`i dam tanglo Nokbe...'

The meaning of this song can be derived from the following lines:

The Dimasa king has designated a messenger to gather information about the activities and settlements of the Karbis, as well as identify any individuals with intelligence gathering capabilities among them. The King had allocated several assignments to assess their capabilities and prowess. Nevertheless, the King had been employing cunning strategies and inflicting various forms of torment upon the Karbis. The tasks were creating garlands using sand and paddy flowers, as well as crafting buffalo horns that were perfectly straight and defect-free. The Karbis effectively accomplished all of these tasks. The king understood the ability of the Karbis to accomplish such jobs. He believed that the Karbis possessed high intelligence and may perhaps pose a threat to the kingdom in the near future. Consequently, he made the decision to assassinate the chief and the courageous individuals of Karbis. The king entered the hall riding an elephant and asked the Maut to count the number using the elephant's trunk. Having completed the counting with *Parok* (which denotes the Dimasa people), the elephant then proceeded to count the Karbi group Aon Nokbe occupied the foremost seat in the first row. The Maut commanded the elephant to first seize Aon with its trunk and then to kill him. Following the act of murdering, the Karbis promptly removed their garments and engaged in combat using bows and arrows. First, they eliminated the Maut, and subsequently initiated a relentless and devastating assault on their adversaries. The Dimasas, lacking any weaponry, quickly dispatched nearly all of their adversaries in and around the designated rendezvous point. The Karbi emerged victorious in the battle, however they mourned the loss of their Chief, Aon Teron.

During this period, Aon Teron, the grandson of Riang, assumed the role of Chief according to custom. Under his guidance, the young individuals were trained in the art of warfare, which ultimately led the Dimasa King to plot the assassination of Aon Teron and his supporters. Unfortunately, Aon Teron and his supporters were killed in this scheme.

Following the demise of Aon Teron, the Karbis encountered the predicament of leadership. In the oral traditions of the Karbi people, there is merely one acknowledged instance of a female Karbi legendary figure, namely Kareng (Runja) Rongpharpi. She is famously referred to as Rongpharpi Rongbe. It is widely believed that she was married to On Teron and had a child named Thong Nokbe Teron. However, the claim must be verified. Under her direction, the Dimasa king was to feed the tiger cubs by providing them with human milk, as they were raised like domesticated animals. It is believed that when Kareng was forcibly demanded to provide her milk to the soldiers of the King, she reacted with intense anger and used an axe to violently kill them. Being aware of the Dimasas' inevitable reprisal for the incurred loss, she advised her people to evacuate rather than engage in combat, recognizing their inability to face the adversary's superior power. Thus, she guided her people to elude the assault of their adversaries by escaping from their territory. This action unequivocally demonstrates Runja Rongpharpi's courage and adeptness in safeguarding the community through strategic means. Nevertheless, the Karbis made the decision to depart from the highlands of Asalu in the current north Cachar region and founded their town near the Kopili River[18].

Thong Nokbe is thought to have fulfilled the role of commander and personal bodyguard of Jaintia king. The Karbis highly regard him as one of their beloved heroes. It is said that the Jaintia troops, motivated by envy, plotted Thong's downfall. The Jaintia troops were unable to tolerate the fact that he was regarded with such great respect. However, the Karbis still hold his name with great reverence and high regard.

Waisong holds great significance in the Karbi legends. He was renowned for his strong physique and striking good looks, earning him the adoration of his subjects. He passionately pursued everything he believed to be right. The Jaintias had a strong aversion towards him due to his unwavering sincerity[19]. They actively sought opportunities to trap him. He was held in bondage for a period of 12 years. He engaged in several significant conflicts and is still revered as a courageous figure.

THE ETYMOLOGY OF KAZIRANGA AND MULTIPLE NARRATIVES

History can be seen as a narrative when it is presented as a story or account of past events, often with a specific perspective or interpretation. Historians craft narratives by carefully choosing, arranging, and analysing historical events to form a cohesive and significant account. By adopting a narrative approach, individuals can gain a deeper understanding and connection to the intricacies of history. However, it is crucial to keep in mind that historical narratives may differ based on the historian's viewpoint and the evidence at hand. Multiple narratives regarding the life of Kajir Ronghangpi could be found on the internet[20]. These legends serve as the basis for the current hypothesis regarding the origin of the name 'Kaziranga' for Kaziranga National Park. However, it is important to verify all internet narratives for accuracy. Besides this, the Karbis have actively challenged the negative perceptions surrounding the legend of Kajir Ronghangpi by preserving and passing down their oral traditions.

The Tale of Love[21]*:* This is the first narrative linked to the tale of love. The name Kaziranga was derived from a heart-wrenching tale of love. Legend has it that a girl named Rawnga, from a nearby village, and a youth named Kazi, from Karbi Anglong, were deeply fascinated with each other. This match was deemed unacceptable by their families, prompting the couple to vanish into the undergrowth of the forest, never to be seen again. As a tribute to their mysterious disappearance, the forest came to bear their name.

The Tale of goat-red color[22]*:* There is another tale that is often connected to the story involving a goat and the color red. The park's name is derived from the native language spoken in the area. Kaziranga derives its name from the local language, with 'Kazi' meaning goat and 'ranga' representing the color red.

The Tale of the Gifted Jacket-Rongai[23]*:* There is an interesting tale about the 30th Ahom King, Rudra Singha, who once stayed overnight at the residence of Chieftain Ranjit Phukan during his journey to Guwahati. During that period, he was captivated by the weaving skills of Kamala Phukan's daughter, who crafted a remarkable silk jacket as a gift for him. Then, the king bestowed upon her the title of Kazi, signifying her expertise in her craft, and generously gifted Rongai and a piece of land to her husband. Over time, the local residents began referring to that piece of land as Kazirongai, which eventually evolved into Kaziranga.

The Tale of a Childless Couple[24]*:* There is another tale that is connected to the tale of the couple who were unable to have children. In that particular region, there resided a couple named Kazi and Rongai who unfortunately did not have any children. The couple explored various healthcare options, as well as spiritual and religious practices, in their quest to conceive a child. Unfortunately, their efforts were unsuccessful. They eventually crossed paths with Madhabdev, the principal disciple of Srimanta Sankaradeva. Madhabdeva encouraged the couple to construct a pool in their neighbourhood, emphasizing the importance of serving the community and leaving a lasting legacy. As Ahom king Swargadeo Pratap Singha strolled by the pond, he was surprised by an unexpected encounter with a fish. To his astonishment, the local chieftain graciously offered him the fish. Curious about the pond's origins, he inquired about it and decided to name it Kaziranga after learning about its varied past and intriguing history.

The Tale of Conversation of the Forest: In 1904, Mary Curzon, the wife of the Viceroy of India at the time, Lord Curzon, urged her husband to take action in safeguarding the vulnerable wildlife, particularly the one-horned rhinoceros, in the Kaziranga National Park[25]. She developed this idea after being unable to find a single Indian one-horned rhinoceros during her visit to the park. During her research, she discovered the necessary measures required to protect the wildlife in the park. After careful consideration and extensive deliberation, on November 4th, 1904, Lord Curzon put forth a proposal to establish a wildlife reserve in Kaziranga. The Kaziranga Proposed Reserve Forest was established on June 1, 1905, spanning an area of 232 square kilometres. The conservation attempt in Kaziranga was initiated in 1908, when it was designated as a 'Reserve Forest', primarily with the objective of safeguarding the Indian Rhinoceros (Rhinoceros unicornis) and its natural environment. Afterwards, it was officially designated as a 'Game Reserve' in 1916, then reclassified as a 'Wildlife Sanctuary' in 1950, and subsequently established as a 'National Park' on January 1st, 1974. In 1985, it received recognition as a UNESCO 'World Natural Heritage Site'[26]. Kaziranga is home to the largest population of one-horned rhinoceros in the world. This population has grown significantly since the early 19th century, making it one of the most successful conservation stories globally.

ORAL NARRATIVES

The following two stories were recently collected from the field by Rengmili Engtipi (2023). She narrated the stories to the authors of this chapter. These stories have provided a fresh perspective on the historical events related to Kajir Ronghangpi.

Kajir Ronghang as 'Brave Lady': As per Noren Singnar, Gaonbura of Bagori and former Executive Member of Karbi Anglong Autonomous Council (KAAC) Benting Terang, Kajir Ronghangpi was the daughter of a Gaonbura whose name they cannot recall. However, it is believed that this Gaonbura was a descendant of either Sai Ronghang or Kania Ronghang. It is believed that the Gaonbura did not have a son, so his work-related responsibilities were inherited by someone else. However, Kajir had a deep understanding of the Kaziranga region. That said, during that period, the name Kaziranga had not yet been established, and the vicinity of present-day Kaziranga was predominantly inhabited by the Karbis. Kajir also had a profound knowledge of different languages and her ability to connect with people from various tribes made her a prominent figure in the region. She demonstrated numerous leadership qualities, so whenever a task or challenge arose, people would seek her guidance. In this context, people would refer to her as Kajir Ronghang, which would later be shortened to Kaziranga.

This argument is supported by the current scenario of the Karbi community's way of life and the practice of giving names to female children derived from Kajir Ronghangpi. There is a belief among certain experts that the name Kaziranga may have originated from the Karbi term Kajir-a-rong, signifying 'the village of Kajir'. Across the Karbi community, the name Kajir is frequently given to female children, reflecting a belief in an influential woman named Kajir who once held power in the region. Fragments of monoliths scattered throughout the area, associated with Karbi rule, provide compelling evidence supporting this claim.

DECODING AJIT TIMUNG'S TEXT OF THE MYTH OF 'KAZIRANGA'

In his renowned four-page work titled 'The Myth behind Name 'Kaziranga', AjitTimung[27] states that according to legend, Kajir Ronghangpi, the daughter of Hok Ronghang, was taken to and raised in the divine realm of gods and goddesses. After achieving divinity and being bestowed with specific divine abilities, Kajir Ronghangpi descended to Earth with the purpose of finding her biological parents and siblings. Kajir Ronghangpi reconstructed the land established by her father within and surrounding the current Kaziranga National Park region. She brought a Rhinoceros named 'Kindu' to assist with tilling. Kajir Ronghangpi returned to the realm of deities, leaving behind the 'Kindu' in their own region. The name 'Kaziranga' is thought to have originated from the revered Kajir Ronghangpi.

Although this document is brief, it is highly relevant to the Karbis today due to its compelling argument regarding the mythical legend of Kajir Ronghangpi. The existence of Kajir Ronghangpi has had a profound impact and continues to shape the collective psyche of the Karbis. The Karbis of today have managed to preserve the different names and objects that were mentioned in his text.

All of these narratives offer distinct interpretations of the derivation of 'Kaziranga'. Each narrative constructs argument with distinct interpretations, influenced by the essence of the 'Kaziranga' myth. This implies that the existence of multiple narratives highlights the complexity of historical events and underscores the importance of critically examining different perspectives to gain a deeper understanding of the Kaziranga National Park through the lens of

Kajir Ronghangpi. Understanding how history is constructed is a crucial part of studying the past. Historians employ various methods to interpret facts and weave them into compelling narratives.

CONCLUSION

When researching historical events or personalities, historians offer distinct viewpoints influenced by elements such as their cultural background, personal experiences, ideological beliefs, or the specific research questions they want to answer. These viewpoints impose a substantial influence on historians' selection and examination of data, emphasis on particular events or personalities, and construction of narratives. This study examines the notion of multiple narratives associated with the mythical legend of Kajir Ronghangpi. By analysing these narratives from an alternative viewpoint, it provides a fresh viewpoint on the historical comprehension of the genesis of 'Kaziranga'. The only way to accomplish this is by reconstructing the event or individual through the use of oral history discourse. This discourse helps us in reconstructing the history of marginalized or overlooked society. Reconstruction is crucial for the proper representation. The process of reconstructing history often gives rise to various interpretations of a particular historical event or historical figures. Gaining insights from several viewpoints is beneficial when examining a past experience. Such historical experiences are negating the dominant narratives. Several viewpoints critique the 'metanarratives', as the Kazirnaga National Park has been constructed on the rulers' or state view points, but the people's narrative has been ignored in the making of the region's history. Therefore, Kajir Ronghangpi's history must be understood from multiple perspectives of the Karbis, which leads to the representation of their voices in the shaping of history.

NOTES

1. Paul Thompson, *The Voice of the Past: Oral History*, Oxford University Press, Oxford, 1978.
2. Jean Francois Lyotard, *The Postmodern Condition: A Report on Knowledge*, Manchester University Press, Manchester, 1984.

3. D.D Kosambi, *Myth and Reality Studies in Indian Culture,* Popular Prakashan Bombay, 1962.
4. B.C Allen, 'Mikir' in Census of India, Vol. IV, Part I. Report, 1901, Assam Government Press, Shillong, 1901.
5. Edward Stack, *The Mikirs*, David Nutt, London, 1908 (This book had been edited, arranged and supplemented by Charles Lyall, 1908).
6. G.D. Walker, *A Dictionary of the Mikir Language*, Mittal Publication, New Delhi (1925), 2022 (Reprint)
7. P.C Choudhury, *The History of Civilization of The People of Assam to the 12th Century A.D*, Guwahati and Delhi: Spectrum publications, 1959.
8. K.L Baruah, *Early History of Kamrup*, Guwahati, 1966.
9. S.K Chatterji, *Kirata Jana Kriti*, Asiatic Society, Revised Edition, 1974.
10. Vulli Dhanaraju and Dharamsing Teron (Ed), 'Introduction' in Karbi History: Past and Present, Mittal Publications, New Delhi, 2020, p.1.
11. Dharamsing Teron, 'Memories of Migration in Karbi Oral Tradition' *in Karbi Studies*, Vol.1, Assam Book Hive, Guwahati, 2008, pp.175-221.
12. VerrierElwin, *When the World was Young*, National Book Trust,New Delhi, 1961.
13. Household Stories from the Collection of the Brothers Grimm (Jacob Grimm and Wilhelm Grimm) (translated by Lucy Crane; illustrations by Walter Crane) 1882. Available at: https://www.encyclopedia.com/children/academic-and-educational-journals/grimm-jacob-and-wilhelm-1785-1863-1786-1859 (Accessed on 10/1/2024).
14. Cited in Linda Degh, 'Folk Narrative' in Richard M. Dorson (Ed), *Folklore and Folk life: An Introduction*, University of Chicago Press, Chicago and London, 1972, p.76.
15. The interview was conducted on November 8, 2020, with Longsing Bey, 70. Time: 04:53pm-5:30pm, village Murap, UmpanaiVothatlangso.
16. A well-known myth explains how the Karbis came to exist. According to this notion, the Karbis previously lived in a place known as 'LonglehAchete,' or the 'Centre of the World,' as described in BarelongTerang's book, *The History of Karbi*, Self-Publication, Diphu, 2003, p.1.
17. Barelong Terang, 2003, op. cit., p. 25.
18. *A Report of Exploration on Dima Hasao District of Assam Under Annual Plan 2015-16*, Directorate of Archaeology, Assam, 2016. Rongbe denote as a person fleeing from the village but from the above narrative it is understood that Rongpharpi Rongbe wanted to safeguard

her people from the danger where she already knows the opponent strength. So, for this very reason the term become little derogatory in Karbi society. So, it will be more suitable to put it as Rongpharpi Nokbe which means Hero or Savior.

19. Phukan Ch. Phangcho, *The Karbis of North-East India*, Anggik Prakashan, Guwahati, 2003, p. 37.
20. 'History about Kaziranga', Available at: https://www.kaziranganationalparkindia.in/history-about-kaziranga.html (Accessed on 20/12/2023)
21. Ibid.
22. Ibid.
23. 'Kaziranga National Park' , Availbel at https://www.newworldencyclopedia.org/entry/Kaziranga_National_Park (Accessed on 14/6/2024)
24. Ibid.
25. 'History about Kaziranga', op. cit.
26. Centre for Wildlife Rehabilitation and Conservation (CWRC), *Annual Report: 2021-2022*, Wildlife Trust of India, Available at: https://www.wti.org.in/ (Accessed on 12-10-2023).
27. Ajit Timung, *The Myth behind the name Kaziranga*, a booklet published by Bhuban Chandra Terang, Integrated Tribal Development Project, Rongmongve Block, Karbi Anglong Autonomous Council, Diphu, 2006.

CHAPTER 12

Kajir Ronghangpi

What Makes her a Mythological Figure in Karbi History

LANGMILI TERANGPI, MIRBIN KATHARPI
and ARNIKA TERANGPI

INTRODUCTION

The Karbi people, who refer to themselves as 'Arleng' meaning men in general, were previously identified as 'Mikir' in earlier times. The Karbis belong to the Mongoloid group and are linguistically associated with the Tibeto-Burman language family. Scholarly investigations suggest that some communities speaking Tibeto-Burman languages were previously located in the western regions of China, particularly near the Yangtze River and the Huang Ho River.[1] The intrepid explorers embarked on a journey along the majestic rivers, namely the Brahmaputra, the Childe Hill, and the Irrawaddy River in Burma. The Karbi people, among others, who migrated to Assam from Central Asia, are commonly recognized as one of the waves of migration[2].

In accordance with the folktales of the Karbi people, it is recounted that in ancient times, their dwelling places were situated along the banks of two prominent rivers, namely the Kalang and the Kapili, encompassing the vast expanse of the Kaziranga region. During the era characterized by the rule of the Kachari King, a significant turn of events unfolded, leading to their migration towards the hills.

Subsequently, a portion of the Kachari population sought refuge in the Jaintia Hills, where they came to reside as subjects under the governance of the Jaintia Kingdom, acknowledging its suzerainty.[3]

In the realm of natural wonders lies Kaziranga, a renowned destination nestled within the boundaries of Golaghat and Nagaon districts. This park has captivated the imaginations of many tourists. In the realm of geographical expanse, this land stretches across a vast territory, measuring a remarkable 430 square kilometres. In the midst of the wild, where the rivers flow and the forests thrive, lies a land renowned for its majestic creatures. Nestled within this enchanting domain, one discovers the abode of the Greater One-Horned Rhino, a magnificent beast that roams these hallowed grounds. Moreover, this sacred land serves as a sanctuary, a haven where the Pelican finds solace and fosters new life.[4] In the context of folklore, it is whispered that the land we now know as Kaziranga was once intertwined with the historical domain of the Karbi people, crafted by the legendary figure Hok Ronghang. According to the tradition, the Karbi people have maintained a steadfast belief that the region acquired its name from a captivating Karbi maiden known as Kajir Ronghangpi. This remarkable young woman was said to possess extraordinary abilities beyond the realm of ordinary mortals.[5] In the vicinity of natural wonders, lies a park that stretches across the lands adjacent to the mystical North Eastern part of the Karbi Anglong district. Behold, it doth boast with great pride of the bountiful array of flora and fauna, bestowing upon its verdant landscape an even greater abundance. In the annals of this land, there emerged a place of great allure, where the convergence of both local and foreign visitors transformed it into a veritable haven for tourism. Year after year, a multitude of wanderers were drawn to the enchanting park, captivated by its irresistible charm.

FOLKTALES

The term 'Folktale' refers to the timeless narratives and occurrences that bear a profound link to the customs and practices of our forebears, resonating with the fabric of contemporary traditional existence. The tales and occurrences in question are relayed through the ancient tradition of oral storytelling. In the course of the ages, the rich tapestry of folktales has expanded beyond the realm of oral tradition, finding its way into the written word as well. Within the intricate tapestry of indigenous cultures, where the written word may not hold sway, the luminous realm of oral tradition takes centre stage. It is in this enchanting realm that the timeless tales of folklore emerge, weaving themselves into the very fabric of cultural heritage. Throughout the ages, a noble custom has endured, wherein the wisdom of yore is passed down to the tender hearts of the young. This sacred duty, undertaken by the esteemed elders of the clan, involves the art of storytelling, wherein tales and legends are woven into the very fabric of their existence. In every community, a varied collection of folktales and folklores integrates itself over time, for such tales do not spring forth in a mere week or fortnight. Oral traditions are valuable sources for societies that lack written sources. Such sources have been passed down through generations.

Some communities around the world have lost their history as a result of a failure to document oral traditions. Once upon a time, in the vast expanse of history, there existed a tribe known as the Beothuk Indian tribe of Newfoundland[6]. Alas, their story is one shrouded in mystery, for no oral tales or written accounts have survived to guide us. In the absence of such records, we are left to ponder the fate that befell this tribe, as they gradually faded away from the tapestry of existence, leaving behind only whispers and echoes of their once vibrant presence. Thus, the Beothuk Indian tribe of Newfoundland stands as a poignant example of how a tribe can, in the course of time, slip into the realm of extinction, their legacy forever lost to the annals of folklore. For these reasons, the Karbis began documenting their oral traditions.

The timeless narrative of Kajir has endured through the ages, captivating the imaginations of countless generations. Within the annals chronicling the rich tapestry of Karbi society, one cannot overlook the enigmatic presence of the one-horned rhinoceros, forever entwined with its human counterpart. This captivating duo has transcended mere existence to become the embodiment of a narrative steeped in the realms of myth and folklore. The enigmatic entity, frequently denoted as 'she,' has captivated the collective imagination, residing in the domain of myth and legend. Over time, the perception of this remarkable figure has evolved, becoming intricately woven into the vibrant fabric of Karbi history. The perception of this enigmatic duo as mythological figures is veiled within the depths of Karbi society's collective consciousness. The Kaziranga National Park was originally designated with the appellation 'Kajir Ronghangpi' as a tribute to an individual by the same name, Kajir Ronghangpi. Nevertheless, it is imperative from a historical perspective to delve into the reasons behind the evolution of this designation, ultimately leading to its recognition as 'Kaziranga.'

MODERN ORIGIN OF KAZIRANGA

The location garnered considerable interest from visitors when Lord Curzon, the Viceroy of India at the time, embarked on a journey to the area accompanied by his wife, Mary Curzon. In 1905, following the counsel of Mary Curzon, a decision was made to designate a specific location as a proposed reserve forest. The primary objective of this action was to safeguard the dwindling population of the One Horned Rhinoceros. Spanning an area measuring 232 square kilometers, this proposed reserve forest aimed to provide a protected habitat for these endangered creatures. In the year 1908, a significant development occurred in the area as it was designated as a reserve forest, encompassing an additional 152 square kilometers.

MYTH ABOUT KAZIRANGA

According to oral tradition, the renowned National Park, which has gained significant prominence, was purportedly believed to have been originally situated within the territorial boundaries of the Karbi community, and was attributed to the visionary efforts of Hok Ronghang, a prominent figure of that era. The current designation of this location is believed to have originated from the captivating tale of a Karbi maiden named Kajir Ronghangpi, renowned for her enchanting beauty and reputed possession of extraordinary abilities. In accordance with the prevailing mythological narrative, it is believed that Hok Ronghang embarked on a migratory journey originating from *Bithi Arlok*, a Karbi settlement situated in close proximity to the Jaintia Kingdom. During a particular period, it is worth noting that the Jaintia community was reportedly involved in a covert conflict with the Karbi people. This clandestine war, unfortunately, led to the tragic loss of numerous innocent lives within the Karbi community.

In the annals of history, it is recorded that the denizens of *Bithi Arlok*, including the esteemed Hok Ronghang himself, were beset by a great tragedy that befell their community. The lamentable loss of their beloved family members compelled them to seek solace and refuge in a hitherto unknown land, which they christened *Tovar Kethom*. Hok, despite experiencing the loss of parental guidance during a covert conflict, matured into a valiant, resilient, industrious, and astute individual. By virtue of his exceptional abilities, he ascended to the esteemed position of *Sarthe* (Headman), and proceeded to augment his dominions through the establishment of his very own Kingdom, which he named Tovar Kethom. In subsequent years, Hok Ronghang entered into matrimony with a woman of comparable intellect by the name of Bong-eh Teronpi. This union bore fruit in the form of three offspring, namely Khoi Ronghang, Kading Ronghangpi, and Kajir Ronghangpi, who were known for their remarkable charm. At around seven years old, Kajir found herself embroiled in a disagreement with her parents. In a moment of emotional turmoil, she made the decision to flee from the comfort and security of her familial abode, seeking solace amidst the untamed wilderness of the jungle. Amidst the dense foliage of the jungle, the intrepid individual ventured towards the meandering river, driven by an insatiable desire to satiate her parched throat. In the course of her journey, the observer beheld a scene of great significance along the banks of the aforementioned river. It was there that she bore witness to the presence of seven celestial beings, believed to be the daughters of a deity, engaging in the act of bathing within the pristine and transparent waters. In a display of profound empathy, the seven sisters, overcome with sorrow, extended their compassion to Kajir and welcomed her into their dwelling. Kajir's upbringing was intertwined with the presence of various deities, among them a pantheon of Goddesses. This auspicious environment fostered her acquisition of diverse knowledge, ultimately shaping her into a resplendent and refined young woman. In the wake of acquiring divine powers, Kajir made the momentous decision to embark upon a visit to her parents, brother, and sister. Kajir's sibling, Khoi Ronghang, matured into a visually appealing young gentleman and entered into matrimony with a woman who was deemed suitable for him. As the passage of time wore on, Kajir's father, Hok Ronghang, found himself succumbing to the inevitable effects of age and infirmity. Recognizing his diminishing ability to effectively govern his territory, he made the momentous decision to entrust the weighty responsibilities and intricate affairs of his domain to his son, Khoi Ronghang. In a manner reminiscent of his esteemed father, Khoi assumed the mantle of leadership and diligently safeguarded his subjects against the incursions launched by neighboring communities.

As a consequence of these events, it is worth noting that a sense of envy and resentment had taken hold among the inner circle of Khoi Ronghang, leading them to conspire and devise a plot with the intention of bringing about his untimely demise. On a fateful day, during Khoi's journey upon a raft as part of his tour, he found himself subjected to a forceful subjugation. His hands and feet were bound, rendering him immobilised, before being callously cast into the flowing currents of the river. In their deep sorrow, Hok Ronghang and Bong-eh Teronpi, burdened by age, found solace in shedding tears. Their days were consumed by the grief of missing their beloved daughter. Growing frustrated, the Ronghang family—comprising the elderly couple, their daughter, and daughter-in-law—decided to abandon their caretaking responsibilities. Motivated by weariness, they resolved to relocate the couple to a remote and desolate place known as *Ritlo*, leaving them to their own devices. In the waning hours of the aforementioned day, Kajir, accompanied by *Chung* and Phang`ok (the Milkyway) descended upon the sacred land known as Ritlo. Upon witnessing the scene, a profound sense of compassion arose within the observers as they beheld a destitute and sorrowful pair, evoking a sentiment of pity. In a moment of contemplation, the individuals known as 'Chung' and 'Phang-ok' engaged in a conversation with the couple, posing a thought-provoking question:

'Between the contrasting sensations of cold and hot, which one do you deem superior?' In this response, the individual suggests that cold weather can be pleasurable when accompanied by the comforting warmth of a fire, while hot weather can be enjoyable when one can cool themselves by fanning and engaging in the tradition of storytelling. Having received satisfactory responses, the individual, having obtained consent from Kajir, resolved to restore the elderly couple's vision. Upon the restoration of their visual faculties, Hok and Bong-eh found themselves consumed by a profound curiosity regarding the mysterious sojourn of Kajir upon the terrestrial realm. In their perception, these three individuals were revered as divine beings, embodying the essence of gods and goddesses.

Upon careful consideration of the available evidence, it became apparent to Hok and Bong-eh that the woman in question was indeed their long-lost daughter, Kajir. This realisation was reached after attentively listening to the narratives she shared. Upon their return, Kajir was filled with an overwhelming sense of joy as she reunited with her family members. However, the fleeting nature of their joy became evident, for their sibling, Khoi Ronghang, remained concealed and overlooked by all. In light of her extraordinary abilities, Kajir resolved to embark upon a quest to locate her sibling, ultimately arriving at the very river into which Khoi had been cast. In her explorations, she chanced upon a sacred tree known as *Alom Bilom*, revered by the Karbi people. This remarkable tree stood proudly on the river's edge, holding within it the secrets and significance cherished by the Karbis throughout history.

In the pursuit of divine favour, Kajir diligently employed a tool known as a *Tari*, possessing a beak-like extremity, to repeatedly strike the tree. In a moment of great ecological significance, it is worth noting that a majestic tree succumbed to the forces of nature, its towering form collapsing into the flowing waters of the river. As a direct consequence, the once vibrant and life-sustaining river experienced a gradual desiccation, its waters diminishing in volume and ultimately ceasing to flow. This event, undoubtedly a testament to the delicate balance of the natural world, serves as a poignant reminder of the intricate interplay between terrestrial and aquatic ecosystems. During that particular era, the individual in question discovered the lifeless body of her sibling within the confines of the riverbed, subsequently proceeding to retrieve it. In a fortuitous turn of events, Khoi, buoyed by divine providence, successfully regained his livelihood and returned to the familiar confines of his abode. In a heartwarming reunion, the various members of the family came together once again. It was during these gatherings that Kajir, a cherished member of the family, would regale her kin with captivating tales of the deities and celestial beings. Following their journey, Kajir, accompanied by Chung and Phang-ok, made their way back to the sacred dwelling of the divine entity. It was here that they pledged to periodically revisit the mortal realm in the future. In light of her profound affection for her kin, Kajir, having duly obtained consent from the divine pantheon, returned to the mortal realm accompanied by Sarsomon Ronghang. Sarsomon's arrival on Earth was driven by the intention to cultivate *Sok*, commonly known as rice. To facilitate this agricultural endeavor, Sarsomon brought with him a formidable creature called a *Kindu*, used for ploughing the land. During this period, the *Kindu* served as a crucial traditional tool in land cultivation, playing a key role in preparing the soil for planting. After ploughing, Sarsomon would sow the rice seeds, a meticulous process essential for ensuring a successful crop. In the context of sustenance, it is worth noting that a multitude of avian creatures, terrestrial mammals, insects, apian species, Lepidoptera, and reptilian organisms congregated in unison, converging upon the rice fields, thus designating the locale as their respective dwelling place. During the course of Khoi's journey, he found himself subjected to yet another assault, as he traversed the landscape following a tour. The individual in question underwent a division of their physical form, resulting in two separate pieces. However, through the utilization of water infused with rice cultivated by Sarsomon, their body was subsequently reconnected into a singular entity. The individual in question experienced a revival of life. After completing his paddy harvest, Sarsomon decided to return to his place of origin. He attempted to bring the '*Kindu*' with him, but the creature, disobedient and unruly, fled into the depths of the surrounding jungle. Sarsomon left for the celestial realm, leaving the *Kindu* behind. It is widely believed that from that moment on, the Kindu became associated with the indigenous inhabitants of Kaziranga. Historians speculate that the presence of a thick, curved object resembling cushioning cloth and rope was used by Sarsomon during ploughing. Over time, the term *Kindu* gradually became associated with rice cultivation.

It is widely believed among the Karbi that *Kindu* represents the revered entity known as *Sok Api*, an animal believed to bring forth a bountiful harvest. Following Sarsomon's rise to power, an incident occurred involving Khoi, wherein he was compelled to consume alcohol during his journey and subsequently suffered a gruesome fate, being severed into two distinct sections. During this period, it was believed that in order to prevent the resurrection of an individual, a specific body part would be subjected to boiling. In the case at hand, it was decided that one piece of his body would undergo this process, as there was a concern that his sister, Kajir, possessed the ability to revive him. In light of the aforementioned event, Kajir ventured to the location with the aspiration of restoring vitality to his existence. However, regrettably, her valiant endeavour did not come to fruition, as a specific portion of the human anatomy was subjected to the process of boiling. The marvel of rice, too, proved to be ineffective. In accordance with the customs and traditions befitting a monarch, she undertook the solemn task of repatriating his remains and overseeing his cremation. Upon Khoi's departure from this mortal realm, he bequeathed a lasting legacy in the form of his two sons. The elder of the two was duly anointed as the successor to the illustrious Karbi throne, assuming the mantle of Karbi King. With his ascension, he assumed the responsibility of governing and presiding over the vast expanse of Karbi territory, ensuring the continuation of his father's reign. Following the passing of Kajir's parents, a significant event occurred in her family's history as her sister, Kading Ronghangpi, entered into the institution of marriage. Kajir, in accordance with the sacred customs of the Karbi people, dutifully conducted the final ceremonial observances for her deceased father, mother, and brother. With her familial ties severed, she resolved to embark upon a pilgrimage to the divine realm, where she believed solace and purpose awaited her. In the moments preceding her ascension to the celestial realm, Kajir Ronghangpi made a solemn declaration. She proclaimed that the land of her nativity shall henceforth bear the appellation of 'Territory of Kajir Ronghangpi,' in perpetuity. This decision was motivated by the profound blessings bestowed upon her, allowing her to reside alongside the divine deities in their sacred abodes. However, her proclamation also carried a sombre curse, foretelling the perpetual absence of unity among the Karbi people. This curse was attributed to the tragic demise of her beloved brother, an act of violence that forever marred her heart. Therefore, Kajir returned to the celestial dwelling place of the deities, abstaining from any subsequent visits to the mortal realm. Reflecting upon their actions, the Karbis came to a profound realization of their misdeeds and decided to take decisive action. As a gesture of repentance and acknowledgment, they chose to name the region after Kajir, a figure of great significance in their cultural framework. The etymology of Kaziranga can be traced back to its indigenous name, 'Kajir Ronghangpi.' Presently, this renowned destination has garnered global recognition primarily due to its population of the majestic One-Horned Rhino.

MYTH ABOUT KAJIR RONGHANGPI

Myths are ancient narratives that have been passed down through generations, believed to be imbued with the essence of cultural creatures and legends. These tales originated from the myths of various civilizations, which were then transmitted orally over time. They reflect the beliefs held by early societies regarding the creation of the universe and its contents.

In the annals of romantic entanglements, there exists a tale that bears witness to the enduring power of love. This narrative unfolds in the realm of antiquity, where two individuals, known to history as *Ranga* and *Kazi*, found themselves inexorably drawn to one another. Their hearts, unburdened by the constraints of societal expectations, embraced a profound affection that transcended the boundaries of time and space. Thus, the chronicles reveal that *Ranga* and *Kazi*, their souls entwined in a symphony of emotions, embarked upon a journey of love. According to historical accounts, it has been posited that Renga originated from what is now known as the Karbi Anglong district. The tale of their love was met with formidable resistance, as the union they sought to forge was met with vehement disapproval from their respective families. The youthful pair thus embarked on a perilous journey into the dense and unforgiving wilderness, their fate forever shrouded in mystery as they eluded discovery. The myth surrounding Kajir Ronghangpi, as documented in various online sources, warrants our attention.

The second narrative delves into the artistry of courage displayed by the subject. According to Naren Singnar, who held the esteemed position of Gaonbura in the region of Bagori, and also served as the former Executive Member of the Karbi Anglong Autonomous Council, it has been relayed that Kajir Ronghangpi, a notable individual, is believed to be a direct descendant of either Soi Ronghang or Kaniya Ronghang. In light of the absence of the Gaonbura's son, the responsibility of managing his affairs fell upon his daughter, Kajir Ronghangpi, who possessed a considerable understanding of the local region. However, during that particular era, the appellation 'Kaziranga' had not yet been bestowed upon the region. The region in question witnessed the settlement of numerous Karbi individuals and various other communities, most notably the Ahoms. As a result of her experiences, she acquired fluency in the languages of various tribes and cultivated the demeanor befitting that of a leader. Due to her notable attributes, the people of the region bestowed upon her the name Kajir Ronghangpi, which has since been abbreviated to Kaziranga.[7]

The historian's perspective on myth as a subject of concern has evolved over time. Initially, there was a tendency to dismiss myth as an unworthy area of study. However, it has become increasingly clear that belief in myth is a pervasive aspect of the human condition that cannot be overlooked by those tasked with unraveling the intricacies of the human narrative. In analyzing the historical event at hand, it becomes imperative to meticulously evaluate the veracity of the various perspectives espoused by the individuals involved. Distinguishing between the authentic and fallacious accounts necessitates a comprehensive examination of the extant information at our disposal. By scrutinizing the congruity between these narratives and the available evidence, we can discern those that align harmoniously with the historical record, as well as those that exhibit incongruity and thus warrant classification as mythical in nature.[8]

CONCLUSION

The accounts surrounding the renowned figure of Kajir Ronghangpi, as recounted in folk narratives and mythologies, exhibit a certain degree of consistency, albeit with notable variations stemming from the diverse recollections, regional perspectives, belief systems, cultural practices, and traditional customs of the people involved. The tales of her extraordinary exploits endured throughout the ages, transcending the passage of time. The passage of time has rendered it elusive and unfamiliar to subsequent generations, as a result of the dearth of documentation and sources available. One must acknowledge that Kaziranga's inclusion within the annals of Karbi history is a matter of contention. The primary factor behind this divergence lies in the inability of our esteemed folklorists and mythographers to ascertain the precise origins and historical trajectory of Kajir Ronghangpi, a figure of considerable significance. Kajir, through her narratives, continues to serve as a source of inspiration, fostering within us a profound connection to our fellow individuals and the collective community. She occupies a significant position within the illustrious Karbi Cultural Heritage, assuming a noteworthy function in imparting knowledge to the younger cohort regarding the opulent Karbi folklore. In an effort to safeguard the rich folkloric traditions of Kajir Ronghangpi, the esteemed authority of the Karbi Anglong Autonomous Council (KAAC), in collaboration with the Department of Art and Culture and Tourism, undertook a series of promotional endeavors. The primary objective of these initiatives was to disseminate knowledge and awareness among diverse segments of society regarding the captivating legend of the Rhino Lady. In summary, the words uttered by the chief of the tribe of the Lushain community, 'We are in pursuit of reclaiming what has been lost,' are presumed to convey their collective desire to restore that which has been taken away.

NOTES

1. Barelong Terang, *The History of Karbi*, Self-Publication, Diphu, 2003, pp.1-2.
2. Ibid.
3. Dharamsing Teron (Ed), 'About Karbis' in Dharamsing Teron (Ed.), *Karbi Studies:Memories, Myth, Metaphor*, Vol.1, Assam Book Hive, Guwahati, 2008, p.4.
4. P. Banerjee, *History of North-East India*, Akansha Publishers, Kolkata, 2016, p.47.
5. Ajit Timung, *The Myth behind the name Kaziranga* , Booklet published by Bhuban Chandra Terang, Integrated Tribal Development Project, Rongmongve Block, Karbi Anglong Atonomous Council, Diphu, 2006.
6. The Beothuk were a North American Indian tribe of hunters and gatherers who lived on the island of Newfoundland.
7. Oral interview was conducted by Rengmili Engtipi in May, 2023 and later narrated it to us.
8. Ian R. Christie, *Myths and Reality in late 18th Century, British Politics*, Macmillan, New York,1970.

CHAPTER 13

The Story of Kajir Ronghangpi via the Memories of the Local People

RAMESH KATHAR and SANGITA DAS

INTRODUCTION

Karbi Anglong District is often considered the heart of Assam. The Karbis are a significant indigenous ethnic group in Northeast India, primarily residing in the hill regions of Assam, which boast a rich cultural heritage. They are governed according to the provisions of the Sixth Schedule of the Indian Constitution. In addition to Karbi Anglong, Karbis can also be found in Dima Hasao, Kamrup Metropolitan, Hojai, Morigaon, Nagaon, Golaghat, Karimganj, Lakhimpur, and Sonitpur Districts in Assam. This picturesque hill district, with its diverse plant and animal life, remains largely unexplored and unexploited. Its lush forests, cascading waterfalls, meandering rivers, and babbling streams contrast beautifully with the rice fields and rolling green hills. Karbi Anglong is rich in cultural diversity, home to a wide range of indigenous tribes and ethnic groups.

Mosera Kehir a prominent genre of Karbi folk narratives recount the origins of Karbi history, including tales of the creation of the universe, the origins of the first Karbi parents, elaborate wedding and funerary rituals, and the trials of migration. In the past, and based on their ancestry, the Karbis referred to themselves as *Arleng*, which translates to 'Men' in the Karbi language. Within this context, it is worth noting the statement made by Lyall: "The name 'Mikir' is that given to the race by Assamese: the origin is unknown. They refer to themselves as *Arleng*". Gopal Chandra Medhi in his work entitled 'The Route of Karbi Migration to Assam' analysed the etymological meaning of the word Karbis or *Arleng*, derived from *Thekar* and *kibi* – which actually is the act of ritual purification after or during worship. According to him, the term *Arleng* is interpreted as a man or hill-slope dweller' while 'Mikir' is derived from '*Mi*' and '*Kiri*'. According to migration history, the Karbis are linguistically connected to the Tibeto-Burman group. It is believed that the original homeland of these people, who speak the Tibeto-Burman language, was located in Western China near the Yang-Tee-Kiang and the Howang-ho rivers. Over time, they travelled along the Brahmaputra, Chindwin, and Irrawaddy rivers, eventually entering India and Burma. According to the folklore of the Karbis, they once resided along the shores of the rivers Kalang and Kopili. Over time, they made their way into the renowned Kaziranga area, which is home to a national park in Assam. Throughout the rule of the Dimasa-Kachari kings, they were compelled to seek refuge in the hills, with a portion of them finding sanctuary in the Jaintia hills. As Karbis migrated to the Northeast, some settled in the Jaintia kingdom while others ventured further, crossing the river Barapani (*Langpi*) and making their way into the Rongkhang range. It was in this new territory that they established their capital, known as *Socheng*. Stack and Lyall state that the Karbis initially inhabited the eastern part of the Khasi and Jayantia hills, near the Kopili River. According to G.C. Medhi (1974), the Karbis initially resided in the mountainous territory ranging from Nagaon to Sivsagar (now Jorhat), which included the Kaziranga forest. According to his narrative, the name Kaziranga is derived from *Kajir-Arong*, which translates as the village of the mythical Karbi lady, Kajir Ronghangpi. According to Ujjal Kumar Sharma's study, the eco-cosmologies of indigenous communities illustrate a profound connection between the human and the natural world. The rituals and ceremonies that stem from these beliefs play a crucial role in the preservation of nature. He also mentioned that 'the culture, specifically the cosmologies and religious beliefs, of an indigenous tribal group called the Karbis, who live near Kaziranga National Park in Assam, India, have established institutions to preserve natural resources'.

According to Karbi legends, Kajir Ronghangpi is a highly revered figure, honoured by having the Kaziranga National Park named after her. For countless generations, the Karbis have passed down their rich history, rituals, culture, customs, social norms, and values through the power of oral tradition. The Karbis revered numerous legendary figures, whose wisdom and loyalty to the community were highly esteemed. Kajir Ronghangpi is one of them. Despite the significant impact of Kajir Ronghangpi's contributions to Karbi society through oral stories and songs, only a select few have a comprehensive understanding of such cultural treasures. Many young people today are unaware of the legendary Kajir Ronghangpi. However, there is a growing curiosity about her in recent times. Due to the lack of comprehensive written records, learning about her often relies on alternative sources. Therefore, the objective of this study is to gather knowledge about Kajir Ronghangpi primarily from local Karbi people who are familiar with her story. This chapter employs the historical method, utilizing a range of primary and secondary sources. Primary data has been collected through interviews, while secondary sources include unpublished materials, books, journals, and magazines.

ORAL TRADITION AND THE KARBIS

Oral tradition is a fascinating method of human communication that involves the passing down of knowledge, art, ideas, and cultural material through spoken word from one generation to the next. Oral traditions encompass a wide range of genres that have been passed down to us by our ancestors through spoken word. These include songs, myths, tales, chants, riddles, proverbs, and more. Through this method, a society can pass down oral history, oral literature, oral law, and other forms of knowledge from one generation to another, even without the use of a writing system. Oral tradition encompasses the recollection and passing down of specific textual and cultural knowledge through spoken communication.

India has a rich tradition of oral history that spans over 3500 years and continues to be preserved to this day. It is fascinating to note that there are a greater number of oral languages in the country compared to those that have a written form. Before the widespread adoption of printing and publishing in the nineteenth century, literature in India primarily thrived through oral traditions. However, many oral literature traditions are now facing the risk of being forgotten as they no longer receive institutional support or are passed down between generations. Recently, there has been a concerning trend where a significant amount of folklore and oral literature is not being passed down to younger generations, putting it at risk of being lost.

THE POPULAR STORY OF KAJIR RONGHANGPI

Legends has it that the name Kaziranga is derived from the name of Kajir Ronghangpi, combining the words *Kajir* and *Arong* (village). Through the collaboration of the village Headman (*Sarthe*) and the local community, a wealth of stories, myths, and tales about Kajir Ronghangpi have emerged, providing valuable insights into their life and accomplishments. Multiple pieces of information have been established through on-site research.

Hok Ronghang (father of Kajir Ronghangpi) made his way from 'Bithi Arlok', a Karbi settlement that bordered the Jayantia kingdom, which is now a part of Meghalaya State. During that period, the Jayantias were engaged in a covert conflict aimed at eradicating the Karbis and their settlements along the borders of the Jayantia kingdom. Unarmed Karbis fell victim to a covert attack resulting in their untimely demise. They were scattered and compelled to escape from their residences and communities, seeking refuge in jungle caves for their security and well-being. The people of Bithi-Arlok often found themselves vulnerable to these covert assaults. Hok Ronghang's family also fell victim to the merciless violence inflicted by Chomang. In his formative years, he tragically lost all of his loved ones in the conflict. As a result, Hok and other Karbi families had to leave their homeland and seek refuge in *Tover Kethom* (Tin-Ali/ three crossed road), which is located in the present-day Kaziranga area. Hok found himself orphaned as a result of the secret war, with no elder relatives to provide care and support. Unfortunately, he was neglected and faced disdain from those around him. However, Hok Ronghang managed to overcome numerous challenges and difficulties and eventually grew up to be a courageous, resilient, diligent, clever, and supportive individual. He had a deep passion for hunting and was highly skilled in his pursuits. The Karbis of that locality were drawn to his bravery, intelligence, and helpfulness, ultimately selecting him as their *Sarthe*. He expanded the Karbi settlement in and around *Tover Kethom* (three crossroads) and governed it with great skill. He was held in high esteem by all the Karbis, who considered him as their ruler. Later, Hok Ronghang married a remarkably intelligent woman named Bong`e Teronpi, and together they were blessed with three wonderfully charming children: Khoi Ronghang, Kajir Ronghangpi, and Kading Ronghangpi.

However, at the age of seven, Kajir left home due to a feud with her parents and cried at the riverbank. Meanwhile, seven celestial daughters descended from the skies to bathe in the earthly waters. They found Kajir alone and crying on the riverbank in the dark jungle. The divine sisters questioned her about the incident and her personal history. Moved by her story, they decided to invite Kajir to their celestial home. In the celestial realm, Kajir was nurtured and developed her singing and dancing abilities while acquiring a diverse range of knowledge and skills. She grew into a beautiful young woman endowed with otherworldly powers by the divine entities, allowing her to descend to Earth and ascend to the realm of the gods. After 24 years, Kajir remembered her parents, brother, and sister whom she had left behind on Earth.

Meanwhile, on earth, Kajir's brother Khoi Ronghang also matured into a handsome and charismatic young man. Kajir's father Hok Ronghang due to age could no longer effectively manage his territory. Thus, on a certain day, he gathered all his subjects and conveyed his desire to pass on the rule and management of his territory to his capable son, Khoi Ronghang. Khoi was chosen to succeed his father as the leader due to his unwavering commitment to Karbi rituals and his remarkable abilities. He upheld his father's legacy by effectively protecting his people and land from rival tribes. However, fuelled by envy, his trusted advisors began to turn his subjects against him and orchestrated a plot to assassinate him.

During one of his journeys, while crossing a river on a raft, Khoi was betrayed by his own friends. They overpowered him, bound his hands and feet, and mercilessly tossed him into the water, leaving him to perish.

Meanwhile, Hok Ronghang and Bong`e Teronpi were devastated by the loss of their daughter Kajir. Overcome with grief, they felt guilty for losing their beloved child, Kajir, who had constantly cried in their memories. They became wholly dependent on others for their basic needs, struggling to see, hear, and even eat or drink without assistance. Their daughter Kading and daughter-in-law grew despondent from caring for them. The elderly couple was frequently blamed for Kajir's death. The prolonged absence of Khoi Ronghang also caused significant distress to his family. Eventually, Khoi's brother-in-law and Kading's lover abandoned the elderly Hok and his wife in Ritlo (a cultivated area), leaving them to face their dire fate alone.

One day, Kajir Ronghangpi, along with her celestial friends Chung and Phang`ok, descended to Earth in search of her family. They arrived at the location where Hok Ronghang and his wife Bong`e Teronpi had been abandoned. Seeing the elderly couple's distress and their desperate need for survival, Kajir, Chung, and Phang`ok approached them. To test the old couple's character, Chung and Phang`ok asked Hok and Bong`e which they preferred: cold or hot temperatures. Hok, unable to perceive his surroundings or sense temperature changes, inquired about the visitors' identities. Bong`e remarked that cold weather might be bearable with a cozy fire and that hot weather could be pleasant with a fan while sharing stories. Impressed by their responses, Chung and Phang`ok sought Kajir's permission to restore Hok and Bong`e's sight, which Kajir gratefully approved. Instantly, Hok and Bong`e regained their vision and saw Kajir, Chung, and Phang`ok as divine beings from the celestial realm. They were amazed and inquired about the purpose of their visit. Kajir explained, "I am searching for my father, mother, and sisters." Hok then recounted his family history in detail, allowing everyone to understand their shared roots. The reunion brought immense joy, and the family was happily reunited, returning to their home.

When Kajir returned home, she was overjoyed to be reunited

with her sister Kading and her sister-in-law. However, the prolonged absence of King Khoi Ronghang was a cause for concern among them. Using her extraordinary abilities, Kajir discovered the whereabouts of her brother and learned about the tragic events that had occurred. Kajir set out to find her brother and arrived at the river where he had drowned. There, she found a sacred tree known as *Alom Bilom* at the river's edge. Using a unique knife called a *Tari*, she tapped the tree and invoked divine favour. Her actions caused the river to dry up, revealing Khoi Ronghang's lifeless body on the riverbed. With the help of divine intervention, Kajir retrieved her brother's body and revived him. Khoi Ronghang was restored to life, and he returned home with Kajir, leading to a joyful family reunion. Kajir shared enchanting stories of the heavenly realms and the divine beings that reside there. Kajir, Chung, and Phang`ok then returned to the divine abodes, promising to visit Earth occasionally. Deeply affectionate toward her family, Kajir requested the divine beings' blessing to visit her loved ones on Earth from time to time. One day, she returned with Sarsomon Ronghang, whose mission was to cultivate rice. Sarsomon brought a rhinoceros named *Kindu* to assist with ploughing the land for rice cultivation.

Meanwhile, Khoi Ronghang was once again brutally assaulted by his companions and tragically dismembered during his journey. Kajir and Sarsomon recovered his remains. By nourishing Khoi Ronghang's body with water mixed with Sarsomon's cultivated rice, a remarkable transformation occurred, and he was revived. After Sarsomon Ronghang completed his rice harvest, he prepared to return to the heavenly abode with his rhinoceros, Kindu. However, Kindu fled into the depths of the jungle and could not be captured. Consequently, Sarsomon had to depart for the heavens without Kindu. It is widely believed that Kindu, the rhinoceros, has since remained on Earth, particularly in Kaziranga.

After Sarsomon Ronghang departed for the divine abode, Khoi Ronghang was once again betrayed by his advisors during one of his journeys. This time, he was brutally killed, and his body was divided into two parts. One part was placed in boiling water to prevent Kajir from resurrecting him through divine means. Kajir, upon learning of the tragedy, descended to Earth in a desperate attempt to save her brother. However, she was unable to revive him due to the severe injuries and the part of the body that had been boiled. The magic of the rice also failed to work on the boiled remains. Respectfully, Kajir returned the body to their home and conducted a cremation ceremony in accordance with Karbi traditions, honouring Khoi Ronghang as a rightful king. Following his death, Khoi Ronghang's eldest son was appointed as the new ruler of the Karbi territory, succeeding his father.

After a few years, Kajir's parents, Hok Ronghang and Bong`e Teronpi, passed away. Her sister, Kading Ronghangpi, had also recently married. KajirRonghangpi performed the final ceremonies for her parents and her brother, King Khoi Ronghang, in accordance with traditional Karbi customs and prepared for her return to her ancestral home. Before departing for the afterlife, Kajir Ronghangpi declared, "This land where I was born shall bear my name and become the territory of Kajir Ronghangpi for generations to come. This land has granted me the privilege of dwelling among the divine beings in their celestial abodes." She also cursed, "The Karbis will never experience true unity among themselves; you took the life of my beloved brother." Kajir then returned to the realm of deities and never again set foot on the earthly plane. The Karbis, acknowledging

FIG. 1: THE ABOVE PICTURE IS THE PLOT WHERE *KAJIR RONGHANGPI'S* RESIDENCE WAS LOCATED.

their wrongdoings, honoured her by naming the area after her, as she had declared before her departure. It is said that Kaziranga received its name from Kajir Ronghangpi. Today, it is renowned worldwide for its population of one-horned rhinoceroses.

Oral Interview-1: Mr. Boronson Tokbi, a resident of Chinthong Tokbi village in Kohora, Karbi Anglong, Assam, recounts that he learned the tale of Kajir Ronghangpi from his ancestors. According to him, during Kajir Ronghangpi's time, she and her friends would often bathe in a picturesque river near their village. When Kajir was around 11 or 12 years old, she was bathing with her friends when the heavenly god Songsar Richo descended from his celestial abode to bathe in the same river. Observers were captivated by Kajir's breath taking beauty, which seemed to rival even the goddesses of heaven. Songsar Richo and his sons frequently descended to Earth, where Kajir would bathe, and they developed a close relationship. One day, Songsar Richo's sons invited Kajir to visit their heavenly home. Kajir was initially hesitant and explained that while they did not have a father, their mother was still alive, and she needed to seek her permission. However, Songsar Richo's relatives reassured Kajir that there was no need for concern. They kindly invited her to visit heaven and see their beautiful home. Kajir agreed and accompanied them to heaven, where she stayed at Songsar Richo's residence. Despite extensive efforts by her mother and the villagers, Kajir's whereabouts remained unknown for a significant period. They became despondent, fearing Kajir had perished in the river. After spending some time in heaven, the Songsar king began to contemplate Kajir's future as a human from Earth. He gently reminded her of her earthly origins and the family she had left behind. Upon receiving this counsel, Kajir willingly returned to Earth to reunite with her mother. After about two years, Kajir's world was shattered when her mother tragically passed away. Hearing of Kajir's loss, King Songsar decided to bring her back to his heavenly residence. Kajir spent some time in the realm of the deities. One day, the Songsar king spoke to Kajir with great concern. He explained that living in heaven was not natural for a human from Earth and advised her to return and embrace a family life. To ensure a smooth transition and help Kajir with earthly life, King Songsar dispatched rhinos to assist in cultivating paddy fields for rice production and other agricultural endeavors. These majestic creatures, introduced by Kajir to Earth at Kajir-Arong (also known as Kajir-Village), made it their permanent home. Due to a lack of understanding of the Karbi language, the Assamese people later changed the name from Kajir-Arong to Kaziranga. Over time, Kaziranga has become renowned for its one-horned rhinoceroses, found in the Kaziranga National Park.

Oral Interview-2: Mr. BinarsonTerang, a resident of Kohora, Karbi Anglong, shared that he learned the story of Kajir Ronghangpi from his grandfather. According to him, one day Hok Ronghang and Bong`e Teronpi ventured across the Lang-Dingpi River to gather vegetables and firewood from the jungle for their home. Unexpectedly, a torrential downpour began and continued relentlessly. At that time, Bong`e Teronpi was expecting. Kajir's parents were devastated when they discovered that their entire stock of raft rice had been washed away by the floodwaters of the Lang-Dingpi River, mixing their bundle of paddy rice with that of the villagers. The water level of the Lang-Dingpi River did not recede. In desperation, Bong`e Teronpi made a plea to the god of the Lang-Dingpi River, promising that after the baby was born, whether a boy or a girl, they would offer it to the god. The river god agreed to this arrangement, providing safe passage and protection for their paddy raft. On the day of Kajir's birth, two rhinoceroses suddenly appeared near their paddy rice stock at night. According to the villagers and Kajir's family, these rhinoceroses were believed to have emerged from the raft rice.

Kajir was always drawn to the Lang-Dingpi River and loved bathing in its waters. She and the Lang-Dingpi River God developed a deep bond. One day, Kajir approached the river god with a concern: a village boy had developed feelings for her and might try to take her away. She requested that the river god marry her to protect her from this situation. Kajir was deeply loved by her family, with a special affection for her brother and parents. She dedicated herself to cultivating the paddy fields, providing rice and other crops for the community, before eventually departing from Earth to her eternal home in heaven.

Oral Interview-3: I had the pleasure of meeting Mr. KohoraTerang, a 68-year-old resident of Phumen Engti village in Kohora. According to Terang, one day Kajir's parents ventured into the jungle early in the morning, around 5 a.m., to gather vegetables and other necessities for their home. That day, a sudden downpour began, lasting for three consecutive days. The Lang-Dingpi River's water level rose dangerously high, with the current flowing rapidly. Due to the high-water level of the Lang-Dingpi River, Hok Ronghang and Bong`e Teronpi were unable to return home. At that time, Bong`e Teronpi was expecting. The floodwaters swept away the paddy rice from the villagers' fields, causing the paddy rafts to become mixed up and unrecognizable to their owners. In desperation, Bong`e Teronpi made a solemn promise to the Lang-Dingpi River God, vowing that if the river god protected their precious cargo of paddy rice and ensured their safe passage across the river, she would offer her unborn child to the river god. However, Hok Ronghang was unaware of this promise. Kajir was born at 1:35 a.m. on the night of Buddha Purnima, which happened to be a Thursday. That same night, Kajir's mother was surprised to see two large rhinoceroses in their backyard. Sar-sermon Terang was eager to marry Kajir, so Kajir shared the details with the Lang-Dingpi River God and requested a swift marriage. Once, a serpent emerged from the depths of the Lang-Dingpi River, only to transform into a human upon reaching the surface. He ventured with Kajir to the depths of the Lang-Dingpi River. Kajir Ronghangpi boarded a golden raft and gracefully approached the river god. She kindly requested the rhinoceroses to stay and explore the riverbank, as she intended to immerse herself in the waters. It was a serendipitous connection, as the rhinoceroses had also appeared on Earth on the very day of Kajir's birth.

CONCLUSION

The Kajir Ronghangpi's oral history, tradition, culture, and rituals have been passed at Kaziranga for generations, existing myths and folktales, folklore, and narratives about Kajir Ronghangpi that are widely held by locals may open the way for greater scientific and methodical inquiry into the subject. Until now, little research has been undertaken on the famous lady Kajir Ronghangpi and textual sources are insufficient for future research. Since this study is based on primary material gathered through interviews with residents, Kajir Ronghangpi's birthplace and home plot are assumed to be located in 'Sepunakuba' village, Kaziranga, Golaghat district. It is located approximately one kilometer from National Highway No. 37. The story is told under mango trees established by Kajir Ronghangpi and her family. There is an intriguing tale about an individual named Kajir Ronghangpi who embarked on a journey into the Lang-Dengpi River after marrying the river deity known as *Lang-Dengpi* (name of the river).

As far as the local people's opinion and also the stakeholders the restoration and preserving historical places like Kajir Ronghangpi is important as they offer a glimpse into our past, showcase cultural heritage, inspire people to know about their legend, serve as valuable educational resources, represent regional pride and identity, and preserve her birthplace for future generation to appreciate. Taking a part in the heritage initiative, spreading awareness of the stories among the people, and hoisting special events, necessary to the restoration and preservation process to sustain the existing form, integrity, and material of a historical property. To assess the condition of the significance and restore the Kajir Ronghangpi's land plot which is believed to be located at Sekunakuba village, Kaziranga, Golaghat District. Therefore, the most immediate and necessary steps need to be taken by the competent authority of Karbi Anglong Autonomous Council (KAAC) to use compatible techniques with the Govt. of Assam and present land owners with materialistic solutions. The locals also appreciate the present KAAC government led by Mr. Tuliram Ronghang Sir for his initiative to preserve the heritage of legend Karbi lady Kajir Ronghangpi by awareness among the people through the installation of Kajir Ronghangpi's statue at Kohora, observing death anniversary at Kajir Ronghangpi Memorial Park, Kohora, hoisting special events, organizing three-day International Conference at the Arboretum cum Craft Centre at Matipung in Diphuon "Oral tradition of the Karbis: Memorizing Kajir Ronghangpi – The Rhinoceros lady".

NOTES

1. Edward Stack, *The Mikirs*, D.Nutt, London, 1908 (This book had been edited, arranged, and supplemented by Charles Lyall, 1908), p. 4.
2. Retrieved from Westkarbianglong.assam.gov.in (1/6/2024).
3. Ibid.
4. G.C. Medhi, 'A Brief Account of Migration Route of the Karbis of Assam', in *Historical Journal*, Diphu Govt. College, Issue-1, 1974.
5. Ujjal Kumar Sarma and Indrani Barpujari, 'Eco-Cosmologies and Biodiversity Conservation: Continuity and Change among the Karbis of Assam', in *the International Indigenous Policy Journal*, Vol. 2, Issue. 4, 2011, pp. 1-10.
6. Aji Timung, 'The Myth behind the name Kaziranga', a booklet published by Bhuban Chandra Terang, Integrated Tribal Development Project, Rongmongve Block, Karbi Anglong Autonomous Council, Diphu, 2006.

CHAPTER 14

The Role of Narratives in Transmitting Traditional Knowledge

Exploring Anomalous Places and Spaces in Karbi Worldview in Context with Kaziranga and Other Places

KARENG RONGHANGPI

INTRODUCTION

The Karbis are a fascinating indigenous community spread across various regions in North East India. In 2016, the district of Karbi Anglong was split into two separate districts: West Karbi Anglong and East Karbi Anglong. The Hills Karbi are primarily located in these twin districts. The Karbi people are categorized into two distinct groups: the Hill Karbi and the Plain Karbi. The plains Karbi and the hills Karbi reside in Karbi Anglong, Ri-bhoi district in Meghalaya, Kamrup, Morigaon, and in the vicinity of Jaintiya Hills, Nagaland, and the borders of Bangladesh. The plain Karbi are also referred to as Dumrali Karbis. This particular group, also referred to as the plain Karbi, is heavily influenced by the customs and beliefs of the Assamese culture. The Hills Karbi maintain a strong connection to the customs and practices that have been handed down through generations although their religious beliefs have undergone several changes over time. The Karbi from the hills and plains have similar rituals, but there are some observed differences in dialect. For instance, the clan names[1] vary between the plains and hill Karbi. The Klien in Ribhoi and Kelleng in Kamrup plains are the same surname derived from the Killing in the Hills of Karbi Anglong. The Tumung in the Kamrup plains is called Timung in the Hills of Karbi Anglong. Similarly, Tron in the plains is referred to as Teron among the hill Karbi.

These changes can be understood as a result of separation during migration that led to a different settlement in different regions. Migration occurred because of various factors such as population growth, internal conflicts, epidemic outbreaks, famine, and in search for greener pastures[2]. The changes in dialect can also be explained as the assimilation with the neighboring community. And also due to the loss of contact with the original language community created a socio-cultural, religious and linguistic chasm among the separated groups[3]. For example, the name of the National Park *Kaziranga* is said to be derived from the Karbi word Karjir Ronghangpi the name of the mythological deity and *Kajir-arong* which means *Kajir*'s village, which later became Kaziranga because this was much easier to articulate than *Kajir-arong* by the neighboring communities.

THE IDEA OF PLACE AND SPACE

Places and spaces are essential ideas that pertain to the tangible and intangible aspects of our being. Although they have some similarities in their overall meanings, there are clear distinctions between the two. Locations are defined by their distinct physical characteristics. They are linked to geographic coordinates, landmarks, and tangible features. Locations can encompass both natural elements like mountains, forests, or rivers, as well as man-made structures like cities, buildings, or parks. They possess a clear presence in space and can be observed and encountered through our senses. Locations frequently carry cultural, historical, or personal importance, influencing our encounters, recollections, and sense of 'self'. Places can evoke a deep sense of significance, connection, and separation, resulting in a place being regarded as sacred, familiar, repulsive, or even unusual[4].

Spaces, on the other hand, have a more conceptual nature and encompass a wider understanding of the environment. They extend beyond physical boundaries and encompass conceptual, social, or metaphorical realms as well. Spaces have a dynamic nature that can be shaped and altered by human actions, perspectives, and engagements. They are shaped by various cultural, social, and psychological elements. Spaces can embody various aspects of human experience, encompassing physical environments like classrooms, markets, or religious gatherings, as well as internal landscapes like personal comfort zones, imaginative realms, or meditative states.

COMPARABILITY IN THE SPACE AND PLACE DOMAINS

Both places and spaces hold significance in our lives. They can evoke emotions, shape our behaviours, and provide a sense of belonging, meaning, and connection. Places and spaces have the power to influence our thoughts, actions, and experiences. They shape our interactions, memories, and relationships, whether it's through the physical environment or the social and cultural dynamics within a space. Places and spaces are subject to individual and collective perceptions. How we perceive and interpret a place or a space can vary based on cultural backgrounds, personal experiences, and social contexts. Places and spaces can carry symbolic meanings and represent concepts, ideologies, or values. They can embody cultural, religious, or spiritual significance and serve as a medium for expressing identity, beliefs, and narratives. Both are critical for comprehending our surroundings and are used to characterize locations. Places and spaces can be understood differently depending on the situation because they are cultural constructs by political, economic, and social forces.

THE DISTINCTION BETWEEN PLACE AND SPACE

Space and place are two concepts that are related but distinct from one another. Places are typically associated with tangible, physical entities and locations, while spaces can be more abstract and intangible, encompassing conceptual, social, or metaphorical dimensions. Spaces are often more flexible and malleable than places. They can be transformed or redefined through human interactions and activities, whereas places are relatively more static in their physical attributes. Places are generally more specific and localized, referring to particular physical locations. Spaces, on the other hand, can have a broader scope, encompassing various dimensions and levels of existence, from physical to social and psychological realms. Places are often context-specific, grounded in a particular physical setting, while spaces can be more contextually versatile, adaptable to different situations, and influenced by cultural or social dynamics. While places and spaces share common elements in their significance and influence, they differ in their tangibility, flexibility, scope, and contextualization. Understanding the nuances between the two concepts provides a more comprehensive perspective on how our environment shapes our experiences and interactions. Space refers to the physical dimensions of an area, while place refers to the social and cultural meanings that are attached to a location. Space can be measured and quantified, while place is more subjective and difficult to quantify. Space is often associated with movement and mobility, while place is associated with stability and a sense of belonging. While space and place are related concepts, they have distinct differences that are important for understanding how we interact with and make sense of the world around us.

INFLUENCE OF NARRATIVES IN SHAPING SPACES AND PLACES

Narrative gives meaning and significance to spaces and places by weaving stories and histories around them. Through narratives, spaces become imbued with cultural, social, or personal significance, transforming them from mere physical locations into sites of emotional connection, identity, and memory. According to Koram (2016),[5] 'local, vernacular narrative functions to order people's lives and beliefs in a coherent manner' because vernacular narratives create imagined realities that can shape our perception of spaces and places. Through stories, literature, or media, we can explore fictional or speculative worlds, altering our understanding of what is possible within a given space. These imagined realities expand our perspectives and influence how we perceive and interact with physical environments. Narratives provide cultural and historical context to spaces and places, highlighting their significance within a specific cultural or historical framework. Narrative functions as a verbal method of instruction to socialize individuals into the local ethos of the place[6]. Historical narratives can reveal the layers of a place's past, preserving and transmitting collective memories and shaping our understanding of its cultural heritage. Cultural narratives can create associations and shared meanings that define a place's identity and character. Through narratives, individuals and communities can connect with shared stories, traditions, and values associated with a particular space. The interactive dynamics of these factors combined with agency, sociality, and reproducibility result in the construction of a distinct place to which individuals claim allegiance.[7] These narratives foster a sense of community and help shape a collective identity tied to the place, strengthening the bond between people and their environment. Narratives influence how we perceive and experience spaces and places. They can shape our expectations, emotions, and interpretations of a given environment. For example, a narrative describing a place as mysterious or haunted can evoke a sense of unease or curiosity when we encounter it in real life, altering our experience and interactions with the space. Narratives often inform the design and architecture of spaces. Whether it's a building, park, or urban development, narratives can guide the creation of spaces that align with a specific story, concept, or cultural narrative. The design elements, symbols, and storytelling within these spaces contribute to shaping the user's experience and understanding of the narrative embedded in the physical environment. Narratives shape spaces and places by providing meaning, creating imagined realities, establishing cultural and historical context, fostering a sense of belonging and identity, influencing perception and experience, and guiding spatial design and architecture. They play a crucial role in shaping our understanding, connection, and relationship with the environments we inhabit.

PLACES AND SPACES IN THE KARBI DOMAIN

In Karbi worldview, the concept of place is crucial. Most of the stories and tales passed on by the Karbi ancestors in the form of narratives have the element of conflict or confrontation with the entities[8]. These confrontations end in the establishment of a pact. The natural habitat such as the forest, mountains, and valleys, manifests a strong connection within the Karbi community and is expressed through various traditions. Keith Basso (1996)[9] has noted that the relationship with place is both reciprocal and dynamic: 'When places are actively sensed, the physical landscape becomes wedded to the landscape of the mind, to the roving imagination, and where the latter may lead is anybody's guess.' 'Places are animated by thoughts, emotions, and memories, place becomes a powerful agent that attracts, inspires and bounds people'. According to Valk and Sävborg's (2018)[10] paper, 'Place-lore is a concept that refers to a symbiotic relationship between traditional communities and their environment, between tangible reality and the story world.' This fundamental phenomenological concept is expanded in Keith Basso's work, particularly in her article 'Wisdom Sits in Places: Notes on a Western Apache Landscape'[11]. He explains that 'environment encompass both created space and myths about place that contribute to the human production of space.' He added that places animate the ideas and feelings of the person who attend to them, these same ideas and feelings animate the places on which attention has been bestowed[12]

The Karbi worldview includes the notion of humans and other than humans co-existing in the same space, and the concept of space/place is significantly integrated into their traditional practices and narratives. Thus, a place can be utilized for settlement, farming, and other human activities if the agency of the place is venerated. There is a distinction between entities such as the ancestor's spirit, wild spirit, and territorial spirit, but mostly they are collectively propitiated, annually or after an interval of time after reaching or arranging a mutual agreement with the entities and these pacts are narrated. These pacts are made in the presence of a 'witness' which is mostly natural resources, such as plants, metals, trees, etc. The Karbi bring this contract into being through verbal communication. Sometimes the entities of place show their interest by disturbing the people through affliction, possession, or through dreams. In such cases, the *Kurusar*[13] further form an agreement with the entity.

In some situations, entities from different communities are also included[14] if they show an interest in being a part of the Karbi belief.

In the Karbi belief systems, places and spaces hold deep spiritual significance. They are considered sacred and are believed to be inhabited by spiritual beings, ancestors, and the divine. The Karbi people often designate certain geographical locations as sacred sites. These sites could be mountains, rivers, caves, or specific natural landmarks. They are believed to be portals to the spiritual realm, connecting the physical and metaphysical worlds. Sacred sites are revered as places of power, where rituals, ceremonies, and prayers are conducted to seek guidance, healing, and spiritual communion. Their belief systems often include spaces for rituals and ceremonies such as space for *Rongker*[15], *Chojun*[16], *Chomangkan*[17], and *Se-Karkli.* These spaces can be within nature or purpose-built structures like sweat lodges or community gathering places. Ritual spaces are considered sacred and serve as a focal point for spiritual practices, honouring the divine, and connecting with the spirit world. They provide a safe and supportive environment for communal worship, prayer, and traditional ceremonies.

The Karbi have a profound connection to their ancestral lands and territories. These lands are not merely physical territories but are seen as living entities with their own spirits and life force. The communities view themselves as custodians of the land[18], respecting and nurturing its resources while maintaining a reciprocal relationship with it. The land provides sustenance, spiritual nourishment, and a sense of connection. The Karbi community have specific places where they gather during significant seasonal events such as the cultural ground, the Karbi youth festival ground (Karbi Riso-Nimso Rong Aje), and the headmen's house. These gathering places facilitate the coming together of the community to celebrate harvests, solstices, equinoxes, or other seasonal milestones. They serve as spaces for cultural exchange, storytelling, dance, music, and the passing down of traditional knowledge from one generation to another. These gatherings reinforce communal bonds, honour ancestral wisdom, and strengthen the spiritual connection to the natural world.

THIRENG-VANGRENG AND THE CONCEPT OF LIMINAL SPACE IN THE KARBI WORLDVIEW

Exploring anomalous places and spaces often leads to intriguing narratives that captivate our imagination. These narratives can delve into mysterious phenomena, supernatural occurrences, or unexplained events. It offers glimpses into the fascinating world of anomalous places and spaces, where the boundaries of what we consider normal and possible are stretched, inviting us to explore the unknown and challenge our perceptions of reality. The Karbi ancestors believed that there is a space that exists in-between the village of the ancestors and the village of the living. According to Karbi scholar Dharamsing Teron (2008)[19],

> In the Karbi context, liminality encompasses the concepts of *thireng-vareng* and *miringrang. Thirengvangreng* (dead alive come alive) is the first person to roam both worlds and cross the barrier of life and death; he is the first person who can be in both places. The other liminal symbol is *miringrang*, which represents the gateway between life and death as well as the space that builds a bridge between the two worlds.

Miringrang is made using three colours during the *Chomangkan*[20]: red, white, black, or black white and red. When hanging, it mimics a rhombus while looking like a square. It is used when the souls are brought from the cremation ground[21] during the *Chomangkan* and are sent back with them, symbolising the closing of the link that connects both worlds. The *miringrang* serves as a portal for *Karjong* (soul) to return to the realm of the living to celebrate with their kin and community members.

KAZIRANGA

It is a renowned national park located in the state of Assam, India. Kaziranga is celebrated for its remarkable biodiversity and is particularly famous for being a UNESCO World Heritage Site and a significant conservation area for the Indian rhinoceros. Kaziranga National Park, composed of marshland and tall elephant grass, is home to various animal species, including the Indian rhinoceros, Asian elephant, Bengal tiger, wild water buffalo, and numerous bird species. The park's distinctive feature is its efforts to conserve and protect the Indian rhinoceros, which is one of the park's primary attractions. Kaziranga has been successful in its conservation initiatives, significantly increasing the population of this endangered species. The park also supports various conservation programs for other wildlife and plays a vital role in preserving the biodiversity of the region.

The name Kaziranga is linked to a number of legends, myths and place-lore. Place-lore consists mostly of narrative lore that is closely related to a toponym, location, or geographical feature. It may also include place, stories, place-bound beliefs, descriptions of customs, historical narratives and memories. According to Ajit Timung (2016)[22] Kaziranga is the assimilation of a Karbi name Kajir Ronghangpi. Kajir is the daughter of Hok Ronghang, she was taken to the dwelling of the deities when she was young and spent 24 human years there. When she came back to earth in search of her parents, she along with Sarsomon Ronghang[23] brought the *kindu*(rhino) to plough the fields and Kaziranga became a place where different species of birds, animals, and insects came to consume the paddy. Legend says that when Kajir went back to the abode of the deities she proclaimed that her birthplace would be known as the territory of Kajir Ronghangpi.

On 15th May, my informant Dilip Ronghang, a farmer from Disama, Karbi Anglong when asked about Kaziranga and if it was sacred, he replied that the Karbis respect every stream and landscape around them and due to its connection to Kajir Ronghangpi and its intertwinement with the local flora, wildlife, and geographical terrain, the place Kaziranga is considered sacred. He also added that the region is sacred since it is where Kajir Ronghangpi was born who brought the rhino and other inhabitants of the area. According to my other informant, the name Kajir Ronghangpi is sacred in itself since she achieved the status of a deity. He further stated that the rhinoceros has been gifted with strong skin and the freedom to roam the sanctuary because of the deity.

According to Dharamsing Teron's continuous discourse[24], she is propitiated in various places as a deity of harvest and wellbeing making Kaziranga sacred and anomalous. My other interlocuter

Kadom Terangpi, a teacher in a government school in Bagori areas of Kaziranga, expressed that there are many places surrounding Kaziranga that are considered sacred but since there are no inhabitants inhabiting the sanctuary at present she does not know if the sanctuary has some anomalous activity, however since the Karbis have strong belief in entities and sacredness of the places it is inevitable that Kaziranga is not considered sacred and anomalous.

RONGBIN

Rongbin is considered a space that exists among us. According to my interlocutor (knowledge sharer), Mr Lokesor Tokbi, from Rongjangphong, Diphu, (*Kurusar*) a ritual specialist, village headman an employee of the state government, *Rongbin* is an invisible village located in the dense forest of Inglongkiri mountain. Inglongkiri Mountain is also the territorial deity, particularly in the immediate vicinity of the greater Diphu localities/region and is propitiated in the East Karbi Anglong. According to Mr. Ronghang, this village used to be a normal village but because of brutal conflict with different tribes, some of the villages decided to bind the community using sacred chants to make the village invisible to the outsider. To clarify, outsiders here also include those Karbi who do not belong to that village. There have been cases where people have narrated their experiences of meeting an individual from *Rongbin*. Such persons have followed the people of Rongbin on the basis of an invitation issued by a village member (of *Rongbin*) and if they follow the instructions, it is said that they would reach home safely or find themselves in the dense forest in case they violate their instructions.

My interlocutor, Sarthe Dera who works as a beat-officer[25] nearby the Singhason area told me about the sighting of women during dawn nearby Elaichi Bagan, Langmili, Silveta, East Karbi Anglong and disappearing in the dense forest. When I asked him if there were any villages nearby, he replied 'No, I have mapped this forest there is none, and there have been several times even other rangers have seen women or clothes hung to dry in the forest, but (they) disappeared'. My informant Mr. Tokbi proceeded to show me the ritual text used for Rongbin, to make a village disappear when asked can you make your village disappear with this ritual, he replied 'this is not in the pure form so it will not make the village disappear but will help partially, for instance, it will make an individual from different village hallucinate or diverge from the location if they attempt to find the village. Klemja Ronghang, a knowledge sharer and resident of Matipung, Diphu, who originally hails from Udharjan, Loringthepi, East Karbi Anglong, has stated that the *Rongbin* people do not have a fixed locality; they keep shifting their village according to their needs or circumstances. He has also expressed occasions where his family member and residence of Jok-an Anglong located at Udharjan have had slight encounters with the people of *Rongbin.* Later in the conversation, he mentioned that the hidden village (*Rongbin*) still exists on the other side of his teak farm at Jok`an Anglong. Occasionally, their presence is felt through sounds and voices, such as people talking or walking. An anonymous informant from Diphu told me about an incident that happened four years ago which made a headline in the local news, an individual from a village fell in love with a girl from Rongbin. According to the family of the boy, they have been speaking for four to five years, and they have been meeting in the stream where they first met and only the boy could see the lady from Rongbin. And later they went to the place where they were invited by the people of Rongbin, 'although they couldn't see them, they could hear voices.'

PHI-PHU ARONG (VILLAGE OF THE ANCESTORS)

After *Chomangkan* (secondary post-mortem festival) has been performed, the souls go to 'Phi-phu Arong', (the village of ancestors). According to Dharamsing Teron (2023)[26], *Phi-phu Arong* is the term often used by the Karbis to refer to the village of the ancestors in the mundane world. Phi-phu Arong is said to have characteristics similar to those of the village of the living; the ancestors are believed to maintain the same status, occupations, and characteristics they had while alive. When a person dies, their *Karjong* (soul) is guided by *Charhepi*, a female dirge singer, who sings songs directing the *Karjong* to the place of the ancestors. The souls must pass through *Vo-mir Anglong*, located near Jatinga village in Haflong, Dima Hasao district[27]. According to my informant Kache Derapi, *Vo-mir Anglong* has its own charm when it comes to plants. It is said that even bamboo grows differently there (referring to the sprout). Hence, when the dead body is taken to the cremation ground all the things are placed rearward. It is believed that plants grow differently and invertedly in *Phu-phi Arong.*

Lt. Khirla Hansepi, a *Charhepi*[28] and *lunsepi* (traditional singer) from Chengbong, Dera Arong, West Karbi Anglong, in an interview in 2020 spoke about her experiences of Vo-mir Anglong. Whenever she visits her daughter in Haflong she would always look at the mountain from her daughter's terrace and admire the hill changing its color. According to the Karbi worldview, one can witness the rice cultivation of the ancestors and the dead kin during the rice plantation on earth. And the plants that resemble rice plants at *Vomir-anglong* would change their colour according to the harvest season. My other informant, the daughter of lt. Hansepi told me about incidents where people would go for trekking and suffer *Manghu* (get confused) on their way back because of the sacredness and concealed energy of the place.

RITLOPHARLA

Ritlopharla is a space for all souls to go after death and for those whose *Chomangkan* (ritual for the dead) has not been conducted. This is the place for the spirits of individuals who died violent deaths, such as death during childbirth, suicide, accidents, etc. The souls known as *Thi-Phalangno* are stranded in a location known as *Ritlo-pharla.* These souls are either bound due to their tragic deaths and the lack of *K-thi kecham/kecham* or *munso padam*, a rite involving purification carried out by *Kakre* (priest), done by the deceased's relatives. Until then, only members of the family are permitted to approach or touch the body. An informant claims that *Ritlo pharla* is located halfway between *Chom-arong* and the place of the residence. The soul of this kind of death keeps wandering around *Ritlopharla* and the world of the living. Because of the nature of their death, they are never at peace and return to trouble the living. This kind of spirit occasionally keeps appearing in people's dreams and bemoans their plight in Ritlopharla, occasionally pleading for food and water, and occasionally even attempting to harm them. After the purification ritual, their souls can be prepared to be sent to *Chom-arong*. After the purification ritual, their souls can be prepared to be sent to *Chom-arong*.

From one of the interviews, I came across a recent incident that happened years ago at Chephongsajir village, Diphu. During my interview about *Karjong*(souls) and *Ritlo-pharla*, I asked her if there were any incidents that had happened recently in the surrounding village. My interlocutor[29] replied:

Ebeng an si do ji, pangthir nang ji, chom arong ta lele, pirthe ta lele, chevang un lo, lasi chevang ham titi lo, cheplang tap cheplang pru varet, aduk do oh oh tangho, 'neke k do kosto oh', apiso accident amat thilot, amat niyom kuri pame me detlo, aron kaprek dunjui amat, amat angbong doh kok lo, harlong var ret lo amethang ahem long, an nang pi tha, neh hem ta ave, ne rit ta ve k, do sung pik, rong isi padosojo lo, dui bosor aprang, rong isi seh charki dun det lo, bhari bhari arlong thepo thepo k var, sang k lang hut si k klang, arve lahai ta van.

Translation and overview of the text: This interview was recorded and written in the Karbi language; however, the interlocutor adopted some words from the Assamese language, such as *kosto*, which loosely translates to 'hardship' in this context. *Niyom kuri* translates to 'rituals/rules' in Assamese, with *Niyom* meaning 'rules' and *kuri* meaning 'doing,' while dui bosor translates to 'two years' in Assamese. This incident tells the story of a woman who tragically died in an accident. Without the customary purification and nourishment, her spirit returned to haunt the villagers in their dreams, pleading for sustenance and lamenting her condition. She even resorted to throwing large stones as a sign of her presence. The entire village was unsettled by this haunting. Some people adhered to the old traditions, performing rituals to strengthen their well-being, while others sought ways to prevent her from haunting them. He also further stated that this type of spirit is trapped between the village of the ancestors and the village of the living, causing them to keep returning to the village of the living. These spirits can assume various shapes and forms, undergo tremendous tribulation, and often express that they are in pain or experiencing excruciating and agonising conditions.

LONGLE KEREM

Longle Kerem is a cursed space that accommodates the soul of the deceased who died due to tiger attacks which are categorized under *Thi-Phalangno*. In this type of incident, if the tiger kills the husband, the woman is referred to as a *me-ang*. The word *me* denotes 'wife' and *ang* – 'cursed',' so it is forbidden for anyone to marry a *me-ang* (cursed wife). The purification of the soul known as *kecham* (purification rite) has to be performed. This type of soul does not get reborn or go to the village of the ancestors even after the *kecham*, instead, they go to a space called *longle kerem,* although there are some exceptions.

According to Dharamsing Teron, *longe kerem* lit. translates to defeated earth. This concept of space which holds the soul of the deceased can be understood as the spatial domain in the Karbi worldview that is only set aside for deaths from tigers. Tigers in the Karbi domain hold a sacred place in their ontology. Hence the tigers are feared and considered sacred. However, some Karbi clans have the power to spiritually connect to animals and tame the body and spirits of the Tigers. The tamers are called *ucha*, (tiger and elephant priests) they have the power to speak, tame and command tigers and elephants to relocate to different geographical locations. and hence, they are forbidden to harm nature to maintain the knowledge that they possess. Hence, humans as much as they are intertwined with non-humans, their interaction can also be fatal not only in this space but also in other spaces such as the cursed space (longle kerem).

CONCLUSION

Shared experiences and stories provide communities with a profound sense of significance and emotional connection to specific locations. The true value of a place is only fully appreciated when its importance is acknowledged by the individuals who live there. Places play a significant role among the Karbi people, holding immense importance and featuring prominently in their belief systems and narratives. Take, for instance, the village of the dead, *Phu-phi arong*, which is situated in close proximity to the living yet maintains its own distinct identity. On the other hand, *Rongbin* exists in the realm of the living, yet it remains hidden and separated from the larger human communities while coexisting alongside them. Kaziranga holds a significant place in the community's shared memory, passed down through generations in stories and oral traditions. It serves as a valuable source of knowledge, offering insights into the past and prompting us to reconsider our understanding of these cultural beliefs.

Rongbin embodies innate knowledge that is transmitted down through meaningful interactions between visitors and the village's community members. Meanwhile, *Phi-phu Arong* serves the idea of life after death and continuity, it also provides a place of secure connection for the entire clan, including both living and departed family members. As the living population occupies the physical realm of Karbi Anglong, including places like Kaziranga, the departed reside in *Phi-phu arong*. This continuity is maintained through regular visits made by both the living and the deceased, as necessitated by the circumstances.

Places such as *Longle Kerem* depict domains that are forbidden or cursed, both for the living and for the *karjong* (souls) of the deceased. Narrative and place-lore often incorporate specific settings to establish a connection with the society.The story of Kajir Ronghangpi and the *Charhepi's* laments provide a compelling example of this approach. This narrative explores the journey of the spirit, drawing inspiration from various landscapes such as mountains and streams. As a result, it shapes the environments of traditional communities, both in their everyday lives and in imaginary worlds. Also, sacred sites often connect the realms of the living and the deceased, as shown in the stories mentioned.

ACKNOWLEDGEMENT

I would like to express my sincere gratitude to my supervisor, Dr Margaret Lyngdoh, from the University of Tartu, for her invaluable guidance and support throughout the process of writing this article. Her expertise, encouragement, and insightful feedback have been instrumental in shaping the direction and quality of this work.

Additionally, I would like to extend my heartfelt thanks to Dr. Dharamsing Teron, the Director of CKS (Center for Karbi Studies), for providing the inspiration and encouragement that motivated me to embark on this endeavour. His vision and passion for research have been a constant source of inspiration and have played a significant role in shaping the ideas presented in this article. I am sincerely grateful to my informant, Klemja Ronghang, and his family members from Loringthepi for sharing their remarkable knowledge and lived experience of Rongbin. I also extend my thanks to Sarthe Dera, Langmili Sub-Beat Officer, Karbi Anglong, for his valuable insights. I thank Lokheswor Tokbi, village headman, traditional belief practitioner, Rongjangphong, Karbi Anglong; Lt. Khirla Hansepi and Kache Derapi for their knowledge and guidance which have been invaluable in enriching my understanding of the subject matter and enhancing the overall quality of this article.

NOTES

1. The Karbi community comprise of five main Kur clans. They are the following: Engti (Lijang), Terang (Hanjang), Enghee (Ejang), Teron (Kronjang), and Timung (Tungjang), each of which is further sub-divided into several sub clans.
2. J. Moshahary, 'Clause Structure in Bodo and Dimasa: A Comparative Study', PhD thesis submitted to Tezpur University, Tezpur, 2013.
3. Ibid.
4. Ü. Valk and D.Sävborg, *Storied and Supernatural Places: Studies in Spatial and Social Dimensions of Folklore and Sagas*, Finnish Literature Society, Helsinki, 2018.
5. Frank J. Korom, 'A Telling Place: Narrative and the Construction of Locality in a Bengali Village' *in Narrative Culture*, Vol. 3, No. 1, Spring, 2016, pp. 32-66.
6. Ibid.
7. Ibid.
8. Entity refers to any kind of visible or invisible non-human being within the Karbi worldview. The word is also inclusive of many non-human biological organisms, such as animals and plants. Among the entities, it is worth mentioning deities (*arnaam*) and spirits, a category used in the present work to include forest entities (*ingnam-api*), the souls

of dead people (*chamburukso*), and other usually non-visible entities (Tita & Ronghangpi, 2023: 118)

9. Keith Basso, 'Wisdom Sits in Places: Notes on a Western Apache Landscape', in S. Feld and K.H. Basso, *Senses of Place*, Santa Fe: School of American Research, 1996, pp. 58-90.
10. Ü. Valk and D. Sävborg, 2018, op. cit.
11. Keith Basso, 1996, op. cit.
12. Ibid., p. 107.
13. Ritual specialist who uses traditional practices to determine the underlying cause of an illness or affliction.
14. Entities of different communities are included through the medium of Karbi propitiation. According to Margaret Lyndoh, Khasi entity *thelen*, is appeased in the neighbouring places of west Karbi Anglong.
15. Ritual performed to placate the local deity in order to protect the village and community from disease, calamities, and occasionally epidemics.
16. Ritual performed by a family or a household for well-being and prosperity.
17. A festival dedicated to the dead kin and ancestors.
18. The unseen forces or nature are the owner of spaces and places, but the Karbi people consider it to be their duty to look after it, according to the *Pirthe keplang asap* (origin narrative of creation).
19. Dharamsing Teron (Ed), *Karbi Studies: Memories, Myth, Metaphor*, Assam Book Hive, Guwahati, 2008.
20. *Chomangkan* is a ritualistic festival for the dead.
21. During the occasion the re-enactment of life and death is performed, the soul and effigy of the body are kept in the house of the host of *Chomangkan*.
22. Aji Timung, *The Myth behind the name Kaziranga*, Booklet published by Bhuban Chandra Terang, Integrated Tribal Development Project, Rongmongve Block, Karbi Anglong Autonomous Council, Diphu, 2006.
23. A deity who accompanied Kajir and helped her plough the fields.
24. Dharamsing Teron delivered a speech in a one-day workshop on 'Approaches to the Study of Kajir Ronghangpi – The Rhino Lady' was held on May 1, 2023, to celebrate the 8th foundation day of the Centre for Karbi Studies, Diphu.
25. Langmili sub-beat office, Karbi Anglong.
26. Dharamsing Teron delivered a speech in workshop, op. cit., 2023.

27. Jatinga has its own mysterious occurrence and is known as the 'valley of dead, migratory birds from all over the world would plummet to their deaths in huge number during the month of September and October. In accordance with R. Pavithra and Kakarla Sai Mitravinda, ornithologists have studied these strange bird deaths, but the causes are still unknown (Mitravinda & R).
28. Dirge singer participates in the Chomangkan ceremony also known as Charhepi. Their role in Chomangkan involves singing and guiding the soul to chom-arong.
29. The identity of the interlocuter has been kept anonymous due to the sensitivity of the interview and also due to the request of the individual.

CHAPTER 15

Kajir Ronghangpi

A Living Myth and Folklore of Other Communities/Regions from Northeast India

BANDITA TERONPI

INTRODUCTION

Myth is Universal. Local artefacts often distinguish popular territories. Identity has been a key focus in geography, folklore, myths, and legends contributing to the unique culture of the beautiful region. What attracts people to the North East of India is its stunning natural beauty, the distinctiveness of the inhabitants who are considered Indians despite their diversity, the unique local food, cultural practices such as folk music and dance, traditional attire, and above all, the captivating folklore and fascinating myths and legends of the region. North–East India is often referred to as 'a heaven for folklore' enthusiasts. There are four theories regarding the presence of myths. There are different theories regarding myths: rational, functional, structural, and psychological. According to the rational myth theory, myths were created to help people comprehend natural events and forces that impacted their daily lives. This theory also explains that the gods and goddesses were in control of all these natural events. This particular myth falls under the category of creation myths originating from various cultures. Creation myths describe the origins of humanity and how people came into existence. The Functional myth theory discusses how myths were utilized to impart moral lessons and guide social conduct. This particular myth explores the repercussions of human actions on individuals and society. Life consists of both positive and negative experiences that one may encounter. It is designed to maintain social order and promote stability within a society. Structural myths are myths originating from human emotion. This variety of myths illustrates the duality of the human psyche, encompassing both positive and negative aspects. [1]This theory of myth leads to another theory that focuses on human emotions originating from the human subconscious mind. All societies around the globe share similar fears and uncertainties related to the natural world, which often remain obscure and mysterious.

Indigenous communities reside within the natural environment, sustaining themselves through a variety of resources from the forests and nature. They have a strong connection to nature, which are reflected in their traditional stories and passed-down knowledge. They come into existence from the natural world. They possess captivating creation stories and beliefs that are truly intriguing. Many of these locations have become popular tourist destinations worldwide. Among the various tourist locations in North East India, I have selected a few that have fascinating myths, which made them renowned. Specifically, focusing on The Karbi community, this community resides along the other communities of the North east India. As mentioned earlier, all communities have many untold mysteries and legends that the world has to know. The Karbis has many living myth and legends like *Ha-imu*: The Rain Goddess, *Thong Nokbe*: The Great warrior, *Serdihun*: The Goddess of weaving, *Mosera*: The Creation or Origin narratives, *Sabin Alun*: The Karbi Ramayana etc.; on which researches are carried on. As for my work, this paper aims to highlight some of Northeast India's legendary tourist locations while introducing an age-old narrative about Kajir Ronghangpi, the legendary figure of the Karbis who claims that the name Kaziranga, famous as a World Heritage site in Assam, was derived from her. It also explores Karbi folklore entailment in determining the relationship between 'Kaziranga' and the legendary Karbi woman 'Kajir Ronghangpi'. The paper will also try to build the substance of 'Kajir Ronghangpi: Kaziranga' a tourist destination like the others destinations famous on Legends and folklore of North East India.

UNFOLDING THE MYTHS OF NORTH EAST INDIA

The North East of India, often known as 'The Seven Sisters with a brother state Sikkim', is today a land of folklore, myths, and tales. Some are unknown, while others are less well known, but all have attracted or continue to attract a vast number of people around the world because of its folklores. My area of focus is identifying those important places based on myths, legends and folklores, while discussing the locations and the reasons behind making them attractive.

The Legend of 'Ka Likai': Meghalaya is the first tourist destination in this category. Meghalaya often referred as the 'Scotland of the East', has become a popular tourist destination throughout the year. Shillong was the capital of earlier Assam, now part of the North East region accounts to be of great historical significances. The 'Nohkailikai Falls' in Meghalaya is situated 90 kilometres away from Shillong city in Cherrapunji, known for being the rainiest region on Earth. It is located in the East Khasi Hills district of Meghalaya state. It is also one of the adjacent states to Assam. This region is renowned for hosting five of the most prominent waterfalls, which have become India's preferred getaways. One of the waterfalls known for its folklore and myth is the 'Nohkailikai Falls'. This autumn marks the return of one of India's highest free-falling waterfalls, measuring 1115 feet (340 meters). According to Khasi tradition, the name 'Nohkailikai' in Khasi language refers to a woman named '*Likai*', with the prefix '*Ka*' indicating the feminine gender. '*Ka Likai*' is required to marry another person following her husband's passing (who died on his way to Sylhet) and a daughter from her prior union. Meanwhile, the husband began to feel envious of the child, because his wife's attention was divided between the child and her career, leaving him feeling unloved. One day, while 'ka likai' was away for work, her husband murdered the baby, dismembered her, and cooked her for a meal. She discovered the reality after consuming the dinner, upon observing her young daughter's fingers. After realizing she had consumed her own daughter, she fled in distress, overwhelmed with sorrow, and leaped from the waterfall's brink. In Khasi, *Noh* translates to 'jump' or 'leap'. The name 'Nohkalikai' refers to the 'Jump of Ka likai', the tallest waterfall that is known for a mythical tragic event. Another misconception is that everything is identical except for the character 'Li kai' slipping and falling off the edge of the waterfalls.[2]

The Myth of 'Tsomgo': Sikkim is a famous tourist destination known for being the location of Mount Kanchenjunga, the world's third tallest mountain. Sikkim is fascinated with the mythology of Tsomgo Lake, a lake known for predicting the future in ancient times. A dark and drab lake suggested impending dismal or gloomy days. The local inhabitants frequently engage in prayer rituals at the Lake. Another legend of the *Lepchas*, residents of Kanchenjunga, is that they are said to have been created by a god from the snow of Mount Kanchenjunga. The book *Khangchendzonga: Sacred Summit* states that Lepchas always stayed within the shadow of their sacred mountain, allowing the Great Mount to be visible from every Lepcha settlement.[3]

The Myth of 'Unakoti': The Lost Faces of Tripura is a mythical tourist destination located in the Unakoti district of Agartala. Unakoti refers to the 99,99,999 stone and rock sculptures carved in the rock faces inside a thick forest, each depicting a god or goddess surrounding a 30 feet tall head of Lord Shiva. According to the myth, 99,99,999 gods and goddesses were traveling with Lord Shiva to Kashi. They rested for the night in a jungle and continued their journey the next morning. None of the 99,99,999 gods woke up the next day, causing Lord Shiva dismayed with anger, popularly known as the Lord of Destruction, to turn all the followers of gods and goddesses into stone.[4]

The Legends of Assam: Assam is famous for Assam Tea, Maa Kamakhya Temple, the Mighty Brahmaputra River, and the Ahom Kingdoms, Mayong the Land of Black Magic, Majuli Island, and Kaziranga National Park. Out of which, three famous tourist destination from the list is selected that are renowned for their legendary and mythical status such as Kamakhya Temple and Mayong, to meet the objective of the study. The third destination of importance, Kaziranga, which is the main focus of the study, relates to a legendary figure of the Karbis called Kajir Ronghangpi, locally known as the 'Karbi Rhino Lady'. At first, the tourist attraction with myths or legends of Assam leads to *Mayong*, known for its black magic practices, is a well-liked tourist spot due to features such as Pobitora Wildlife Sanctuary and its association with occultism. Stories of persons vanishing, transforming into animals, and illnesses being healed through magic attract tourists due to their curiosity. The name Mayong is derived from the Sanskrit word *Maya*, which means 'illusion'. The Mayong Central Museum houses several ancient artefacts related to dark magic.

The Legend of Kamakhya Temple: According to Gutimali Goswami and Minakshi Das (2020)[5] in their article 'Rajaswala Kamakhya: An Eco-Feminist Analysis of Menstruation in the Man from Chinnamasta', the Kamakhya Temple in Assam is a well-known pilgrimage destination in India. One of the most renowned legends associated with the temple involves Lord Shiva and Goddess Parvati, where Lord Shiva, in a fit of anger over his wife's death, carried her body and performed the Tandav (dance of destruction). Lord Vishnu stopped her by dismembering her body with his chakra, causing the fragments to scatter across 108 spots in the country known as the Shakti Peeths. The reproductive section is said to have fallen into the Kamakhya Hills location. The Kamakhya Temple was then built in the area for devotees worldwide to seek blessings from Goddess Kamakhya (*Ambubachi*).

The above two famous tourist attractions of Assam, is based on their famous folklore or legends, which makes them different from other tourist destinations of Assam making a person curious to know about them. Now, the third tourist destination is famous for the one horned Rhinoceros, but very less people know about its existence connected to the folklore or oral narratives of 'Kajir Ronghangpi', whom from the term 'Kaziranga' was derived.

THE MYTH OF KAZIRANGA

Kaziranga National Park, a UNESCO World Heritage Site, is renowned for its population of one-horned rhinoceros. It is a vast wildlife sanctuary located in the Golaghat and Nagaon districts of Assam, bordering the Karbi Anglong East and West districts, together occupying an area of 10,434 square kilometers, the largest in the state. The documented history of Kaziranga, may be dated back to 1904, at the start of the twentieth century. It was referred to as the game sanctuary of the British administrators in colonial India. In 1950, Forest Conservationist P.D. Stracey renamed it to 'Kaziranga Wildlife Sanctuary.' The area covered is 429.93 square kilometers. In addition to the one-horned rhinoceros, the area also has a high concentration of tigers, elephants, wild Asiatic water buffaloes, and swamp deer. Birdlife International has acknowledged Kaziranga for its conservation efforts towards avifaunal species. In 2006, it was designated as a Tiger Reserve.

Kaziranga does not have its origins among the Assamese people of Golaghat and Nagaon. There are no references or archival sources available that may provide information on the origin or etymology of the term. Several assumptions in this regard as whether the term is derived from a thing, a person or some mythical or legendary figure. Researches on the history of it is getting a well-known attraction. According to the legend of the Karbi community, a divine being named Kajir Ronghangpi is said to have transported a Rhinoceros, known as *Kindu*, from heaven to earth as her pet as per the oral narratives of the commmunity. However, available internet sources recount a legend about a village girl named *Ranga* and a young man named *Kazi* from the Karbi community who fell in love[6]. Their parents did not approve of their romance, so they disappeared into the forest and were never seen again. Subsequently, the woodland was named 'Kaziranga' by the people. Though this statement achieved from the internet source is not related to the Karbi Narratives, yet the legend on 'kajir' is different from the Karbi prospective. Another tradition tells of Ahom King Rudra Singha, who once slept overnight at the residence of Chief Ranjit Phukan during his voyage.[7] He was delighted to receive a handwoven silk jacket as a present from Phukan's daughter, Kamala. In return, he praised her as a 'specialist' and gifted a piece of property in Rongai to her husband. The residents nearby began referring to that location as 'Kazirongai'. Another tale associated with Kaziranga is Madhabdev, a prominent follower of the Mahapurush Srimanta Sankardeva in the 16th Century. Madhabdev blessed a childless couple named Kazi and

Rangai, instructing them to dig a large pond in the area to ensure their legacy. During the 17th Century, the fourth legend, Ahom King Pratap Singha, was impressed by the taste of fish in the pond of Kaziranga. The sixth narrative involves a Karbi woman named *Kajir*, and Kaziranga is thought to have originated from the Karbi term *Kajir-a-rong*, which translates to 'the village of Kajir' (*Kajiror gaon*). Kajir, a youthful Karbi woman, formerly governed the region. Remnants of monoliths linked to Karbi governance were discovered around the region, confirming the claim.[8] Now, this claim has been further trodden by the folklore of the Karbi Community.

FOLKLORE OF KAZIR RONGHANGPI

The Karbi people claims that it is from their legendary character 'Kajir Ronghangpi', that the term 'Kaziranga' had its origin. There is less research data available about this specific community. However, the British officials documented information about the Karbi community as 'Mikirs,' as it was the earlier name for the Karbi people[9]. This statement has been included to make the reader understand the fact that the following secondary source of data written by the British officers will be as 'Mikirs' and not 'Karbi'. The fact is that oral tradition has been a primary medium through which knowledge and values have been transmitted in Indian society. From ancient times, storytellers known as bards or sages have orally transmitted important texts and scriptures, such as the epics Ramayana and Mahabharata.[10] Karbi ancestors also carried their migration story as they moved and established themselves in different areas. While not mentioning the Mosera, which presents a different origin theory of the tribe, official data indicates that the Karbis, after entering the Indian territory in the North East region in pre-historic times, began their settlement journey from the North Cachar, Khasi and Jaintia Hills to Kamrup, the plains of Nowgong, the north of the Brahmaputra in Darrang, Sonitpur, Kaliabor, and Kaziranga, according to records documented by British administrators. The Karbis who carried their journey continued, the rest chose to settle, leading to the presence of the Karbi Community in the district of Karbi Anglong as well as in Kamrup, Morigaon, Sonapur, Jagiroad, Nagaon etc. of Assam, including neighbouring states like Meghalaya, Nagaland and Arunachal Pradesh.[11]

Oral narratives or folklore is crucial in Karbi society for recreating and comprehending their history. In his book, Edward Stack noted that the Karbi people have a reputation for storytelling. The Karbis possess an enduring cultural legacy of oral narrative, which is greatly esteemed and held in high regard.[12] Kajir Ronghangpi, a 'mythical legendary' in folklore, is associated with the renowned Kaziranga National Park area. 'Kajir' is a revered deity among the Karbi people, believed to possess extraordinary abilities bestowed by the Gods. She is honoured and commemorated annually on the 5thof December in Kohora, near Kaziranga, by the community and organised by the Karbi Anglong Autonomous Council (KAAC). 'Kajir Ronghangpi', according to Karbi mythology, was Hok Ronghang's daughter, raised up by deities. Upon her return to the earth, she introduced the *Kindu* (Rhinoceros) into the Kaziranga region.

COLONIAL DOCUMENTS AND THE PRESENCE OF KARBIS IN KAZIRANGA

Valid evidence or documentation is crucial to substantiate the presence of the Karbi community in the area where the Kaziranga National Park is situated and to establish its connection with the Karbi community or Kajir Ronghangpi. To have a comprehensive understanding of the history of Kaziranga, it is important to not only research articles authored by local writers but also to study material written by British officials that discusses the presence of the Karbi community in the Kaziranga area.

In his book, William Robinson[13] gave a brief description of the 'Mikirs' that were located in the surrounding area. 'Mikir or Mikir Hills' is the title of the book that was used to acquire this information. He stated that the first division is composed of hills, the largest group of which within the valley is that of the Mikir Hills, which stand out in the plain, insulated from the southern mountains by the valley of the Jumna River. These extend from east to west about 63 miles, and are in breadth about 27 miles, occupying some area of 1700 sq.

miles. The hills projecting into the valley at Gowhatti, and extending from Nowgang to the Kamakhya Parbut.[14]

Another description from the book that describes the presence of Mikir or Mikir Hills is that:

> On the south bank of the river ... is greatest immediately east of the Dhansiri. The great projection to the north of the Mikir hills, ... being the cause of the Brahmaputra 'at that point taking a northerly direction, a deep plain has been preserved on its southern bank, extending from the river back –to the Naga hills, and comprising a breadth of about thirty miles'[15]. Yet another statement that adds to the relevance is that 'Mikir Hills – That division of the Nowgong district known as the Mikir hills occupies a tract of – hilly country covering some area of 1710 sq. miles. These hills are inhabited by a fine athletic and industrious race of people, called Mikirs. Living as they do in a I' due state of society, and possessing no written ...[16].

These descriptions are the evidence of the presence of the tribe or tribes that had settled in the area, as of all other tribes of the then Assam, it is only the Mikirs, Rengma Nagas and Kacharis that records their presence in the said belt.

During the course of my inquiry, I came across other official records that were published by Major John Butler[17] and J.P. Mills[18]. Many scholars, while writing about the tribes of Assam frequently acknowledge these two colonial ethnographers. J.P. Mills notes that the Rengma people continue to reside in Karbi Anglong, which was originally referred to as Mikir Hills, and this has been recorded. Around the beginning of the 1800s, the Rengmas migrated to the Mikir Hills. There is also the possibility of tracing the migration of the Rengmas through the books wrote by J.P. Mills. In the book 'The Angami Naga,' it is stated that:

> About a hundred years ago or more of the western Rengmas migrated North-West to the Mikir Hills, where they are still living.[19]

Further information that John Butler mentioned in his book was that beyond the Kuleanee River the Rengma boundary commences and terminates with the Dhunseeree river, separating Now-Gong from the Seebsaghur district.[20]. This record of Butler indicates the presence of Rengma Naga tribes' concentration along with the

Mikirs in the area. Edward Stack, in his book 'The Mikir,' published in 1908[21], not only provided a description of the Mikir people, but they also provided more information of the region in Assam where this particular tribe resided at the time. He stated that:

> The Mikirs were undoubtedly one of the most numerous and homogenous of the many Tibeto-Burman races inhabiting the province of Assam. From Sibsagar to Sylhet in the present Bangladesh the Mikirs inhabited this long stretch.[22]

Several excerpts from the book 'Census of India' Volume 1 written by E. A. Gait in the year 1891 offer proof that Mikir people were present in the Kaziranga area. He stated that The Deputy Commissioner of Tezpur Reports that he visited a Mikir village in which he found the numbers of the houses written on the drums of the occupants, who had been forbidden by their enumerator to use these instruments again until the census was over.[23] As the area of Kaziranga was diagrammed later, the whole stretching of the area along with the study of the population living in the area is crucial to find the probable origin of the legendary Kajir or the Karbis. Karbi population in the Kaziranga area settled firmly through the following lines, which demonstrate their economic transactions via waterways. As that,

'It's inland floating population is proportionately more numerous than that of any other district. As already explained, the whole of cotton from the Mikir Hills is brought down the Kallang by boat, and this channel is also extensively used, in preference to the Brahmaputra, by boatman who brings down mustard from the Majuli to Gauhati.'[24] It is also interesting to note here that the present name of the River *Kollong*, has been previously noted by the British Deputy Commissioner as *Kallang* indicates the name being termed by the Karbi people as *Lang* in Karbi means water. Again, the following statement in the records testifies it.

'The characteristic dements of Mikir topographical nomenclature are *Lang*, river water; *Langso,* small stream; *Inglong*, mountain; *Long*, stone; *Rong*, Village; *Sar,* chief. In the isolated mountainous block which fills the triangle between the Brahmaputra on the north, the Dhansiri valley on the west, these names are found everywhere, as well in the southern part now inhabited by the Rengma Naga from the hills across the Dhansiri as in the northern portion included in the Nowgong district and known more particularly as the Mikir hills.'[25]

THE WORD 'KINDU': THE FIRST MIKIR DICTIONARY

At the arrival of British colonial officers and Christian Missionaries, two different types of documents began to be documented for the history of the region, unlike many tribes in the northeast region of India. The primary sources include official records, data, and personal diaries of the officers sent to the region. The secondary sources consist of writings on the vocabulary of the tribes by missionaries who worked in the area. To comprehend the language for communication and spreading religion or education, Christian missionaries began documenting and creating dictionaries for all tribes in the region with whom they interacted. The evolution of new vocabulary is a natural process within every community, including the Karbi Community, as things and concepts develop. It is worth mentioning that creating a dictionary during that time was quite challenging due to limited communication and technology. The vocabulary in the dictionary of the time was restricted to words that were well-known within the community. In 1878, Rev. R. E. Neighbour published the first dictionary on the Mikir language titled 'A vocabulary in English and Mikir.' The inclusion of the term *Kindu* meaning 'Rhinoceros' indicates the community's familiarity with the rhinoceros.[26]More importantly, the information collected suggests that the Karbis were familiar with the species, which is significant considering that rhinos are not seen in every place due to their lack of widespread distribution. Another piece of evidence that supports the earlier occurrence is the presence of the term 'Kindu-Rhinoceros' in G.D. Walker's Dictionary of the Mikir Language, which was published in 1925.[27]

The outcome of the evidences presented above suggests that the name of the heritage site, 'Kaziranga National Park' was special in order to pay tribute to 'Kajir Ronghangpi', the legendary Karbi woman who was the daughter of King Hok Rongkhang, as stated in the Karbi Folklore. It is proved that the 'Mikir,' which is now known as the Karbi, resided in the area that is now known as Kaziranga National Park, as per the substantial sources from the colonial authorities. The research would not have been possible without the substantial supports that the documents provide. The existence of the Karbis have been documented by a number of foreign and British officials in a geographical range that stretches from the Brahmaputra in northern Assam to Sylhet in Bangladesh. This territory includes the Patkai Hills, which include the Kaziranga National Park or the forest tracts. There are still a significant number of Karbi people who live in the highlands or deep forests, where they are forest residents. There are many people who still maintain the old karbi religious and cultural practices, which allow them to preserve a deep connection to forest resources. Also, as a result of the 'Mikir Hills' being designated as a 'partially excluded area, governed by British Governors' a number of terms in the language known as 'Karbi' are now being identified or termed. These names have been adopted from languages such as Assamese, Khasi, and others. The inclusion of the term 'Kindu' (Rhinoceros) in the first dictionary, which was published in 1878, indicates the strong basis of Rhinoceros's relation with the Karbi.

CONCLUSION

Therefore, it can be concluded that the investigation on Kajir Ronghangpi: the Kaziranga is supported by multiple valid reasons. Firstly, the official documents produced by various British Officials confirm the presence of the Karbi People in the area. The second ground is the presence of the term *Kindu*, which is the Karbi word for rhinoceros. This term, found in the first vocabulary of the Karbi language compiled by RE Neighbor, a Christian missionary, in 1878, is clear indication of the Karbi-Rhino relationship in the area. Again, the statement becomes more strong as Karbi tribe glorifies and celebrates their legendary Kajir Ronghangpi, a Karbi princess annually at Kajir Ronghangpi Memorial Park at Kohora, a geographical area adjacent to the World Heritage Kaziranga National Park. Therefore, if the myth of *Ka Likai* folklore attracts attention to the famous *NohKaLikai Falls* in Meghalaya, the origin of the *Lepchas* from the snow of Mount Kanchenjunga, the myth of the predicting lake in Sikkim, the vanishing of humans into thin air or their transformation into animals in Assam's *Mayong* – 'Land of Black Magic,' and the legend of Lord Shiva and Goddess Sati Parvati and the 'Kamakhya Temple' are all based on significant cultural narratives with widespread beliefs and acceptance, then the mythology of Kajir Ronghangpi, linked to Assam's world-renowned heritage site 'Kaziranga National Park,' also stands firm. She is a living myth similar to all others of North East India.

NOTES

1. Renu Rani, 'Introduction of various Modern Theories of Myth' in *International journal of English Language, Literature and Humanities*, Vol. 3, Issue II, April, 2015, pp. 439-445.
2. 'Meghalaya Tourism (Signboard)', See at www.meghalayatourism.co.in (Accessed on 27/7/2023)
3. Pema Wangchuk and Mita Zulca, *Khangchendzonga: Sacred Summit,* Little Kingdom, Gangtok, 2007.
4. 'Tripura Tourism', See at www.tripuratourism.gov.in (Accessed on 27/7/2023).
5. Gutimala Goswami and Minakshi Das, 'Rajaswala Kamakhya: An Eco-Feminist analysis of menstruation in the man from Chinnamasta', in *International Journal of Management(IJM),* Vol. 11, Issue 3, March, 2020, pp. 967-975.
6. 'History about Kaziranga', Available at: https://www.kaziranga-nationalparkindia.in/history-about-kaziranga.html (Accessed on 12/6/2024).
7. 'Kaziranga National Park' , Availbel at https://www.newworldencyclopedia.org/entry/Kaziranga_National_Park (Accessed on 2/6/2024)
8. Available at www.google.com/amp/s/Timesofindia.indiatimes.com (Accessed on 2/6/2024)
9. Edward Stack, *The Mikirs*, David Nutt, London, 1908, p.36. (This book had been edited, arranged and supplemented by Charles Lyall, 1908).
10. Language and literature by Indian culture team, posted on November 16, 2023 https://indianculture.com/the-significance (Accessed on 6/6/2024).

11. Phukan Ch. Phangcho, *The Karbis of North-East India-The Karbis: A Spatio-Temporal Analysis in Tribal Geography* ,Angik Prakshan, North Sarania,Ghy-3, 2003,p. 26.
12. Dharamsing Teron, *Karbi Studies: Reclaiming the Ancestor's Voices*, Vol. 2, Assam Book Hive, 2012, p. 40.
13. William Robinson, *A Description Account of Assam: With a Sketch of the Local Geography and a Concise History of The Tea-Planter of Assam – A Short Account of the Neighbouring Tribes*, Sanskaran Prakashak, 1841.
14. Ibid., p. 20.
15. Ibid., p. 22.
16. Ibid., p. 329.
17. John Butler, *Travels and Adventures in the province of Assam*, Smith Elder, London, 1855, p. 307.
18. J.P. Mills, The Rengma Nagas, Macmillan and Co., London, 1922, p. 419.
19. Ibid., p. 2.
20. John Butler, op. cit., p. 126.
21. Edward Stack and Charles Lyall, op. cit., 1908.
22. Ibid.
23. E.A Gait, *Census of India, 1891,* Vol. 1, The Assam Secretariat Printing Office, Shillong, 1892, p. 32.
24. Ibid.
    Ibid., p. 88.
25. Ibid., p. 219.
26. Rev. R E Neighbor, *A Vocabulary in English and Mikir*, Baptist Mission Press, Calcutta, 1878, p. 56.
27. G.D. Walker, *A Dictionary of the Mikir Language,* Mittal Publication, New Delhi (1925), 2022 (Reprint), p. 84.

CHAPTER 16

Myth and Identity Formation

Revisiting the Oral Tradition of Kajir Ronghangpi

MONGOLSING RONGPHAR and THEJANI-I POHENA

INTRODUCTION

Every culture possesses its own distinct traditions and rituals that are deeply ingrained in their daily lives. However, at times, these narratives or behaviors may appear illogical or challenging to elucidate to individuals from different external groups or identities. These stories or rituals are a reflection of human experiences and are handed down from one generation to the next. The Karbis possess a wealth of cultural myths, although some of them may be uncertain due to a lack of historical records. Despite the importance of oral tradition in Karbi culture, the absence of proper documentation has made it challenging to safeguard these valuable cultural practices. One particular myth that warrants a closer examination is the myth of Kajir Ronghangpi, which deserves a fresh perspective. Throughout history, myths have had a profound impact on shaping both personal and collective identities. They offer narratives that give individuals and communities a sense of meaning, purpose, and belonging. This chapter aims to analyse the connection between myth and the shaping of identity. It delves into the process of myth creation, transmission, and interpretation, and explores their impact on individuals and communities. The focus is on the surviving narratives of the legend of Kajir Ronghangpi, which have been primarily passed down through oral traditions. Given the significance of myths in shaping identity of the community, this chapter aims to explore how myth influences a community's collective consciousness, worldview, and understanding of history.

The relationship between myth and identity formation is a vital aspect of human culture because 'myth is closely related to the cultural identity of places and the culture of its people'[1]. Within this context, oral tradition serves as a significant source for the creation, transmission, and interpretation of myths. Through generations of oral storytelling, myths have played a crucial role in shaping personal and collective identities, providing individuals with a sense of belonging and offering communities a shared narrative framework. Every culture has a unique mythology, a set of sacred stories about divine beings and events with cosmic significance, from the start of life to what happens after death. These myths have been passed down the generations to make sense of the world and their own lives. These myths have fascinated people for centuries with their variety and interesting tales. People read mythologies because of the insight they provide about human nature, interpersonal dynamics, and societal norms.

According to Clyde Kluckhohn (1959)[2] in his essay 'Recurrent Themes in Myths and Mythmaking' while discussing the Navaho Mythology suggests the similarities in myth and noted that it usually incorporates a 'separation from both parents at an early age' and 'antagonism and violence toward near kin, though mainly siblings or father-in-law'[3] and further presented that the 'hero's achievements are realized by his immediate family, and redound in some way to their benefit and that of the larger group to which the family belongs'[4]. The myth of Kajir Ronghangpi imbibes the same. In Ajit Timung's *The Myth behind the Name of 'Kaziranga'* (2010) Kajir Ronghangpi was separated from both parents at an early age and her kin, immediate brother, Khoi Ronghang had to suffer from his fellow men[5]. Similarly, William Bascom (1965)[6]in his article, 'The Forms of Folklore: Prose Narratives' proposed comprehensive characteristics of myth, legend and folktale. According to Bascom, myth is believed to be a fact of a remote past of a different world or other or earlier and considered to be sacred with non-human qualities. Kajir Ronghangpi, in The Myth behind the Name of 'Kaziranga' ascended to heaven with the human body. Sarsomon Ronghang aided her when she was back to earth for a momentary stay in bringing back her brother Khoi Ronghang to life, reminding us of Doctor Faustus, a Renaissance hero in the play Doctor Faustus by Christopher Marlowe, who takes the help of Mephistopheles in performing the art of magic.[7] In this exploration, the paper will delve into the oral tradition of Kajir Ronghangpi, after whom the Karbi people believe that Kaziranga National Park has been named after her keeping in mind how it influences personal and collective identity as well as its role in contemporary society from the lens of mythology.

There are various theories concerning myth, however, not all theories are equal or express similar ideas because each describes a distinct aspect of myth. It is difficult to grade mythological theories. There are various hypotheses concerning the beginning of the myth, but none of them provides definitive solutions to the question of how the myth came to be. To Robert A. Segal (2004)[8], '...myth is just a story' but to folklorists, it's about the creation of the world. Greek mythographer Euhemerus's concept of myth, known as Euhemerism, proposed that myths originated from historical events and individuals who were later deified and mythologized[9]. True, that Euhemerus' works have been lost, but his ideas were influential and inspired subsequent scholars to further explore and develop his theory. Although it has had a significant impact, it is not the only or prevailing method of studying myths in contemporary times. Contemporary scholarship acknowledges the complex and diverse aspects of myth, including its psychological, symbolic, and cultural dimensions.

KARBI ORAL TRADITION AND THE MYTH OF KAJIR RONGHANGPI

Alessandro Portelli in *The Death of Luigi Trastulli and Other Stories: Form and Meaning in Oral History* (1991)[10] explores the use of oral history as a means of understanding and interpreting collective memory, social movements, and cultural change and further highlights the power of oral history in capturing marginalized voices and challenging dominant historical narratives. He argued that 'oral sources are a necessary (not a sufficient) condition for a history of the non-hegemonic classes...Nevertheless, the historical discourse remains firmly in the hands of the historians[11].' This is true in the case of Karbis as well. This is rightly reflected in their songs or rituals. The tones, verse and accents of the oral discourse convey the history and identity of the Karbis. Jan Vansina in *Oral Tradition as History* (1985)[12] states that oral tradition plays a vital role in the reconstruction of historical events and the understanding of the past in societies where written records are absent or scarce. He asserts that oral tradition are 'messages' not only a source of the 'past but historiography of the past' and has a crucial role to 'play in the reconstruction of the past'. He further asserts that it should not be dismissed as unreliable or mythological; rather, it should be approached as a valuable and distinct source of historical information that can offer unique insights into the past as it provides a dynamic and living connection between past and present, offering a rich tapestry of narratives, cultural practices, and historical perspectives that might otherwise remain hidden.

In the oral tradition, myths are born from the collective imagination and experiences of a community. Anthropologist Claude Levi-Strauss (1966)[13] illuminates this process, stating, myths are made of words, but words whose resonances, silences, absences, and equivocations form part of their meaning. Oral narratives undergo transformations as storytellers incorporate their own interpretations and experiences into the stories. The oral tradition enables myths to remain dynamic, adjusting to the needs and values of every generation.

The Karbi people, also known as *Mikir* or *Arleng*[14], are an indigenous community predominantly residing in the northeastern region of India. They have a rich cultural heritage and a vibrant oral tradition that has been passed down through generations. The oral tradition of the Karbi people plays a significant role in preserving their history, cultural practices, and beliefs. It encompasses various forms of storytelling, folk songs, myths, legends, and proverbs. The oral tradition serves as a means of education, entertainment, and a way to transmit knowledge from one generation to another.

Storytelling is an essential part of Karbi oral tradition. Elders and respected community members often narrate stories to teach moral lessons, share historical events, or explain natural phenomena. Folk songs and chants are another integral aspect of the Karbi oral tradition. In fact almost every tale told is in verse or metrical form[15]. These songs are sung during festivals, rituals, and social gatherings. They reflect the community's joy, sorrow, love, and aspirations. The songs often revolve around themes such as agricultural activities, love, nature, and cultural identity. The Karbi oral tradition also encompasses myths and legends that explain the origin of the universe and the Karbis, and the relationship between humans and nature. These myths often incorporate elements of animism and spiritual beliefs. They depict the close connection between the Karbi people and the natural environment, emphasizing the need for harmony and respect for nature. The myth of Kajir Ronghangpi is one such tradition that provides a dynamic and living connection between nature and the Karbis, offering a rich tapestry of narratives, cultural practices, and historical perspectives. It is believed that the Karbis resided in the Kajiranga area, which is now known as the Kaziranga National Park. Remnants of shattered monoliths, bearing a striking resemblance to the historical Karbi traditions[16], can still be found in the region. In order to delve into the oral traditions of Kajir Ronghangpi, it is crucial to shed some light on the narratives or legends surrounding the origin of the word Kaziranga. The origin of the name Kaziranga is surrounded by multiple myths, as found in local legends and historical records and the official website of Kaziranga National Park.

Myth 1: TThe second mythology surrounding this park concerns Rudra Singha, the 30th Ahom King, who spent the night in Chief Ranjit Phukan's home while travelling to Guwahati. He was amazed by Phukan's daughter, Kamala's weaving skills at the time because she had fashioned him a magnificent silk jacket as a present. The chief referred to her as Kazi, which is another word for 'an expert in a field'. Chief Ranjit Phukan impressed by her work gave her a husband, Rongai and a land. Eventually, locals began naming that land Kazirongai, and eventually, it became Kaziranga[17].

Myth 2: There was a barren couple in the area. That couple tried numerous medical procedures as well as spiritual and religious practitioners to bear a child, but nothing was successful. They eventually met Madhabdev, the principal disciple of the illustrious Mahapurush Srimanta Shankardeva[18]. To ensure that their name would live on even after they were gone, Madhabdev urged the couple to dig a pool in the area so that it benefits the locals thereby their name living perpetually. 'Testimony to the long history of the name can be found in some records, which state that once, while the Ahom king Pratap Singha was passing by the region during the seventeenth century, he was particularly impressed by the taste of fish, and on asking was told it came from Kaziranga[19].'When he discovered the beginnings and development of the pond, he named it Kaziranga.

Myth 3: The word *Kazi* in the local language (Karbi) means 'Goat' and Rangai means 'Red'. Kaziranga thus means the 'Land of red goats (Deer) [20]. However, the word *Kazi* does not bear any meaning in Karbi Language. It may be a corrupted word or mispronunciation for the word *Karjo*, meaning a wild goat in Karbi.

Myth 4: Many historians believe that Kaziranga might have been derived from the Karbi phrase Kajir-a-rong, which means 'the village of Kajir' (kajiror-gaon). Kajir is a popular name among the Karbis for a girl child, and it was formerly thought that a Kajir-named woman governed the region. This claim appears to be supported by fragments of Karbi-related monoliths that have been found around the region[21].

The fourth myth and its descriptions suggest that there was a person with the name Kajir Ronghangpi. Now what makes it interesting is the fact that there are several narratives around the legend Kajir Ronghangpi. These narratives speak of extraordinary abilities and character, whose deeds and virtues have become woven into the fabric of Karbi folklore. According to the oral tradition, this individual possesses an indomitable spirit, a force that transcends the ordinary. The accounts vary, but many speak of a commanding presence, a figure of remarkable stature and strength. Despite the absence of written records, the oral tradition keeps the memory of this legendary figure alive, emphasizing their impact on the communities and societies they encountered. One of the first written records of

Kajir Ronghangpi is found in *The Myth Behind name 'Kaziranga'* by Ajit Timung (2010)[22], of Lorulangso, Diphu. According to Timung, Kajir Ronghangpi, her sister Kading Ronghangpi, and brother Khoi Ronghang were the children of Hok Ronghang and Bong`e Teronpi. Hok Ronghang was a village headman, who expanded his kingdom in and around *Tovar Kethom* after fleeing from the notorious treatment of the Jaintia kings. This narrative tells about the migration of Karbis from the Jaintia settlements to *Kajiranga* and its surrounding areas, in the story mentioned as *Tovar Kethom.* Kajir Ronghangpi is portrayed as a divine being with the ability to control the elements and possesses supernatural powers and is closely associated with nature and its forces. The myth highlights the significance of unity and cooperation among the people while imparting moral values such as compassion, and resilience and encourages individuals to act selflessly and with integrity with a sense of recognizing that their actions have consequences that extend beyond themselves. In the myth, Kajir Ronghangpi's extraordinary deeds and moral character lead to her ultimate ascent to heaven. This signifies her transformation into a divine being and serves as a symbol of reward for her selfless actions and contributions.

Another narrative of Kajir Ronghangpi was narrated by His Highness Harsing Ronghang, the 41st Karbi King and recorded by Elwin Teron (2023)[23], a well-known public figure among the Karbis. The narratives deviate from that of Ajit Timung's writings. According to this narrative, Kajir Ronghangpi's parents were Sereng Ronghang and Kare Engtipi. Sereng Ronghang had a brother named Dok Ronghang. The Couple had two daughters; Kareng Ronghangpi and Kajir Ronghangpi and a son. The daughters were known for their aesthetic beauties which caught the attention of the Medhibura. Upon rejection of the proposal for marriage by Kareng, she was killed by the Medhibura. Fearing Medhibura and his associates, that they might come for Kajir as well, a solution was poured on her which turned her into a red color. Hence, Kajir Ranga, *Kajir* (Name) and *Ranga* (Red Colour). The narrative later reveals that Kajir Ronghangpi was also murdered by the Ahoms.

The above narratives reveal Kajir Ronghangpi lived somewhere in the present Kaziranga National Park however, the names of her parents are different in both the narratives. Further investigation and research may reveal more oral narratives and each narrative may be distinct from each other. That's the reality of myth and orality. However, through the power of oral tradition, the legend persists, binding generations together and reminding us of the enduring power of storytelling to preserve the memory of extraordinary individuals who have left an indelible mark on the collective consciousness.

MYTHS AND IDENTITY FORMATION

Myths not only shape personal identity but also contribute to the formation of collective identity. Based on this, sociologist Émile Durkheim (1995)[24] argues that myths are to societies what dreams are to individuals, collective representations of society's deepest values and aspirations. Myths bind communities together, reinforcing shared values, customs, and traditions. They provide a cohesive narrative that helps establish a sense of belonging and solidarity within a collective identity. Myths also play an important role in shaping collective identities, as they are often associated with cultural or national identity. Myths can serve as a means of reinforcing cultural values and traditions and can provide a sense of cohesion and unity within a group.

The myth of Kajir Ronghangpi holds enormous significance in the identity formation of the Karbi community as it not only reinforces their reverence for the natural environment but also plays a vital role in shaping their collective consciousness and understanding of their place in the world. It can be seen as a form of cultural resistance and empowerment for the Karbis. As an indigenous community, they have historically faced marginalization, loss of land, and cultural assimilation due to external forces. The myth acts as a tool for asserting their distinct identity and reclaiming their connection to the land. By portraying Kajir Ronghangpi as a powerful guardian and protector, the myth challenges dominant narratives that undermine or dismiss the significance of indigenous cultures and their relationship with nature. It plays an important role in shaping collective identity, as they often provide a shared cultural narrative that reinforces a group's sense of identity and belonging. It enriches a sense of belonging and shared identity that individuals feel as members of a larger social group, such as a nation, ethnic group, or cultural community. Collective identity is shaped by a variety of factors, including shared history, culture, language, religion, and values. Since collective identity is shaped by shared experiences of oppression or marginalization, the myth of Kajir Ronghangpi may be used to challenge dominant cultural narratives and to assert alternative perspectives on history and identity. The civil rights movement in the United States used myths of resistance and heroism to challenge the dominant narrative of white supremacy and to assert the value and dignity of Black lives. Similarly, the myth is also reconsidered as the Karbis revisit the narratives of how and why the community has not been credited, despite being the original settlers of the place.

Cultural theorist Stuart Hall (1997)[25] suggests, 'if meaning is the result, not of something fixed out there, in nature, but of our social, cultural, and linguistic conventions, then meaning can never be finally fixed.' Similarly, as societies evolve; new interpretations of myths emerge, reflecting contemporary concerns and challenges. Reinterpreting myths ensures their continued relevance in shaping identities and addressing the needs of changing communities. Robert Segal (2004)[26] in *Myth: A Very Short Introduction* echoes that of Hall that myths are dynamic and can be adapted to new contexts; they are not static, unchanging, or uniform. Myths are not static and can be interpreted and reinterpreted over time. As societies change and evolve, myths can be adapted to reflect new social, cultural, and political realities. However, reinterpretation can also lead to the loss of original meanings and values and can result in the creation of new myths that may not reflect the original cultural context. Levi-Strauss, (1967)[27] in his essay 'The Structural Study of Myth', has laid the basic idea that myths are passed down through generations, not arbitrary or random but rather organized according to specific structures. He argues that these structures can be analyzed and understood through the examination of binary oppositions; contrasting concepts or ideas, such as life and death, male and female, and nature and culture. He further contested that myths can be understood as systems of signification, similar to language. Just as words gain meaning through their relationships with other words, myths gain significance through the relationships and patterns created by the binary oppositions they contain. The myth of Kajir Ronghangpi, has been interpreted and reinterpreted by individuals and has been passed down from the generations based on the necessities and cultural assimilations. Therefore, variations in the oral narration of the same have been found in different places among the Karbis.

In contemporary society, myths continue to hold significance, albeit in different forms. Cultural historian Joseph Campbell (1991)[28] asserts the function of mythological symbols is to give you a sense of 'Aha! Yes. I know what it is. He states that 'Myths are clues to the spiritual potentialities of the human life.' Myths, whether in traditional oral narratives or modern storytelling mediums, provide individuals with a sense of meaning and purpose. They offer insights into the human condition, provide moral guidance, and offer perspectives on existential questions.

Myths continue to play an important role in contemporary society, shaping personal and collective identities in a globalized world. With the rise of digital media, myths can be shared and transmitted across cultures and borders, leading to new forms of identity formation. However, the proliferation of myths in contemporary society also raises questions about authenticity, appropriation, and cultural ownership. The role of myths in contemporary society is complex and multifaceted. On the one hand, myths continue to play an important role in shaping personal and collective identities, providing individuals with a sense of purpose, guiding values and beliefs, fostering a sense of belonging, and offering comfort and resilience in difficult times. However, in today's globalized and interconnected world, myths are also subject to new forms of appropriation, reinterpretation, and commodification. The myth of Kajir Ronghangpi exemplifies how myths can shape cultural identity, instil a sense of pride, foster environmental conservation, and maintain collective memory.

It holds immense significance in the identity formation of the Karbi people. It serves as a cultural emblem, reinforcing their deep-rooted connection to the land, wildlife, and ancestral heritage. By identifying themselves with Kajir Ronghangpi, the Karbis establishes a sense of belonging and pride in their unique cultural identity. The myth becomes a narrative thread that links them to their environment, their history, and their shared values.

The myth of Kajir Ronghangpi not only shapes cultural identity but also acts as a catalyst for environmental conservation. The connection with nature inspires the Karbi people to view themselves as guardians of the land and its biodiversity. The myth promotes a sense of responsibility and reverence for the environment, motivating the community to protect Kaziranga National Park, known for its population of one-horned rhinoceroses. It is a common belief among the Karbis that *Kindu* (Rhinoceros) is *Lokhi Api*[29]. An apparition of Rhinoceros in a dream is believed to be a good fortune for the Karbi people. As the myth narrates Rhinoceros was used for cultivating then. Kajir Ronghangpi was believed to have been looking after the Rhinoceros after Sarsomon Ronghang failed to take it back to heaven.

Myths serve as vehicles for cultural transmission, ensuring the continuity of traditions, values, and beliefs. In today's scenario, the myth of Kajir Ronghangpi has been treated as an integral part of the Karbi community's storytelling traditions. Through oral retellings, the myth is passed down from one generation to the next, fostering social bonds and reinforcing the shared cultural heritage. This collective memory sustains the Karbi people's connection to their past, preserving their unique identity and providing a sense of continuity amidst the changing dynamics of contemporary society.

The Karbi myth of Kajir Ronghangpi and its association with Kaziranga National Park vividly demonstrates the profound role of myth in contemporary identity formation. This myth serves as a cultural anchor, providing the Karbi community with a sense of belonging, pride, and environmental stewardship. By linking their identity to this myth, the Karbi people maintain their cultural heritage, nurture a conservation ethic, and pass on their traditions to future generations. The power of myth extends far beyond the Karbi community, as myths worldwide continue to shape individual and collective identities, instilling a sense of meaning, connection, and purpose in the modern world.

CONCLUSION

The oral tradition, with its inherent flexibility and adaptability, has played a crucial role in the formation, dissemination, and understanding of myths. These stories, in turn, shape personal and collective identities, fostering a sense of belonging and guiding individuals in navigating life's complexities. As time goes on, the re-evaluation of myths guarantees that they remain meaningful and impactful. In today's world, myths still play a significant role, offering people a sense of purpose and linking them to a larger shared story. Postcolonial theorists such as Franz Fanon, Edward Said, Homi Bhabha, and others delve into the psychological and political consequences of colonization on those who were colonized. The story of Kajir Ronghangpi can be interpreted as a rebellious response to the marginalization imposed by external forces. It enables the Karbi community to reclaim their indigenous knowledge, rediscover their ancestral land, and question the prevailing narratives imposed upon them. Although the myth may have different versions, they all agree that there was a woman named Kajir Ronghangpi and the Karbis settled in the Kaziranga area. *The book, The Mikirs* by Edward Stack and Charles Lyall, published in 1908, provides evidence supporting this conclusion.[30] The myth also highlights and encourages the fight against gender-based discrimination and oppression. It examines the possibility of significant change within the Karbi community. It sheds light on the gender dynamics within the Karbi Community. Kajir Ronghangpi, a young girl who defies societal expectations and questions established norms. The myth empowers Karbi women and contributes to the formation of a gendered identity that challenges societal norms.

Thus, the legend of Kajir Ronghangpi functions as a cultural repository that preserves and passes down shared recollections. Through the oral traditions, the Karbi community upholds a vibrant link to their history, guaranteeing the perpetuation of their cultural customs, principles, and convictions. This vibrant process of cultural transmission nurtures a feeling of connection, collective past, and intergenerational unity within the Karbi community. The oral tradition of the Karbi community highlights the significance of myth as a form of alternative storytelling, a means of defiance, and a storehouse of shared recollections. Through a careful examination and thoughtful analysis of myths, we can uncover valuable insights into the intricate processes of shaping identity, preserving culture, and driving societal change. The story of Kajir Ronghangpi serves as a powerful example of how myths can shape and reinforce identities in the midst of external challenges and the evolving dynamics of the contemporary era.

NOTES

1. Jenny Gil Sousa, 'The Myths of the Origin and the Cultural Identity: The presence of D. Dinis in the imagination of the people of Leiria'. Available at https://europe-nations.estudosculturais.com/pdf/0171i.pdf . (Accessed on 28/04/24).
2. Clyde Kluckhohn, 'Recurrent Themes in Myths and Mythmaking', in *Daedalus*, Vol. 88, No. 2, Spring, 1959, pp. 268-279.
3. Ibid.
4. Ibid.
5. Ajit Timung, *The Myth behind the name Kaziranga* , Booklet published by Bhuban Chandra Terang, Integrated Tribal Development Project, Rongmongve Block, Karbi Anglong Autonomous Council, Diphu, 2006.
6. William Bascom, 'The Forms of Folklore: Prose Narratives', in *The Journal of American Folklore*, 78(307), pp. 3-20.
7. Ajit Timung, 2010, op. cit.
8. Robert A. Segal, *Myth: A very Short Introduction*, Oxford University Press, Oxford, 2004.
9. Wikipedia contributors,'Euhemerism' in *Wikipedia, The Free Encyclopedia*. Retrieved 19:20, May 20, 2023, from https://en.wikipedia.org/w/index.php?title=Euhemerism&oldid=1150721271(Acccessed on 19/4/2023).
10. Alessandro Portelli, *The Death of Luigi Trastulli and Other Stories: Form and Meaning in Oral History*, State University of New York Press, New York, 1991.
11. Ibid., p. 56.
12. Jan Vansina,*Oral Tradition as History*, The University of Wisconsin Press,Wisconsin, 1985, pp. 197-200.

13. Claude Levi-Strauss, *The Savage Mind*,(Published by Weidenfeld & Nicolson), University of Chicago Press,Chicago, 1966, pp. 15-17.
14. Teron Dharamsing, 'Migration memories in Karbi Oral Tradition' in Dharamsing Teron (Ed.) *Karbi Studies: Memories, Myths and Metaphor*, Assam Book Hive, Guwahati, 2008, pp. 180-189
15. Ibid.
16. New World Encyclopedia, 'Kaziranga National Park', https://www.newworldencyclopedia.org/entry/Kaziranga_National_Park#cite_note-2. (Accessed on 29/04/24).
17. NewWorld Encyclopedia, 'Kaziranga National Park', https://www.newworldencyclopedia.org/entry/Kaziranga_National_Park#cite_note-2 . (Accessed on 29/04/24)
18. Available at Kaziranga National Park Website, https://www.kaziranganationalparkindia.in/history-about-kaziranga.html . (Accessed on 29/04/24)
19. Vinod Bihari Mathur, Ashok Kumar Verma, Nigel Dudley, Sue Stolton, Marc Hockings and Robyn James, 'Opportunities and Challenges for Kaziranga National Park , Assam over the next Fifty Years' (2005), Available at:https://www.semanticscholar.org/paper/OPPORTUNITIES-AND-CHALLENGES-FOR-KAZIRANGA-NATIONAL-Mathur-Verma/2af8105eb0830789f77256fb3bed56758e9d306c (Accessed on 8/9/2023).
20. Mathur, V.B.; Sinha, P.R.; Mishra, Manoj, 'UNESCO EoH Project_South Asia Technical Report No. 7–Kaziranga National Park' http://www.enhancingheritage.net/docs/UNESCOEoH_Project_South_Asia_Technical_Report_07_v1.pdf, p.14-15 (Accessed on 29/04/24) .
21. New World Encyclopedia, op. cit., (Accessed on 29/04/24).
22. Ajit Timung, op. cit., 2010.
23. Teron, Elwin, 'Kajir Ronghangpi: The legends in Rongkhang', Unpublished Work, 2023.
24. Emile Durkheim,*The Elementary Forms of Religious Life*. (Translated in English by Karen E. Field), The Free Press, 1995.
25. Stuart Hall (Ed.), *Representation: Cultural Representations and Signifying Practices,* Vol. 2, Sage Publications, New Delhi, 1997, p. 24.
26. Robert A. Segal, op. cit., 2004.
27. Claude Levi-Strauss, Claude, 'The Structural Study of Myth'. *The Structural Study of Myth and Totemism*, Tavistock Publications, London, 1967, p. 58.
28. Joseph Campbell, *The Power of Myth*, Anchor Books, New York, 1991, p. 8

29. Lokhi-Api – harbinger of good harvest. The Karbi considers Kindu as harbinger of good harvest.
30. Edward Stack, *The Mikirs*, David Nutt, London, 1908, p. 36. (This book had been edited, arranged and supplemented by Charles Lyall, 1908), p. 2.

Contributors

AMPHU TERANGPI, Research Scholar, Centre for Folk Culture Studies, University of Hyderabad, Hyderabad, Telangana.

ANJANA ENGTIPI, Research Scholar, Department of History,. Assam University (Central University), Diphu Campus, Assam.

ARNIKA TERANGPI, Assistant Professor, Department of History, Bokajan College, Assam.

BANDITA TERONPI, Assistant Professor, Department of Political Science, Lumding College, Lumding, Assam.

BARASHA RANI DAS, Assistant Professor, Department of Geography, Sibsagar Girls College, Sivasagar, Assam.

BARNALI SARMAH, Assistant Professor, Department of Political Science, L.G.B Girls' College, Tezpur, Assam.

BEENA RONGPIPI, Assistant Professor, Department of Commerce, Diphu Govt. College, Diphu, Assam.

DHARAMSING TERON, Director, Centre for Karbi Studies, Diphu, Assam.

JUNMONI HANSEPI, Assistants Professor, Department of History, Bhattadev University, Assam.

KADOMBINI TERANGPI, Assistant Professor, Department of History, Diphu Govt. College, Diphu, Assam.

KARENG RONGHANGPI, Assistant Professor, Department of English, Diphu Govt. College, Diphu, Assam.

LANGMILI TERANGPI, Assistant Professor, Department of History, Semson Sing Engti College, Baithangso, Assam.

MAGGIE KATHARPI, Assistant Professor, Department of English, Diphu Govt. College, Diphu, Assam.

MIRBIN KATHARPI, Assistant Professor, Department of History, Bokajan College, Assam.

MONGOLSING RONGPHAR, Assistant Professor, Department of English, H.P.B. Girls' College, Golaghat, Assam.

NITYANANDA DEKA, Associate Professor, Department of Geography, Gauhati University, Assam.

RAMESH KATHAR, Assistant Professor, Department of Political Science, Eastern Karbi Anglong College, Assam.

RASHMI ENGTIPI, Assistant Professor, Department of History, Don Bosco College, Diphu, Assam.

RENGKA TIMUNGPI, Assistant Professor, Department of Education, Diphu Govt. College, Diphu, Assam.

RESENMENLA LONGCHAR, Assistant Professor, Department of History, ICFAI University, Nagaland.

RUPALI RONGPIPI, Assistant Professor, Department of History, Lakhipur College, Goalpara, Assam.

SANGITA DAS, Assistant Professor, Department of Sociology, Eastern Karbi Anglong College, Assam.

SERDIHUN TERONPI, Assistant Professor, Department of English, Diphu Govt. College, Diphu, Assam.

SUMI DAA-DHORA, Assistant Professor, Department of Sankaradeva Studies, Nagaon, Assam.

THEJANI-I POHENA, Assistant Professor (English), Department of Law, Assam University (Central University), Silchar, Assam.

VULLI DHANARAJU, Professor, Department of History, North-Eastern Hill University, Shillong, Meghalaya.

Index